THE
KNOWLEDGE
MACHINE

THE

KNOWLEDGE MACHINE

ARTIFICIAL INTELLIGENCE AND THE FUTURE OF MAN

Donald Michie and
Rory Johnston

WILLIAM MORROW AND COMPANY, INC.
New York

PREFACE

THE MESSAGE OF THIS BOOK has implications not just for technology but for every sector of our society. We want to reach as wide a readership as possible, both inside and outside the technical community. In considering who our readers are, we are conscious that the explosive growth of computing in recent years has enormously widened the number of people who are acquainted with the concepts involved, many using computers in their work, in education, or at home. At the same time, there are many people to whom this technology is still strange. We need to address both groups, because they are equally concerned with the future of society. Not only that: the "two cultures" divide between technology and the arts shows little sign of narrowing, and we are convinced there is a need to open a new dialogue between the two sides.

Our requirement, therefore, has been to make the book understandable to the intelligent layman. At the same time, we have tried to avoid bogging down the argument by continually returning to first principles, and to provide enough detail to satisfy the technical reader's need to be convinced. To do this, the book is structured in an unusual way. Detailed knowledge of computer technology is not necessary for understanding it, but familiarity with the concepts is, so an appendix is provided to introduce these concepts. Readers with no experience of computing should start there and then proceed to Chapter 1. This chapter is largely background, much of which will be familiar to technical readers, but they may find it a useful summary. The central theme of the book starts with Chapter 2.

Our subject matter is specialized, and it would be counterproductive to avoid using the language of the specialism, which has been evolved to express precisely the ideas at hand. Technical ideas are explained as they arise in the text. However, non-scientist readers may occasionally encounter unexplained terms that are new to them, included to provide extra detail for the initiated. In all cases we have been careful to ensure that these are not central to the argument, so readers need feel no concern about skipping over them, getting the general sense from the context. Anyone curious to know more will find these terms explained in full in the Glossary.

On the other side of the coin, scientific readers will find that for the sake of comprehensibility, arguments are not gone into with the rigor that would be expected in a report of research. For those wishing to investigate more deeply, references to the scientific literature are given. By this approach, we aim to capture the imagination of both groups of readers.

As would be expected with any novel subject matter, the ideas in this book are not easy. But we are certain that the educated layman will be able to follow and appreciate them, alongside readers with technical backgrounds, and will be especially well placed to assess their social significance and to take steps to see that the opportunities here offered are not missed. The book will also, we hope, give a glimpse inside the fascinating world where these developments are taking place.

CONTENTS

8 / THE KNOWLEDGE MACHINE

INTRODUCTION

THE WORLD IS SLIDING precariously close to disaster. This conclusion follows from any sober analysis of the state of the planet. Economic stagnation, poverty, rampant inflation, massive unemployment, overpopulation, political strife, terrorism, wars and rumors of wars, and the threat of Armageddon permeate every corner of the globe. Of course, mankind has always faced problems, and present ones naturally seem more formidable than those in the past, but we do appear now to have reached a point where something very substantial will have to give. The height of irony is that much of the blame is now being laid specifically on mankind's systematic efforts to find solutions to its problems—that is, on technology.

Technology has been around for millennia and is nothing more than man's cumulative search for means to improve his lot. Now, however, some claim that technology is making his life worse, not better. The problems laid at its door range from the social upheavals caused by technical change, unemployment, pollution, and the threat of nuclear extinction, to alienation and the loss of job satisfaction and fulfillment. To these can be added the very real possibility that the complexity induced by technology is to blame for the intractability of our economic malaise, and the substantial danger that technical systems are getting so complicated that soon their human operators will lack the knowledge and understanding to control them.

In the face of this array of problems, we ask from where might answers come? Could inanimate creatures of technology possibly produce solutions to the problems it has spawned, and to myriad others that afflict humanity? Could machines themselves conceive solutions that have eluded human minds? The message of this book is that in principle they can, and that in the world of tomorrow they will.

This assertion is not simply dreaming by technological optimists. It is based on fact—in the shape of discoveries that are beginning to emerge from some of the world's advanced computer laboratories. It has long been wrongly assumed that you can only get out of a computer what you put in. This notion is certainly justified in the case of most of the workaday data processing of the last three decades. Now, however, it has been demonstrated incontrovertibly that something new can come out of computers, and that new something is knowledge. That knowledge, in turn, can be original ideas, strategies and solutions to real problems.

As yet, the knowledge that has been generated by machine is of little practical use to the deeper afflictions of the world. This is to be expected—the biologist who first synthesizes life will come up with possibly a virus, not a full-grown horse. But the implications are clear and important. Eventually it will be possible to set computers going on the search for solutions, not to the winning of games, but to the harsher problems that confront society, and solutions will be found.

Certainly this will take a long time, but equally certainly, given human resolve, it will happen. We can foresee the day when poverty, hunger, disease, and political strife have been tamed through the use of new knowledge, the product of computers acting as our servants, not our slaves. In addition, the mental and artistic potential of man will be expanded in ways as yet undreamt of, and the doors of the human imagination will be opened as never before.

Taking the opportunities will not be easy. It will require a complete reversal of the approach traditionally followed by technology, from one intended to get the most economical use out of machinery to one aimed at making the processes of the system clearly comprehensible to humans. For this, computers will need to think like people. Unless the computer systems of the next decade fit the "human window," they will become so complex and opaque that they will be impossible to control. Loss of control leads merely to frustration as far as many applications now are concerned, but when society becomes more dependent on computers, and where such things as military warning systems, nuclear power stations, and geopolitical and financial communications networks are operated by them, loss of control can lead to major crisis.

The prospect of machines becoming as capable and powerful as we describe can be daunting, even frightening. The notion of something non-human applying thought and judgment appears to encroach on what the human holds most dear: his consciousness. The creative computer has artistic, religious, political, and emotional associations of all kinds. But it is important that these philosophical considerations, interesting as they are, do not confuse our commitment urgently to seek to exploit the beneficial potential of the new technology. With it, our future looks brighter than we can imagine. Without it, we may have no future at all.

THE
KNOWLEDGE
MACHINE

1

BRUTE FORCE AND IGNORANCE

AMID THE EUPHORIA that followed man's first landing on the moon in July 1969, there appeared in the London *Evening Standard* the following letter:

> Watching the Apollo 11 Moon Shot with enthralled and uncritical admiration, I am particularly amazed (as we all must be) with the sheer technological brilliance of the whole thing, and wonder why computers cannot be used to solve our economic problems. Is it because the men who program them would tend to "build in" their own prejudice and shortsightedness? Our human experts seem to be full of both and have been most unsuccessful to date.

A few days later came another letter in reply:

> A computer is nothing more than a very elaborate adding machine, and it cannot solve any problem that the programmer does not know exactly how to solve already. Every one of the calculations involved in navigating Apollo 11 could have been solved by hand, but, of course, it would have taken far too

long. A computer is a slave that does exactly what we tell it—it will do all our tedious arithmetic and correlation of data, but how to solve our economic and social problems—that, unfortunately, will have to be worked out by people.

Some would disagree with the work *unfortunately* in that last sentence, but the second letter reflects a view that is widely held, especially among those who have spent many long hours programming computers, making a machine perform to their will. It is satisfying to see a complicated mechanism obey one's instructions faultlessly and uncomplaining for hours, months, or years on end. The natural conclusion to reach is that since no less can come out than you expected, no more can either—a point ofter expressed as, "You only get out what you put in." This seems so obvious in the light of personal experience of programming.

It is already apparent, however, that what seemed obvious is not obvious at all. Computers can create, and what they create could constitute solutions to major problems. To be sure, the creative computer is still far from being able to tackle the sort of problem raised by the *Evening Standard's* correspondent. The level of difficulty of a problem is often deceptive. Getting a robot to guide a spacecraft to the moon is today straightforward. A difficult problem would be to get the robot to go down to the corner of the road and buy a pack of cigarettes. Compared to that, even sorting out the economy may turn out to be simple.

THE NEED FOR CREATIVITY

The fundamental difference between the task of controlling a spacecraft and that of walking to the street corner is the need to deal with unforeseen occurrences. If the number of things that can possibly happen is relatively small, the computer program can be told what to do in the event of each of them. In real-life situations, however, the range of possibilities is so enormously large that they could never all be thought of beforehand. Consequently, the machine has to be able to store an internal model of its world from which to derive its own solutions to problems. Beyond that, it must be able to adjust or extend the model as experience accumulates and thus, on occasion, to be creative.

It also has to be intelligent in another but related sense. If a robot tries to pick something up and burns its hand because the object is hot, it must realize that the next thing to try is *not* picking it up with the other hand. Simple "chronological backtracking" will not do.

As yet, the ability of machines to solve problems is very limited. A prime example is the near disaster of Apollo 13, which was successfully piloted to earth after an explosion had crippled the main engine and power systems. Only the ingenuity of men, overriding the computer, saved the day, although all credit should be given to the system design that supported this overriding. On top of this, there are much more basic tasks that are so commonplace that human beings are seldom conscious that they are showing remarkable capability in carrying them out, but which computer technology in its current state can barely tackle at all. These include using natural language (English, French, etc.), deciphering speech, and making sense of the physical world through sight. Since these are fundamental to most human activities, the abilities to cope with them are of high priority in computer research and development. But there are other less obvious faculties that computers ought to have. There is common sense—an essential human attribute. Take the two sentences: "Clyde is an elephant"; "Clyde is sitting in the back row of the cinema." A useful computer ought to be able to say, "Now, *wait* a minute!" In the late 1950s, John McCarthy, one of the great pioneers of the scientific quest for the intelligent computer, posed as the central problem the construction of a mechanizable logic of common-sense reasoning. Through a quarter-century of fitful but accelerating progress, this has remained the central technical challenge.

INTELLIGENCE BY MACHINE

The finding of solutions to such problems is the *raison d'être* of the branch of computer science that is known by the rather strange title of Artificial Intelligence. Quite apart from the subject matter, the name itself is controversial. Some people hold the view that intelligence is an essentially human attribute and that therefore "artificial intelligence" is a contradiction in terms. Others are convinced that however clever computers become, they will never produce anything that is genuinely intelligent. This leads to problems of definition. How would you tell if a computer *had* produced something intelligent? An answer put forward in the early days by Marvin Minsky of MIT is that the machine is being intelligent if the task it is carrying out would require intelligence if performed by humans. To test this notion, we ask, Does a human use intelligence when doing arithmetic? Of course! Then, according to the definition, machines became intelligent with the first floating-point arithmetic package, a nonsensical conclusion.

Another phenomenon in the controversy concerns understanding. "Would it be intelligent if a machine could read a newspaper and give you a summary of its contents?" asks the AI scientist.

"Certainly!" concedes his critic.

"My student," replies the AI man, "has just written a program to do that (and it does not cheat simply by printing out the headlines)."

"But how does his program work?" asks the critic with an air of suspicion. After a spell with blackboard and terminal he decides that his suspicion was justified. "So that's all! I don't call that intelligent."

There appears to be a feeling that if one understands how something works, then it is not intelligent. This leads to the idea coined by Larry Tesler that "Artificial Intelligence is whatever hasn't been done yet," placing AI workers in a "no-win situation."

It is not altogether surprising that there is a problem with names here, since we have no sound definition of natural intelligence either. Some psychologists define it thus: "Intelligence is what intelligence tests measure." So what then are intelligence tests? In the absence of anything more rigorous for the time being, we are going to have to define intelligence in machines in the same way that Justice Potter Stewart described pornography: "I can't define it, but I know it when I see it."

ROVING ON MARS

Quite apart from the general problems described above, there are specific areas for which the need for machines with built-in intelligence is strikingly clear. One example is the Mars Rover project under development at the U.S. National Aeronautics and Space Administration. Since landing a man on Mars is out of the question for the foreseeable future, the idea is to have an unmanned robot vehicle that can be landed on the planet. The robot then drives around, taking pictures and soil samples and sending the data back to earth. The conventional way of operating this would be by remote control, with a technician at base watching the television pictures sent back by the Rover and returning radio signals to the steering mechanism on board. When the vehicle is on Mars, however, it takes between four and twenty minutes for the TV signals to reach earth, depending on the relative positions of the two planets in their orbits, and the same time again for the control signals to get back. Clearly if a chasm appears in front of the Rover, by the time the "Stop!" command arrives from earth, the machine will long since have crashed. Inescapably, a great deal of real intelligence will have to be built into the Rover in order for it to look after itself, getting only its broad strategic instructions from earth. As a result, the space roboticists at the Jet Propulsion Laboratory in Pasadena see their problem as primarily one of Artificial Intelligence.

Closer to home, the enormous growth in air travel has placed so much strain on air-traffic-control systems that in some parts of the world these systems look ready to break down altogether. The operators can only be relieved of the requirement for unblinking vigilance and its accompanying tension by computer systems of the kind of dependability and resourcefulness associated with intelligence. The scale of the catastrophe that might ensue from a computer mistake brings home to us how reliable both the hardware and the software must be.

The hostile environment of the North Sea provides an application for automatic unmanned submersibles capable of carrying out the hazardous tasks of inspecting and repairing oil platforms, currently done by human divers with all-too-frequent loss of life or injury. On land there are jobs for which intelligent "gofers" would be useful (gofers are people detailed to "go for coffee, go for the mail . . . ."). These would be "find and fetch" mobile robots capable of laying pipelines in the Libyan desert, working in mines, and faultfinding inside nuclear reactors oblivious of deadly radiation.

In the developing countries of the third world, the need for expert medical care is acute, and the fundamental shortage is that of trained staff. Sometimes money is not the problem at all. British medical visitors to Saudi Arabia and neighboring territories report widespread purchase of the latest and shiniest American equipment, which the local level of medical and technical education is not adequate to put to use. Computer systems are needed that incorporate the expert knowledge of specialists in the developed countries, so that not only can correct diagnoses be made by less skilled people in remote areas, but those people can acquire more of the knowledge itself through machine-aided training.

The computer industry worldwide and consequently business as a whole face a continuing "software crisis" in the shortage of skilled programmers and the ever-increasing cost of designing and writing systems. This will become worse as the new micro-chip technology of Very Large-Scale Integration floods the market with faster and cheaper computers. On present showing, the software industry, even at the highest imaginable rate of recruiting, will be unable to provide programs for all these machines. The story is told in Figure 1.

DATA PROCESSING INDUSTRY TRENDS[1]

Indicator	1955	1965	1975	1985
Industry growth	1	20	80	320
Hardware performance/cost	1	100	10,000	1,000,000
Programmer productivity	1	2.0	2.7	3.6

Figure 1.

If the markets of the booming microelectronics industries are not to collapse from program starvation, radical innovation—not just improvement—is needed in automatic programming. This means the development of systems capable of producing software from only a general statement of the user's requirements, perhaps using a stored sample of expert decisions—in effect very high-level languages with built-in intelligence.

TUA CULPA

Another crying need in the field of computers is for "error tolerance." Most computer systems still require their users to provide commands with every jot and tittle in exactly the right place. A comma missing or a single character wrong in a command word will cause a whole instruction or request for data to fail completely, a source of much irritation for fallible humans. "It was obvious what I meant!" we cry, but to the machine it was not obvious. Add to this the difficulty of errors in data that has already been stored. Suppose a word in an information retrieval system has been misspelled: "guage" instead of "gauge," for instance. When a user puts in a search for that word, unless he happens to make the same mistake himself in keying in his request, the answer to his retrieval query may *never* be found. Improved forms of "fuzzy" matching are needed, together with a more flexible understanding of language on the part of the machine.

"Fault tolerance" is an even bigger problem. In any machine with millions of components, it is inevitable that some of the components will be faulty. A complex system of redundant parts is often needed to avoid catastrophe. A failure can easily be far more serious than the fate of the cetologist in *Catch-22* who was posted to the army medical corps by a defective anode in an IBM machine. Even more alarming is the fact that in a large computer program—say, a Fortran compiler of 150,000 instructions—some of the instructions will inescapably be wrong. There will *always* be some that are wrong, because changes to fix errors can have unforeseen adverse effects on other parts of the program. Work is being done in the area of fault-tolerant software, notably by Brian Randell's team at Newcastle University, so far taking the rather long-haul route of providing duplicate software routines that do the same job in a different way, on the principle that it is unlikely they will both be wrong.

DOMAINS NOT REDUCIBLE BY BRUTE FORCE

Transcending all these examples, the fundamental need for a new form of intelligent computing is in the subject areas that simply cannot be handled by the traditional approach of data processing, best characterized as "brute force." These include such complex, open-ended tasks as route-finding, scheduling, and allocation of resources, network design, and most of the "real world" problems we have been discussing, where it is simply not practicable to foresee all possible eventualities. The idea is best illustrated by comparing two games: tick-tack-toe and chess. To make a computer play tick-tack-toe all a programmer has to do is work out every possible game situation and tell the machine what to do in each case. There are only a few hundred of these, and the number is further reduced by symmetry. This is why tick-tack-toe is basically a boring game. Chess on the other hand has 10^{120} different possible games, and although a complete strategy for play is trivial for a mathematician to formulate, it has the drawback, as Claude Shannon pointed out in 1950, that it would take 10^{90} years of processing on a super-fast machine to select one move.[2] The age of the solar system is but a flash by comparison, a mere 10^{15} years or so. Perhaps we could harness all the atoms in the universe into a giant multiprocessor and bring the time for one move down to 10^{40} years! However one does it, the attempt to construct a "tree" of all possible moves by saying, "If I move here, he might move here, or here, or I could move there . . ." rapidly leads to what has been called the "combinatorial explosion" (Figure 2). One can of course limit the number of moves ahead that are examined, and there are chess-playing programs that work entirely by "look-ahead" in this way, but in order to match a human player who uses his intelligence (combined with experience), the computer still has to calculate *millions* of possible moves. Either the storage capacity of even the largest machine is exceeded, or the program takes an impossibly long time to run. Consequently, progress requires a more selective approach. In chess playing, as in most other problem solving by computer, brute force and ignorance are the wave of the past.

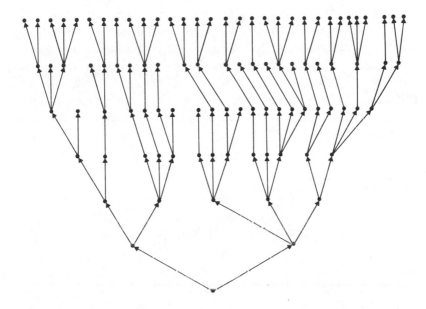

Figure 2. A look-ahead tree

A GIFT OF TONGUES

Looking at the limitations of current computing technology in more detail, an obvious area to choose is speech. Talking and listening are such basic human activities that it would clearly be useful for computers to be able to do them. As it turns out, talking is not difficult. Cheap speech synthesizers are available now that produce a Dalek-like but nonetheless recognizable voice. Pronunciation is carried out according to general rules about the sounds of letters and letter sequences in English, with an "exception dictionary" for words that are pronounced irregularly. This dictionary is never a hundred percent complete of course, and it is not unknown for instance to hear a synthesizer pronounce *guide* as "gwee-duh." That may not present a problem, but distortion of meaning can. Take a sentence from an advertising poster seen in London: LIVE AT THE BARBICAN. Whether the *i* in *live* is long or short depends on the meaning of the sentence, and that depends on knowledge of the world, namely, what the Barbican is. But even that is not sufficient, because the Barbican is both an arts center and a housing complex and the sign could belong to a show promoter or to a real-estate agent. The clue comes from the preceding part of the poster. Complete, it reads: INDIA. LIVE AT THE BARBICAN, and it is only this that tells us the *i* is long. Knowledge, a very considerable amount of knowledge, is the key to successful handling of this task by machine.

EARS FOR HEARING

Listening by computer, or speech recognition as it is called, is a very different matter. Human speech patterns are very complicated, and not only are there many different words that sound the same, but the same word can be pronounced in different tones and accents. The biggest problem, though, is detecting the breaks between the words. We imagine when we hear speech that there are clear gaps between the words, but in fact there are not—our brains supply them as we listen, through our knowledge of the language. A computer has to have that knowledge to make sense of the sound too. There is only an infinitesimal difference between the sounds of "She was a tanker" and "She was at anchor," and it usually has to be worked out from the context, including prediction of what is expected next. Prediction can run into problems too. Imagine the machine hears the syllable "six." That's fine. Then it hears "teen." Quick backtracking is needed to change the number from 6 to 16. Then the machine hears "agers." Ah, six teenagers! The six was right after all. Confusion is never far away.

If the number of words that has to be deciphered is relatively small, the problem can be manageable. If all you are talking about is chemicals, then you can be confident that what you heard was *nitrate* and not *night rate,* and common sense could tell you that *abominable* is seldom *a bomb in a bull.* But as the world gets larger and we try to make our machines more versatile, the problem compounds.

Current commercial speech recognition devices are limited to a vocabulary of a few hundred words, and usually the words have to be spoken with deliberate gaps in between. Also the machine has to be "trained" for every person whose voice is to be deciphered. The user has to say every word several times over into the machine.

Some experimental systems can accept continuous speech of, say, three or four words in length without gaps, but with commensurate reduction in the size of the workable vocabulary. Others take many times longer to process the speech than it took the human to say it—these are obviously of limited practical use, since they continually get further and further behind. The day of a typewriter that can be talked at to produce good English text is certainly a long way off, although in countries where there is a phonetic alphabet, such as Japan, the idea is more of a practical proposition.

CHATTING WITH A COMPUTER

Most communication with computers at present is by means of typewriter or video terminals with keyboards, and this avoids the problem of handling sound. It still would be very useful to be able to converse in ordinary English rather than the extremely stilted and strict syntaxes of existing programming and data-base query languages. Again, a general solution to this problem is thwarted by how little we know of how humans understand language. A few years ago it was thought that a comprehensive theory of parsing sentences was just around the corner, but it has turned out to be much more difficult to find a unique parsing of a sentence than was realized.

Take the two sentences: "Helmets must be worn," and "Dogs

must be carried." They are identical in form, yet mean totally different things. The would-be traveler on the London subway needs to know several unspoken things about the way the world works to be confident that he does not have to acquire a dog before boarding the escalator. Again, extensive knowledge of the world is essential to making sense of language.

Despite this, it is surprisingly easy to make a computer carry on a plausible conversation (by screen and keyboard) so long as the domain of discourse is strictly limited. One of the earliest and best-known programs to do this is called Eliza, written by Joseph Weizenbaum at MIT.[3] This simulates a Rogerian psychotherapist, encouraging the human "patient" to type in his troubles, in ordinary sentences, while the machine makes supposedly helpful comments in reply. A dialogue could look like this:

> Patient: MY FATHER HATED ME.
> Computer: TELL ME MORE ABOUT YOUR FAMILY.
> Patient: I REMEMBER MY CHILDHOOD IN BOSTON.
> Computer: DO YOU OFTEN THINK OF YOUR CHILDHOOD
> IN BOSTON?

and so on. The program is actually very simple. It looks for certain key phrases in the "patient's" statements, and for each key it has a preset reply. In the last two examples, the key phrases are "my father" and "I remember." Sometimes the part of the patient's sentence following the key phrase is included in the machine's reply, with the pronouns and verb forms swapped round: "I" for "you," "are" for "am," and so on. It does this without having the slightest understanding of the content of what it is repeating. Given this very crude procedure, it is uncanny how plausible the "doctor's" conversation is. Only occasionally does the grammar come out wrong, and sometimes the machine will say something silly—such as, in reply to:

> I CAN'T SLEEP AT NIGHT

it will say:

HOW DO YOU KNOW YOU CAN'T SLEEP AT NIGHT?

Eliza is nothing but a very carefully worked out parlor trick. Weizenbaum intended it as a joke—a parody—and was appalled when established psychiatrists took it seriously and started talking about the possibility of automated psychotherapy. Perhaps this tells us more about psychiatry than it does about computing.

In contrast, there is a great deal of practical value in the program Intellect produced by the Artificial Intelligence Corporation of Massachusetts. This is a system for interrogating a commercial data base, using ordinary English so executives do not have to learn tiresome sets of special instructions. The user can type: "WHICH SALESMEN HAVE PASSED THEIR TARGETS THIS YEAR?" and the program will produce a paraphrase of the question in its own terminology to confirm it understood and then display the requested information in tabular form. If the program misunderstands, this can be seen from the paraphrase, and since, unlike Eliza, Intellect has no game to give away, if it cannot make sense of the query at all, it says so.[4]

In the absence of any general theory of grammar, the method used is distinctly "hammer and tongs." The system includes a dictionary of several thousand words, with instructions to the program as to what to do with each word should it appear in the query. Another well-known natural language interface system was Ladder, developed at Stanford Research Institute as an experiment in helping U.S. naval officers get information on operational resources from a computer without having to know about the technology.[5] This program does not even attempt to classify words as nouns or verbs. Rather, it tries to match the query against a large range of expected sentence patterns, such as:

WHAT IS THE <ATTRIBUTE> OF <SHIP>

rather than the more general:

<NOUN-PHRASE><VERB-PHRASE>

One notable power Ladder has is to remember earlier queries and assume that pronouns or elliptical queries refer to them. However, the essential feature of all these systems is that they only work within a very limited domain of disclosure (e.g., sales reports, disposition of ships). Were their worlds to get substantially larger, the crude methods they use would require their programs and dictionaries to be expanded beyond the bounds of present-day practicality.

Similar problems arise with computer translation of natural language (English into German, Russian into English, and so on). Funny stories abound of the howlers that attempts at computer translation have produced such as "water sheep" for "hydraulic ram." The difficulty comes back to knowledge. The translator (human or machine) needs a detailed mental model of the world being described in the text, and providing computers with such knowledge in the form of such models is one of the key tasks of Artificial Intelligence.

Despite the serious limitations of present-day natural-language processing, the fact that a machine appears to be able to converse impresses lay people more than practically anything else in computer technology. One assumes that if something can talk, it is human, or humanoid. A detailed examination of the workings of Eliza is an excellent antidote to this delusion.[6] Most importantly, people must not be distracted by the natural-language frills a program has from grasping the significance of its substantive core.

EYES FOR SEEING

The general purpose home robot after which we hanker, and the imminent arrival of which is regularly announced in the less informed press, will have a fundamental requirement aside from the ability to receive instructions—namely, vision. If it is to vacuum the living room, it will have to be able not to run over the cat. If it is to weed the garden (nonchemically), it must be able to tell the difference between flowers and weeds. Obviously this is difficult (it is difficult enough for human beings). Much research has been done into the problem of "pattern recognition," some of it with computers trying to make sense of television images of scenes consisting of simple geometrical objects: blocks, pyramids, boxes, etc. Sometimes the computer manipulates the objects with a robot arm. Among the things the machine has to understand are: the sight of an object can be obscured by another in front of it; everything must be supported by something or it will fall; some things the machine can be told to do are possible (such as "Put the ball in the box") while others are not ("Put the box in the ball"). As soon as the objects become real—that is, not regular—things start to get out of hand.

Central to the problem is the fact that a picture contains an enormous amount of information. One television frame contains over two million bits, and this is repeated twenty-five times a second. A computer has even more difficulty in keeping up with this torrent of information than it does in speech recognition. In fact it is out of the question to do this processing with a conventional computer, because essential to the principle of such a machine is that it processes everything in a strict sequence, one item of data after another, and present circuits just cannot move fast enough. Owing to this "von Neumann bottleneck," for image processing in particular, information must inescapably be processed many bits at a time—that is, in parallel.

Research into the workings of animal eyes seems to indicate that this is how nature processes pictures too. A celebrated paper by Lettvin, Maturana, McCullough, and Pitts was called "What the Frog's Eye Tells the Frog's Brain."[7] Their general conclusion was that most of the practical chore of vision, including virtually all the calculation involved in recognizing simple objects such as bugs, was carried out in parallel processors in the frog's retina rather than by sequential operations in its brain. For machines to do this, a completely new type of hardware is needed.

THINKING IN PARALLEL

Nor is it practicable simply to take a bank of processors and somehow divide the task up between them. As Michael Duff of University College London explains, multiple processors introduce overheads in the amount of time needed to do the housekeeping and sort out which processor is doing what. With as few as twelve processors working together they can spend all their time talking to each other and get no real work done at all. Duff's solution is to build a special-purpose machine with processors laid out in a rectangular array, onto which the picture to be processed, from a television camera, is superimposed. This is called the Cellular Logic Image Processor, and the falling cost of integrated circuits allows the latest operational model, CLIP4, to incorporate no less than 9,216 separate microprocessors.[8]

A picture broken up into 9,216 dots is still fairly coarse, but all the processors can work simultaneously, giving a speed-up of four orders of magnitude. Each processor is connected to its eight immediate neighbors (see Figure 3). The significance of this arrangement is, for example, that it is easy to detect where the picture changes, by seeing where adjacent processors have different levels of light rather than the same. Thus the machine can directly find edges of objects, a fundamental task of image processing (Figure 4).

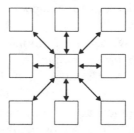

Figure 3. *(After Michael Duff)*

There is still a long way from finding edges and other local features to recognizing actual objects, especially if the objects are as complex as, say, human faces. It is to tackle this problem of recognition that a quite different device called Wisard has been built at Brunel University. This is entirely purpose-built electronics that can match an image it receives against a set of perhaps three or four that it has previously been "taught" about, and decide

Figure 4. *(After Michael Duff)*

which is the closest. The machine can cope with slight variations in the images, such as in the angle of presentation of the object, or in the expression on a face, because in the learning process it is shown a series of images of each object, not just one (Figure 5). What it stores is not the images themselves but an ingenious internal representation of what they have in common. Connected to a voice storage device, the machine can be made to say, as a person sits down in front of it, "Hello, John" or "Hello, Mary" as appropriate—an unnerving experience for the person. Still, it is important to remember that Wisard can only *recognize* images, it cannot *process* them further as CLIP4 can.

Parallel processing turns out to be useful for other purposes as well as vision. Some computing tasks are so enormous that to make any real advance in the technique, things will have to be done in parallel. For example in weather forecasting, data from thousands of monitoring stations have to be merged using complex equations of physics to predict how the weather is going to change.

In the field of information retrieval, the quantity of data similarly threatens to swamp those handling it. Keeping track of scientific research, changes in the law, and many other human endeavors is the object of the giant bibliographic data bases that are now proliferating, and to get information out of them it is necessary to match up records with index terms fed in by an inquirer. For instance, one may wish to find out about discoveries to do with copper-doped germanium. It is not sufficient, however, simply to search the data bank for that string of characters because it would

Figure 5. To recognize a face, Brunel University's Wisard is "taught" with a series of television pictures of the face, all slightly different (top and middle rows). In "recognizing mode" (bottom row), the machine displays above the head a bar chart showing how close a match it senses between the image it is seeing and that which it "knows." At the bottom left, the length of the lower bar shows matching of over 90 percent. With the different face in the middle, matching has gone down to 40 percent. On the right, when the subject covers his beard with his hand, recognition goes up slightly, but it is still clearly distinguished from the "learned" face. Likewise, removing his glasses makes hardly any difference. The upper bar of the histogram shows how closely the image matches an empty picture. *(Photos: Tony Firshman)*

fail to match against, for example, "germanium doped with copper." Thus, the substantive words need to be searched for separately, disregarding their order. But then a search for "general powers of attorney" will mis-hit against "powers of the attorney general."

Where computing overall is falling behind the amount of work that needs to be done, parallel processing can give a much needed boost. For instance, much computing involves operations in logic. Suppose we need to work out whether A is true, and we know that in order for A to be true, B and C must both be true. Thus, we need to find out whether or not B and C are true, but we can do these both at the same time rather than one after the other, speeding up the process considerably. In the same way, if A is true when *either* B *or* C is true, again working out B and C simultaneously will save time.

CONNECTIONS

An interesting new use of parallel processing is the subject of a project being carried out by some engineers from MIT, in an attempt to deal with the problem mentioned earlier of how to give a computer common sense. As we said, fundamentally this involves knowledge, and knowledge held not in a random fashion but in a complex interconnected structure. This can be represented by what is known as a "semantic network," by which objects and attributes are linked. Figure 6 is an example of part of a semantic network dealing with fruit. The network consists of *nodes* (junction points) and *links*. Danny Hillis's team at Thinking Machines, Inc., believe that to automate this properly, every node and every link in a network should have its own processor. Naturally, to have a semantic network of useful size, this will be an enormous task. Undaunted, they are proceeding to build a machine with one million processors, each admittedly much cruder than a normal microprocessor, containing only about 100 bits of memory. These units are being built into custom-designed chips, 64 per chip, so there will be 16,000 chips in the complete machine. Predicting how the

"Connection Machine" is going to work is difficult, explains Hillis. Simulating it on a conventional computer, it takes all night to get through one clock cycle!

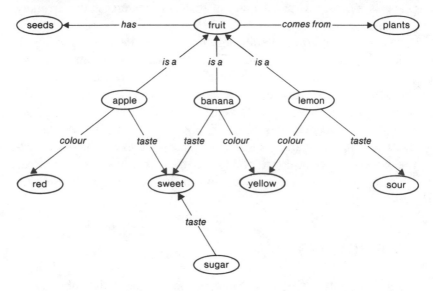

Figure 6. A semantic network *(After Danny Hillis)*

WHAT IS CREATIVITY?

The notion of connections brings us back to that of creativity. It is not at all clear exactly what creativity is, and that contributes to the reverence in which it is held. We stand in awe of the works of Bach or El Greco or Faraday, and the awareness that we would have no idea how to do what they did increases our awe. But it may be that creativity is not as amazing as it seems. To a great extent it appears to consist of noticing connections between things where no connection had been seen before. When Shakespeare says:

> How sweet the moonlight sleeps upon this bank!
> Here will we sit, and let the sounds of music
> Creep in our ears: soft stillness and the night
> Become the touches of sweet harmony.

on the face of it he is talking nonsense. Moonlight does not sleep; sound does not creep; stillness and night cannot become touches. But Shakespeare sees connections between these things that never occurred to us before and so produces poetry that moves us in a way that a less original assertion never can.

Newton based his laws of motion on the conjecture that both heavenly bodies and objects on earth were subject to exactly the same physical laws. This notion seems to the untutored observer absurd—the planets behave totally differently from the things close around us. Yet, as Newton realized, this is only because the environments are different.

Even the box of transistors that implements some state-of-the-art image-recognizer finds connections in that it assembles all the features and attributes that are the same in the images it is learning from and then makes connections with the image it is meant to recognize.

There is also a form of creativity that consists of building up new structures that are more complex than the preceding ones. Aaron Sloman, in considering creativity mainly from the viewpoint of the formation of new ideas, describes three layers on which creativity can take place: semantics, syntax, and notation. On the semantic level, new meanings can be attributed to existing words or whatever material is being dealt with. Lower down, the syntactic rules by which these are connected can be changed—an example of this could be discoveries of new techniques of harmony in music. At the most basic level, and possibly the most creative, new notation can be invented, for instance the tempered scale in music, or tensor calculus, which opened up a whole new way of dealing with physical phenomena. In any case, he says, there is no single metric of degrees of creativity.

Not all creativity is momentous. Indeed, Sloman points out, there is plenty of creativity in ordinary life, as for instance in recognizing a face we have not seen for a long time: We have to imagine what the ravages of time would have done and fill in the gaps for those things only half remembered. What we must beware is the view that if we understand it, it cannot be creative. (The reverse is also clearly fallacious: it often happens that nobody understands exactly what is going on inside large computer systems, yet the output is for the most part not creative.) It should be possible to recognize creativity entirely by output, not by origins or by whether the mechanism that produced the output was organic or electronic.

Creativity will be a vital attribute of the computers of the future. Without it they will be unable to generalize to solve problems, to act on their own new descriptions and concepts rather than the ones provided by the programmer. They will be unable to make the connections that are an essential part of even the most mundane tasks. Most serious of all, they will be unable to learn from examples, the only practical way of supplying them with the vast amount of knowledge that we have seen is essential if they are to be really useful. This way, computers can become valuable assistants and not slaves.

Knowledge is indeed the key. How one constructs computer systems based on knowledge is the subject of the next chapter.

2
COMPUTERS JOIN THE EXPERTS

THE MACHINES BUILT BY the pioneers of computing in the 1940s were popularly known for a long time as "electronic brains." The name "computer" when it took over was more appropriate because the machines were very far from being able to do any of the things we consider important as far as the brain is concerned; all they could do was numerical calculation. Computers now are routinely programmed for handling nonnumerical information, but they are still for the most part stuck with dealing with explicit *facts*, hard-and-fast objective data about which there is little, if any, uncertainty, and which can be filed and retrieved directly. This is a major drawback, because much of the information used by humans in their daily lives is far from clear-cut and certain. We did not want just to ask computers questions like: "What is the square root of 35,769?" We want to ask: "What is wrong with this patient?"; "Would this be a good spot to drill a well?"; "Are there precedents for this application of patent law?"; "What is the likely molecular structure of this compound?"; "What would be a good way to synthesize insulin?"; "Who killed the sheriff?" The information involved in these questions is the stock-in-trade of those knowledgeable and respected people we know as "experts."

Computers up to now have been largely confined to doing tasks that can be specified in exact detail—mindless and predictable work that would otherwise be done by clerks. To overcome this limitation and tackle the sort of problems that hitherto could only be dealt with by highly skilled experts such as doctors, engineers, lawyers, and accountants, Artificial Intelligence researchers have developed the programming technology known as "expert systems."

THE EXPERTS' LORE

Edward Feigenbaum of Stanford University explains the idea thus: While conventional programs deal with facts, expert systems handle "lore." By this he means the rules of thumb, the hunches, the intuition, and facility for judgment that are seldom explicitly laid down but which form the basis of an expert's skills, acquired over a lifetime's experience. Often the lore does not appear in the textbooks; it is seldom even discussed or brought to view. Commonly, the expert himself is not even conscious of it and has little understanding of how it works. For instance, much of the time, a doctor does not know why his treatment is effective; he just knows that it usually is. Yet despite the intangibility of expert knowledge, it has been found possible to encapsulate it in computer programs that can then rival the competence of highly skilled human practitioners.

Expert systems that have been constructed so far advise on such diverse areas as the diagnosis of infectious diseases, mineral exploration, analysis of organic compounds, income tax, and the operation of an area defense system. Each of these subjects not only involves imprecise information but is also highly complex, making it difficult to deal with using a conventional computer program but ideally suited to an expert system. In each case, the knowledge has been acquired from a human expert in the form of *rules*, typically many hundreds of them, which together make up the computer's "knowledge base." The expert system consists of this knowledge base together with an "inference engine," a program that works out the logical consequences of all the rules taken together. Some rules are unequivocal, in the form for example: IF this AND that, THEN some result. Others are vaguer and involve probabilities: IF (to some degree) this AND (to some degree) that, THEN (to some degree) result. It is here that the ability to deal with lore rather than facts comes in most strongly. The machine works through the rules, asks for appropriate information, and then announces its conclusions.

OIL AT SEA

A good example of an expert system is one developed at the Machine Intelligence Research Unit at Edinburgh University to help diagnose faults on North Sea oil platforms, commissioned as a feasibility study by British Petroleum. Each oil platform is a maze of pipes, pumps, and storage vessels, and to ensure the highest possible level of safety, there are a large number of sensors and emergency trips that shut down production automatically should anything go wrong. When this happens, the engineers on the spot have to get production going again as quickly as possible, but the system is so complicated that they can often have great difficulty in working out what exactly has failed. Lost production time is lost revenue, so BP was interested to see whether an expert system might help the engineers trace the fault quickly.

The Edinburgh pilot system carries on a dialogue with the engineers via a screen and keyboard. It asks such questions as:

HOW CERTAIN ARE YOU THAT THE V-01 PRESSURE CHART IN THE CENTRAL CONTROL ROOM INDICATES THAT THE RELIEF VALVE PRESSURE WAS REACHED?

The engineer replies with a number in the range +5 (meaning "I am completely sure it is true") to −5 ("I am completely sure it is not true"), with 0 meaning "I have no idea." For example, he might type "4.5." The machine then goes on:

Computer: HOW CERTAIN ARE YOU THAT GAS FLOW NOISE OR COOLING IS NOTICEABLE NEAR THE V-01 RELIEF VALVE?

User: 0

And so on until the computer reaches a conclusion, such as:

> AFTER CONSIDERING ALL RELEVANT QUESTIONS, THE PROBABILITY THAT AN UNSOLICITED CLOSURE OF ONE OR MORE OF THE SCRUBBER INLET VALVES CAUSED HIGH SEPARATOR PRESSURE INITIALLY WAS 0.002. IT IS NOW 0.909. CERTAINTY FACTOR IS 4.55.

Note that already we are dealing with information that is inexact and uncertain, as is so much in normal life.

LANGUAGES FOR ADVICE

Constructing the expert system is a long, involved process. An expert human practitioner in whatever field sits down with a person called a "knowledge engineer," who corresponds to the programmer in conventional computing. Together they work out in laborious detail what all the rules should be and how they interrelate. These are drawn up as an "inference network," similar in some ways to the semantic network described in Chapter 1. An example from the oil platform system is shown in Figure 7.

Formidable as this appears, it only covers a small part of the whole system. Each box represents a *belief*, the truth of which implies other beliefs in a pattern that can be seen from the diagram. The figures above and below each arrow are the "sufficiency factor" and the "necessity factor"—that is, they show to what degree the second box *must* be true if the first is and to what degree the second *cannot* be true if the first is not. When the network is finished, the knowledge engineer rewrites the rules in a special-purpose "advice language," which the computer can accept—in the Edinburgh project this language is called AL/X, as shown in Figure 8. He includes with each rule a piece of English text, which the computer inserts into the question it asks the user when that rule is encountered, such as the words "THE RELIEF VALVE HAS LIFTED." A fixed routine in the expert system outputs the words "HOW CERTAIN ARE YOU THAT," the text for the individual rule follows, and a question mark is tagged on the end: "HOW CERTAIN ARE YOU THAT THE RELIEF VALVE HAS LIFTED?" Thus, a fairly natural conversational mode of working is provided for the user.

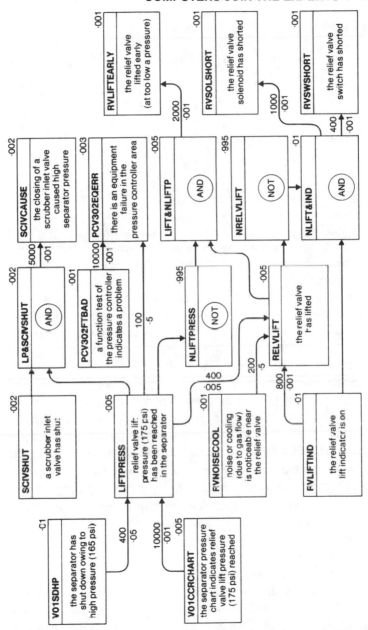

Figure 7. A small part of the inference network for an oil-platform expert system *(After John Reiter)*

```
space relvlift
        text    description
/* the relief valve on V-01 has lifted*/
        inference
                prior .005
                rules antecedents ( rvliftind ls 800 ln .001
                                     liftpress ls 400 ln .005
        control                      rvnoisecool ls 200 ln .5 )
                goal

space rvliftind
        text    description
/* the V-01 relief valve lift indicator is on (on the CCR, MOL
room, or separator panel)*/
        inference
                prior .01
        control
                askable
```

Figure 8. A sample of the "advice language" by which the human knowledge is fed to the computer. Drawing up the rules in this form is the job of a skilled "knowledge engineer." (*John Reiter*)

In operation the rules are dealt with in order, according to priorities specified by the knowledge engineer. However, the user can volunteer information that he knows is relevant by interrupting the machine's sequence and directing it to ask a particular question for which he has the answer. He needs of course to be quite familiar with the particular expert system to be able to do this.

After being put together an expert system needs "tuning," in interaction with the human expert, until he is happy with it. It is unlikely ever to be "finished," because the expert's own knowledge of the subject may grow, so the system needs to be continually adaptable. The process of putting the rules together has to be exhaustive (and so, exhausting). For example, as can be seen from the network, the fact that the relief valve lift indicator is on does not mean for certain that the relief valve has lifted. It only means it probably has, because there might be something wrong with the indicator.

One surprising aspect of this process is that the knowledge engineer typically has great difficulty in getting the expert to articulate his knowledge. Experts tend to underestimate the amount of knowledge they possess and to overestimate their own ability to describe it. At the same time, all kinds of curious facts and practices come out that never appear in the official operating manuals. At one point the expert will say, "Oh, we never trust those gauges!" so the network has to be adjusted to allow for that. Normally, rules are given "certainty factors," reflecting how confident the expert is that the given rule itself is valid. Then sometimes the expert is more surprised than anyone by what emerges in the knowledge-engineering process. He had knowledge and was following practices that he was not aware of.

EXPLAINING ON DEMAND

To help the expert and the knowledge engineer find their way through all the confusion that can easily result from this complex process, an essential feature of expert systems is the ability of the computer to explain on demand what is going on. Examples of this can be seen in Figure 9, which is a sample dialogue with one of the best-known expert systems, Mycin. This was developed at Stanford for diagnosing infectious diseases such as meningitis.[1]

Computer:	22. WAS ANY CHEMOTHERAPY RECENTLY BEGUN SPECIFICALLY TO COMBAT ORGANISM-1?
User:	NO
Computer:	23. IS JEREMIAH SAMPLE (PATIENT-1) A BURN PATIENT?
User:	RULE
Computer:	RULE047

IF: 1. THE SITE OF THE CULTURE IS BLOOD, AND
2. THE IDENTITY OF THE ORGANISM IS NOT KNOWN WITH CERTAINTY, AND
3. THE STAIN OF THE ORGANISM IS GRAMNEG, AND
4. THE MORPHOLOGY OF THE ORGANISM IS ROD, AND
5. THE PATIENT HAS BEEN SERIOUSLY BURNED

THEN: THERE IS WEAKLY SUGGESTIVE EVIDENCE (.4) THAT THE IDENTITY OF THE ORGANISM IS PSEUDOMONAS

User:	NO
Computer:	24. IS THE PATIENT'S ILLNESS WITH ORGANISM-1 A HOSPITAL-ACQUIRED INFECTION?
User:	YES
Computer:	25. DO YOU CONSIDER JEREMIAH SAMPLE (PATIENT-1) TO BE A COMPROMISED HOST? (ALCOHOLIC, IMMU-NOSUPPRESSED, ETC.)
User:	NO
Computer:	26. HAS JEREMIAH SAMPLE (PATIENT-1) HAD ANY GENITO-URINARY SURGERY OR MANIPULATION OF THE URINARY TRACT? (E.G. INDWELLING CATHETER, CYSTOSCOPY, ETC.)
User:	WHY
Computer:	I AM TRYING TO FIND OUT ABOUT THE IDENTITY OF THE ORGANISM. I ALREADY KNOW THAT:

THE PORTAL OF ENTRY OF THE ORGANISM IS UPPER-GU

THE MORPHOLOGY OF THE ORGANISM IS ROD

THE STAIN OF THE ORGANISM IS GRAMNEG

THE SITE OF THE CULTURE IS BLOOD

THEREFORE, IF:

1. THE PATIENT HAS NOT HAD A GENITO-URINARY MANIPULATIVE PROCEDURE, AND

2. URINARY-TRACT-INFECTION IS NOT A PROBLEM FOR WHICH THE PATIENT HAS BEEN TREATED

THEN:

THERE IS SUGGESTIVE EVIDENCE (.6) THAT THE IDENTITY OF THE ORGANISM IS E. COLI (RULE156)

Figure 9: Excerpt from a consultation with Mycin

Information about the patient is fed in by a doctor or medical assistant in answer to questions from the computer. Most of these answers are simply YES or NO, but instead of answering, the user can type RULE, and this will cause the machine to display the rule that it is currently evaluating. This gives the user an idea of what is happening. For a more detailed explanation, the user asks WHY and gets a summary of the logical process that is being worked through. The "explain" facility is one of the most important aspects of expert systems, and one with profound implications for the rest of computer technology. This issue we discuss in greater depth in the next chapter.

The explanations are composed from the English text that is held in the machine in conjunction with each rule; the rules that the machine actually operates are held internally in advice language. Some expert systems allow the user to volunteer information in simple English sentences. Again, this is not too difficult for the system to cope with because the subject area in question is always narrow, so the possible interpretations of words are few. Experts tend to use jargon and stereotyped ways of expressing things, with the result that text templates and simple parsing routines will usually work. When they do not, the program will simply say, "I don't understand."

Mycin does its logical reasoning by a simple process called "backward chaining." This enables a large number of interrelated rules to be dealt with together. To see how this works, consider the rule

If A is true and B is true, then F is true

where A, B, and F are all beliefs. This can be represented in the form

$$A \ \& \ B \rightarrow F$$

where the ampersand stands for the logic "and" operation and the arrow is read as "implies." Suppose we have a whole set of rules such as:

1. $A \ \& \ B \rightarrow F$
2. $C \ \& \ D \rightarrow G$
3. $E \quad\quad \rightarrow H$

4. B & G → J
5. F & H → X
6. G & E → K
7. J & K → X

In a particular case, we are told that beliefs B, C, D, and E are all true, and we need to work out whether X is true. By backward chaining, we look to see which beliefs imply X by finding where X is on the right-hand side of a rule. Then we look at the left-hand side of those rules and work out how to tell whether they are true, and so on until we arrive at facts that we know to be true or false.* The advantage of this over forward chaining is that we do not waste time working out lots of unwanted conclusions or asking questions irrelevant to the goal. For dealing with probabilities rather than clear cut "true/false" facts, a more complex inference process of the same general kind is needed, using the laws of statistics to work out combined probabilities of events.

Mycin can also contain "metarules," that is, rules about rules, that help in working out the conflicts of rules and uncertainties of priority that inevitably arise with a large knowledge base. For example:

METARULE 2
IF:
1) THE PATIENT IS A COMPROMISED HOST, AND
2) THERE ARE RULES THAT MENTION IN THEIR PREMISE PSEUDOMONAS, AND
3) THERE ARE RULES THAT MENTION IN THEIR PREMISE KLEB-SIELLAS
THEN:
THERE IS SUGGESTIVE EVIDENCE (.4) THAT THE FORMER SHOULD BE DONE BEFORE THE LATTER

The output of Mycin is suggested diagnoses, but it can also recommend antibiotic treatment. In one trial, ten difficult cases were selected and detailed clinical summaries of these were presented to a group of nine doctors of varying levels of experience

---

*In the example, X works out to be true.

and to Mycin. The prescriptions they came up with were given to a panel of meningitis experts to assess, with no clues as to the identities of the prescribers. The highest score was achieved by Mycin.[2]

To help construct expert systems in other spheres, the disease rules were taken out of Mycin, leaving a general-purpose system called Essential Mycin, or Emycin. Using this, a quite separate expert system was constructed to diagnose lung disease. This is called Puff and has been in routine use at the Pacific Medical Center in San Francisco. It takes data from a spirometer, a machine that measures air flow rates and volumes as the patient breathes in and out of a tube. It also asks questions about the patient's history—how many cigarettes a day and so on—and then, using a knowledge base of about a hundred rules, produces a detailed description of the patient's apparent condition and a diagnosis of disease. The doctors who check all of Puff's reports sign 85 percent of them unchanged.[3] With medical expert systems, as with those in other fields, the story is the same: the systems consistently perform as well as human clinicians.

PROSPECTING FOR BURIED TREASURES

In a completely different area, an expert system has been exciting interest among mining corporations as well as in U.S. government agencies concerned with the energy problem and with exploitation of natural resources. SRI's Prospector takes in geological data about the rocks and ores observed in a given area of land, levels of erosion, and so forth, and produces forecasts of what valuable minerals might be found there.[4] It can display its forecasts as a colored map on a computer screen, as shown in Figure 10. With its 1,600 rules, Prospector uses an inference network of hypotheses, which it tests out according to the evidence. One hypothesis might be: "The alteration of hornblende suggests the potassic zone of a porphyry copper deposit." The hypotheses are tested by asking appropriate questions, and with much juggling of probability factors, they are confirmed or refuted. They can also be linked by "context constraints." These say in effect: "Don't even consider hypothesis A unless the probability of hypothesis B falls within such and such a range.''

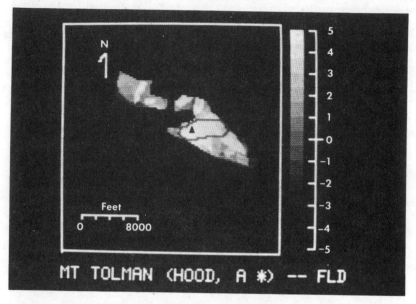

MT TOLMAN (HOOD, A *) -- FLD

Figure 10. Prospector's graphical display showing a map of where it predicts molybdenum deposits around Mount Tolman in Washington State. The favorability scale on the right shows the likelihood of deposits by brightness. The triangle marks the summit of the mountain. *(SRI International)*

Prospector can also reason intelligently about the information it holds. For instance, using a separate "taxonomy network" it can know that pyrites are a type of sulfide, so if it already has some information about pyrites it can avoid asking redundant questions about sulfides. Similarly, if the user tells it, "There are pyrites present," and then "There are no sulfides," the machine can say, "Hold on! There's a mistake there."

An important issue the designers of Prospector had to tackle was that of sensitivity. The user does not want slight variations in the certainty of his input to cause wild fluctuations in the conclusions the system reaches. As evidence of the effectiveness of the SRI team's design, Prospector has succeeded in finding a major deposit of molybdenum, previously unknown, in the Mount Tolman area of Washington State. Drilling at the site has uncovered ore in remarkably close correspondence with Prospector's forecast.

Other fields in which expert systems are now being applied include:

Defense: At the U.S. Naval Ocean Systems Center a 400-rule expert system called TECA, for Threat Evaluation Countermeasures Agent, has been developed. This is to help officers work out whether blips on a radar screen are hostile ships or planes, what the supposed enemy might be trying to do, and which of a large number of possible defensive actions has the highest chance of success.

Organic chemistry: Stanford University's earliest excursion into expert systems was Dendral, used to work out the molecular structures of complex organic compounds. From the user, the program gets the chemical formula of the compound and data from mass spectrometer analyses, and then it suggests the most likely arrangements of the atoms in each molecule from the vast number possible.

Discovering a structure is quite a different task from diagnosis, which has been the purpose of most of the expert systems discussed so far. Thus, Dendral works rather differently and is one of a class of expert systems based on *searching*, using rules to narrow down the searches to manageable numbers. Eliminating whole sections of a search tree in some way is aptly called "pruning," as in Figure 11.

Producing a *plan* is yet another possible task for expert systems; an example of this is Molgen.

Genetics: Molgen is an expert system for helping molecular geneticists plan experiments that involve the manipulation of DNA, the basic carrier of heredity. This entails cutting up the very long molecules of DNA, joining pieces together, inserting new materials in a myriad different possible places, and keeping track of the biological consequences and the chemical tools and instrumentation required. Molgen produces a plan, often thousands of steps long, to organize all these. It has been used effectively in a number of experiments, including one notable one involving gene cloning in rat insulin, and will doubtless become an important part of the promising and controversial field of genetic engineering.

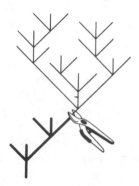

Figure 11. "Pruning" a search tree. The shears indicate a place where the system could have grown a whole extra sub-tree in its search but was saved the labor by intervention of a pruning criterion that indicated lack of promise in that direction. *(After Mark Stefik)*

Computer fault-finding: IBM is cooperating with Stanford to produce an expert system for diagnosing component failures in computers and networks, a job which is often very difficult, requiring highly skilled engineers, who are always in short supply. The expert system requires an internal "model" of the computer system, and much of the research work involves defining an adequate "machine-definition language" in which the computer can be described.

Computer system planning: Related to this, Digital Equipment Corporation, following on from work at Carnegie-Mellon University, has devised expert systems to help work out the best configuration of a computer system to meet the customer's requirements and, having done that, to fit the hundred or so components into the various cabinets so that all the necessary electrical connections can be made.

Structural engineering: Some expert systems are even experts *about* computer programs. For example, civil engineers use in designing structures a very complex set of programs called the Finite Element Analysis Package. The instruction manual for this alone is four inches thick. The expert system Sacon has been put together to guide engineers and provide them with plans for their use of the analysis programs.

Political-risk assessment: SPL International in Abingdon has produced for Shell an expert system to assess the advisability of investing in a foreign country, according to the likelihood of war, riot, nationalization, and so on. It asks questions along the lines of: Has there been civil commotion? Is the government left-wing? How big is its majority? The program then makes hypotheses and produces recommendations. The major problem the system has is assessing how much reliance to place on the judgments made by the humans in answering its questions.

Benefits and tax: An offshoot of work at the Rand Corporation in the U.S. is an expert system called Demsoc, for helping people work out their eligibility for Social Security benefits. Similar to this, several projects are afoot to build expert systems that advise on how to arrange one's business affairs in order to minimize tax. Working at the University of Illinois as a graduate student, Robert Michaelsen, who is also a professional accountant, put together an expert tax adviser using Emycin as inference engine. Taxadvisor generates shrewd proposals for each given case. The next step will be to feed these into a separate simulator program that faithfully encodes the intricacies of the tax system so that the financial consequences of alternate proposals can be precisely computed. This is to select out the best scheme put forward by the "adviser."

MS. FRIDAY TO THE RESCUE

Some such pool of electronic sanity in the proliferating jungle of tax regulations is certainly overdue. A senior partner in one of the longest established accountancy firms in the City of London has confided that the suicide rate among accountants is exceptionally high. The reason, he explained, is that accountants by character tend to be lovers of orderly precision, cautious, exact, upset by sudden change or tendency of things to fall apart. Imagine such neat and rigid personalities under the full blast of successive waves of revisionist hysteria propagated from new regulations— unintelligible, voluminous, ambiguously drawn, and tested in a welter of mutually inconsistent court decisions!

Certainly business as a whole is a field ripe for the introduction of intelligent systems. So far, computers in offices have been used mainly to get marginal increases in the efficiency of typing and the planning of appointments. An expert system in the office should enable the Girl Friday to make a more substantial contribution than simply protecting her boss from unwanted telephone calls. That accountant who is just about to jump off the window ledge is no less important to the small business than the medicine man is to the small village. The chief executive and the company secretary bicker dejectedly among the ruins.

After consultation with her desktop computer, Friday sweetly intones: "If I might suggest . . . we could form a subsidiary, which in turn could act as a holding company for certain of our assets. The new company goes into temporary liquidation, is bought by an educational charity consisting of the original directors, and meanwhile transfers its trading address to the Bahamas. The old company sacks its board and reengages its directors as consultants who promptly sue for emotional damage. The costs of the company's out-of-court settlements are written off as expenses, and the directors donate their compensation payments to the charity."

"Say no more, Ms. Friday! Write me a very short memo. Oh, and if it works, take an increase in your expense allowance!"

WHERE THE OLD WAY IS BEST

There are still of course very many fields of human endeavor for which no expert systems exist as yet. Indeed, there are plenty for which these techniques are just not suitable. Richard Duda and John Gaschnig give an example:

Although a mathematician possesses specialized knowledge, the additional knowledge needed to function in that role is far more extensive than current knowledge-based expert systems can handle. On the other hand, where there are well-defined mathematical procedures for solving a problem, knowledge-based expert systems are unnecessary.[5]

Douglas Lenat of Stanford relates how the expert systems company set up by him and his colleagues was visited in its early days by a gambler from Las Vegas who wanted to build a system for shooting dice. He rattled off 50 to 100 rules along the lines of, "If there has been a six, hold the dice *this* way." They were just the sort of rule that knowledge engineers need. The Stanford people listened in fascination. Eventually, as Lenat comments, "It was only our fundamental beliefs in the workings of the universe that got us to push him out the door."

It is important to remember that not all problems involving knowledge need as an expert system, or even a computer, to solve them. For instance, what to do if your car won't start (check the battery leads, check the plugs . . .) is better shown to you by a printed flowchart than with a computer. To be suitable material for an expert system, a subject area needs to be large and to include uncertainty and incomplete knowledge.

The uncertainty leads to another feature of expert systems, which John McDermott of Carnegie-Mellon brings out in referring to R1, the computer-layout system he designed:

It is not clear that all (or even most) of R1's supporters realize that R1 will always make mistakes. The problem is that at least some of R1's supporters think of it as a program rather than as an expert. There is, of course, a big difference between programs and experts. Finished programs, by definition, have no bugs. When experts are finished, on the other hand, they're dead. During the last two years, I have hammered on the theme that a knowledge-based program must pass through a relatively lengthy apprenticeship stage and that even after it has become an expert, it will, like all experts, occasionally make mistakes. The first part of this message got through, but I suspect that the second has not. My concern, then, is whether, as this characteristic of expert programs is recognized, Digital (or any large corporation) will be emotionally prepared to give a significant amount of responsibility to programs that are known to be fallible.[6]

The tendency to confuse expert systems with programs using very large data bases of useful scientific facts is widespread. The difference is that a question can be answered only by reference to a data base if the answer is already stored. An expert system, which may itself have access to one or more data bases, answers questions by reasoning and intelligent conjecture. What is stored consists not only of individual facts but also of more general patterns, rules and "theories" from which it infers its answers.

INTELLIGENT DATA BASE AT THE ZOO

Having said all that, we have no doubt that the techniques of knowledge-based systems will come to be applied in areas where they are not strictly necessary. Pat Winston of MIT gives a light-hearted example of a rule-based system for identifying animals.[7] This could actually be incorporated in a data base kept by a zoo of details of all its stock: their pet names, keepers, cages, diets, ages, dates of acquisition, health records, and so on, as well as descriptive features ("lays eggs," "swims," "has dark spots") and genus names ("penguin," "tiger"). An extra feature of the system would be that it could infer facts from fragmentary observations.

The zoo manager calls up from home. "This animal that seems to have gotten into my backyard—I don't know what it is or whether it belongs to our collection. Connect me to the new system and I'll try to find out." Using his home terminal, he has the following conversation with the computer:

Manager: CALL TAXONOMY
Computer: TAXONOMY HERE. TELL ME SOME FEATURES
Manager: DARK SPOTS

Computer: IS IT A CARNIVORE?

Manager: I HOPE NOT

Computer: DOES IT HAVE POINTED TEETH?

Manager: I DON'T KNOW

Computer: DOES IT HAVE CLAWS?

Manager: WHY?

Computer: I AM TRYING TO ESTABLISH WHETHER IT IS A CARNIVORE. DOES IT HAVE CLAWS?

Manager: NO

Computer: DOES IT HAVE HOOVES?

Manager: YES

Computer: DOES IT HAVE VERY LONG LEGS AND NECK?

Manager: YES

Computer: THEN IT IS A GIRAFFE. WANT TO KNOW WHICH RULES GOT THAT?

Manager: YES

Computer: RULE 7. IF ANIMAL IS A MAMMAL AND ANIMAL HAS HOOVES, THEN ANIMAL IS AN UNGULATE.
RULE 11. IF ANIMAL IS AN UNGULATE AND ANIMAL HAS LONG NECK AND ANIMAL HAS LONG LEGS AND ANIMAL HAS DARK SPOTS, THEN IT IS A GIRAFFE.

The inference network for Pat Winston's toy system is shown in Figure 12.

We have been aiming to make clear the distinction between rule-based systems and conventional programming—this is summed up schematically in Figure 13.

For expert systems, using rules instead of programs provides four basic advantages:

- It is easy to add rules and change existing ones to expand and improve the system.
- The system can easily be made to explain itself by printing out the rules it is acting on. This is useful both for those building the system and the eventual "real" user.
- The system can be made introspective, that is, it can check rules for consistency, and it can modify rules and learn new ones.

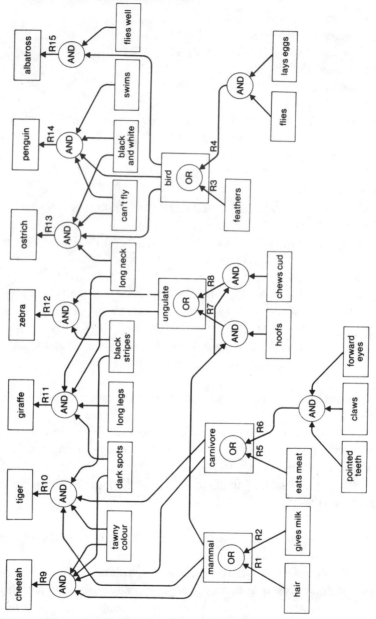

Figure 12. A possible inference network for an animal-classification expert system[8] *(After Winston, Duda, and Gaschnig)*

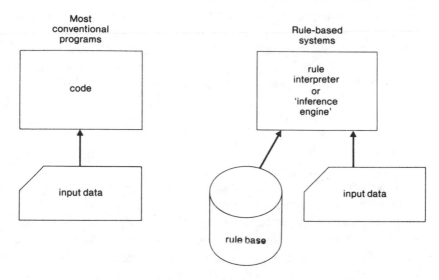

Figure 13. The difference between conventional programs and rule-based systems *(After Duda and Gaschnig[9])*

- The same knowledge base can be used for different purposes by changing the software.

Admittedly, as yet rule-based systems exhibiting these useful characteristics are not all that large. How they will behave and whether they will continue to be manageable when they get 20,000 or 100,000 rules remains to be seen.

TOOLS FOR BUILDING

The big problem holding up the development of new expert systems is the work involved in discovering and encoding the rules. This can take anywhere from a couple of man-months to several man-years. First of all, it requires the attention of a highly skilled knowledge engineer, and there are not nearly enough of these around. Training more runs up against the shortage of people to teach them. In the U.S. especially, the growth of the whole computer industry is being held up because the universities find it hard to hang on to skilled technologists to do the teaching in the face of the leap-frogging salaries being paid by industry. This is like nothing so much as ripping apart the carriages of the train in order to stoke the engine, but it shows no signs of changing. Second, the time of a valuable domain specialist has to be taken up for most of the knowledge-acquisition process and often for much longer than he expects.

It is not just the content of the rules that varies from one expert system to another. It would be nice to be able to lift the rules out of a system and just slot in those for another subject domain, but differences in the types of output of systems, according to their purposes, mean that there often has to be wide variation in the syntax of rules. This forces knowledge engineers, despite themselves, to make changes throughout their software. In an effort to get around this and produce an all-purpose framework for future expert systems, Stanford has been working on a package called AGE, or Attempt to Generalize. This provides a selection of modules that can be incorporated in the new expert system, including facilities for forward or backward chaining and a knowledge-representation package known as UNITS. AGE coaches the user on how rules should be laid out: what should be on the left-hand side, the right-hand side, and so on. Other tools that have been developed for those constructing expert systems are the advice language AL/X with its associated rule-generator ACLS ("Analog Concept Learning System") and the interface builder RITA and model builder ROSIE from the Rand Corporation.

However, it is essential in the long run that expert systems be able to acquire their own rules automatically, from data or key *examples* they are given. In other words, the problem is one of language: instead of *telling* the machine things, we want to *show* it things and have it understand their significance itself. A picture, as we know, is worth a thousand words because what the picture can be used to convey is a key example. Just how it is possible for a computer program to learn by example is something we go into in Chapter 5.

An additional and very promising use for expert systems is in teaching humans about the subject domain. Guidon is a variation of Mycin with extra rules added to direct a dialogue with a student so he can learn about the infections in question and the techniques of diagnosis. With Puff's rules instead of Mycin's, the system has also been teaching about lung disease. The IBM computer fault-diagnosis system is similarly expected to be used for training human field engineers.

While new subject areas for expert systems are being worked on, changes in technology are promising to make the systems not only more powerful but more accessible. Expert system packages are now available to use on microcomputers, putting them within reach of private individuals and of small businesses and organizations. At the other end of the technological scale, research into what is known as Dataflow architecture will open up new vistas for expert systems. The Dataflow work, notably at Manchester University and MIT, is an attempt to get around the von Neumann bottleneck in general computing with a machine in which instructions do not simply wait until they are activated in sequence, one at a time. Instead, each "fires" independently as soon as the data it requires is available. This speeds things up, since much work can get done in parallel, but naturally, it requires a far more complex structure of machine to keep track of everything that is going on. The advantage for expert systems is that a rule can be made to trigger whenever its preconditions are satisfied rather than waiting to be called specifically by a central controller. The process of extracting patterns also becomes easier.[10]

EXPERT SYSTEMS AND SOCIETY

It looks as if it will not be long before people will be able to buy knowledge bases in their local Rexall's as easily as they pick up a magazine. Interactive as these will be, many people will find them more attractive and easy to use than passive books and papers. Other knowledge bases will be held on large central computers, easily accessible by anyone with a telephone and a television-set-cum-terminal. But would this necessarily be a good thing?

There are doubts. Researchers envisage terminals in public libraries that, in return for a few coins, would provide diagnoses of all and sundry health problems. Doctors may be uneasy about some aspects of this. Despite the obvious attractions of getting scarce medical skills to the third world, the prospect of "Mycin for the Eskimos," with paramedics taking over the work and responsibilities, is a possible cause for concern among qualified practitioners. There is a fundamental problem of responsibility. At the moment, all output from medical systems is checked by doctors, but presumably there will come a time when it is not. What then if (or rather when) the system makes a mistake?

Alternatively, if a doctor is relying on an expert system for specialist advice, what happens if a malpractice suit arises? Assuming that he did not use the "explain" facility or he cannot remember what it said or he trusted the system's facts to be correct, he is in difficulty if all he can say to the court is, "I took this action because the box told me to." Thus, doctors might well be reluctant to use computer-based diagnosis. Nevertheless many are not, and have cooperated enthusiastically in providing knowledge for their development. In Great Britain, Royal Sussex County and Brighton General hospitals on their own initiative asked Sussex University, in collaboration with Tim de Dombal of Leeds University, to construct a system for diagnosing acute abdominal pain. Its principal use so far is in helping to train junior surgeons.

Certainly there is a rational element in the fear of expert systems putting highly paid professional people out of work. Hitherto the threat from new technology has always hung over the low-skilled and the low-paid—those in factory or clerical jobs. Whether professionals will really be seriously affected is in some doubt, but there are those who are sure that lawyers, for instance, could be replaced by computers and that an expert system, albeit a very big one, could actually do the job better. It is true that finding chains of consequences in laws and finding where laws contradict each other are ideal tasks for computers and are often done poorly by humans at the moment. An improved legal service to the public would be an undoubted boon. Still, plenty of legal barriers as well as technical ones stand in the way of these developments, such as changes in the law that have to be made for computer output to be admissible as evidence in trials. The day is yet to come when the opinion of a computer, and perhaps its reasoning, are admitted. Then if it is an expert system with an "explain" facility, it will at least be possible to cross-examine it!

Not all expert systems are doing work that humans are happy to be doing. The computer layout task at Digital for instance is extremely boring as well as being difficult, and resistance there to the R1 system was based not on self-interest but on skepticism about whether it would work. R1 has now been accepted as a useful assistant and one that provides interest to humans in the task of improving it.

Overall, there is little doubt that the world's demand for experts will continue far to outreach the supply. Ronald Clark of the Inter-Bank Research Organization points out that each individual branch bank manager is supposed to be able to provide his customers with knowledgeable advice on any of three to four hundred services he can offer. So fears of deskilling can be balanced against the fact that it is normally not humanly possible to have all the skills that ideally one needs. The human race needs all the knowledge sources it can get.

3

THE HUMAN WINDOW
ON THE WORLD

A FEW SECONDS AFTER 4:00 A.M. on March 28, 1979, an alarm echoed through the No. 2 control room at the nuclear power station at Three Mile Island, Pennsylvania. The operators were unperturbed at first, as minor breakdowns were not uncommon, but it was only a few minutes before they realized that this one was far from minor. A tiny valve in the pneumatic system had stuck, causing the plant's supply of secondary cooling water to be shut off. Within seconds the uranium core of the reactor started to overheat, and despite everything the operators tried in order to contain the problem, it became steadily worse. A relief valve stuck open, spewing radioactive water and steam into the reactor building and from there into the atmosphere outside. A bubble of hydrogen collected at the top of the reactor vessel, threatening to explode at any minute. The possibility arose of the uranium core itself melting. Either of these occurrences would cover the Pennsylvania countryside with radioactivity.

Over the next few days, the operators together with experts from the Nuclear Regulatory Commission struggled to get the reactor under control, while a horrified world looked on. Pennsylvania's Governor Richard Thornburgh ordered the evacuation of children and pregnant women from the area, and large numbers of other people started to leave of their own accord. It was a week before the owners, the Metropolitan Edison Company, announced that a cold shutdown of the reactor was finally in sight and life in Pennsylvania started gradually to return to normal. Cleaning up the Augean Stables of the reactor buildings has taken several years.

Figure 14. President Jimmy Carter visiting the Three Mile Island control room at the height of the crisis on April Fool's Day, 1979 *(AP)*

Dispute still simmers over how much radiation was released into the atmosphere during the incident, how dangerous was the 50,000 gallons of radioactive waste water that was dumped into the Susquehanna River, and how near was the ultimate catastrophe of a meltdown. The repercussions have been enormous, with "Three Mile Island" a rallying cry for the anti-nuclear movement the world over, together with the slogan "We all live in Pennsylvania." But one point over which there is no dispute is why a problem that should have been containable almost became a disaster. President Carter's commission, reporting on the causes of the accident, said: "The major factor that turned this incident into a serious accident was inappropriate operator action." In turn, that was caused, as the commission put it, by one thing: "confusion."[1]

This is hardly surprising considering the circumstances. Within the first few minutes, between one and two hundred alarms went off. As Bill Zewe, the shift supervisor, described it afterwards:

> I noticed that we had every alarm, just about every alarm, on panel 15, which monitors most of the ICS parameters for feed water limited by reactor, reactor limited by feed water, BTU limits, and so on. Most of these were lit.[2]

The experts from the Nuclear Regulatory Commission were in the same plight. Reactor inspector James Higgins told a Congressional committee:

> There was a tremendous amount of activity going on in the control room. A lot of people were involved with a lot of different problems, and that [an indication that some hydrogen had exploded] was one of many things. Operators were— alarms were going off; pumps were being started and stopped; valves were being cycled, and this was just one of a myriad of those things that was occurring throughout the entire day. And I was thoroughly not able to follow what was going on. And I did not pick it up at all.[3]

A committee chaired by Dr. Thomas Malone investigated the human factors of the incident and reported:

> . . . the operator was bombarded with displays, warning lights, print-outs and so on to the point where the detection of any error condition and the assessment of the right action to correct the condition was impossible.[4]

The President's commission agreed, stating that "lack of attention to the human factor in nuclear safety" was to blame. The lesson is clear: unless a technical system is designed in every detail so as to be comprehensible to the humans operating it, unless the way information is presented fits in with the way human eyes and minds work rather than the way the machinery works, then once the system starts to malfunction, it will tend to become unmanageable.

TROUBLE AT STEEL MILL

In 1975 the Dutch steel company Estel Hoogovens installed a highly automated new hot strip mill at its plant in Ijmuiden, on the coast near Amsterdam. Expecting productivity to be given a boost by this advanced equipment, the management was shocked to see the output of the mill actually fall. Consultants from the British Steel Corporation were called in, and their report laid the blame squarely on the design of the interface between machine and operator. *New Scientist* summed it up thus:

> The operators became so unsure of themselves that, on some occasions, they actually left the pulpits used for control unmanned . . . the operators also failed fully to understand the control theory of the programs used in the controlling computer, and this reinforced their attitude of "standing well back" from the operation—except when things were very clearly going awry. By intervening late, the operators let the productivity drop below that of plants using traditional control methods. So automation had led to lower productivity and operator alienation simultaneously.[5]

Matters were made worse by the fact that, in the new design, the path of the steel strip being rolled had been enclosed so the operators could not even see the material they were supposed to be working on. The consultants' report firmly asserted that among other things the operators had to be put in closer touch with the process and that information displays should help them *understand* the decisions taken by the automation, instead of just indicating the state of a process.

Air-traffic control is causing worries to planners and travelers alike in North America and Europe. Near misses in the air have become alarmingly commonplace, along with breakdowns in the complex radar and computer equipment that can leave controllers helpless for vital seconds or even minutes. According to the Co-ordinated Science Laboratory at the University of Illinois, American computerized air-traffic control is getting so complicated that operators have serious difficulty in telling what is going on. As for the future, there is controversy about how replacement systems should be designed. Some experts call for even more automation to eliminate the uncertainty of the human element, and others argue for schemes in which humans and machines share the load in a kind of partnership. Whatever way it is done, there will always arise the case where something goes wrong and a human has to intervene. If the system is not designed so that he can understand it, his intervention is likely to be too little and too late.

THE END OF THE WORLD, ALMOST

Within an eight-month period over 1979–80, three false alerts were sent out to United States forces that the country was under attack from Soviet missiles. These alerts came from the North American Air Defense Command's control center deep inside Cheyenne Mountain, Colorado. The first was an operator error, when a data tape intended only for exercise was inadvertently fed into the system. The second was a component failure of a single integrated circuit. The third was, apparently, deliberate—an attempt to reproduce the conditions of the second as a test.[6]

Happily, the false alarms were all cancelled within a few minutes, but the nerve jangling they caused has hardly subsided yet. Clearly, a system that can literally bring about the end of our world has to be very carefully designed to avoid the possibility of misunderstanding between man and machine.

The moral in these stories is the same: as technical systems get more complicated, they become more and more difficult to understand and therefore to control. This applies especially to computing systems, which have to be complex even to do the simplest things. As we strive to give them power to handle substantial tasks from the real world, we increase their complexity to a level outside the ability of a human or even teams of humans to grasp fully. This is happening already: as we have described, large computer programs and operating systems are getting increasingly unmanageable both for their designers and their users.

If technologists carry on designing computer systems as they do now, adding more and more power to an already shaky architecture, there is little doubt that the machines of the 1990s will become unusable—uncontrollable and demoralizing—the Sorcerer's Apprentice on a global scale. Our society, which is becoming dependent on these machines, will be faced with a crisis of monstrous proportions. Computers in their present form have in a sense gone as far as they can go. No longer can they be built with the central aim of maximizing performance and making the best of machine resources. Instead, they will have to work on a totally different basis—one designed to be anthropocentric. To make computers comprehensible, we must build them in the image of the human mind.

THE INSCRUTABLE PLANET

One can take the baleful scenario very much further by recalling the view of the future that has appeared and reappeared in science fiction ever since Samuel Butler: a world being taken over by machines. This tends to be discussed by technologists as nonsense. But is it nonsense? Consider the computers that are already being used to run our cities. Include not just City Hall but the public utilities, sanitation, medical and education services, the banks, the airline system, the traffic-control system, the building and planning authority, and so on. There comes a point when their computing networks begin to talk to each other, initially for quite simple pragmatic reasons. If the road is being dug up, refuse collection must be rerouted. When someone is booking a flight, the airline needs to check the validity of his credit card.

Extend these ideas to the year 2010, when the city administration network and the medical network and the news media network and the bank network and the traffic-control network have considerable intelligence built into them so that they are smarter than people for most tasks. They also have their own radio-linked free-moving effectors. The networks are all communicating quite richly and densely with each other. Imagine then an eventual situation in which computer control networks for entire cities have their own goal setting, in which nobody can be found anymore who can understand even the documentation, let alone the systems themselves. Each person sees only one little pathway in the electronic jungle. We will then have to be certain that all evaluation functions and heuristic rules are tuned just right, because an electronic city will have to do all the normal administrative trading and bargaining with other electronic cities. Each city controls certain resources and can make certain concessions. One city wants something done about the water supply, but another's control system can make that cheap or expensive for them. In exchange, if the traffic system could be altered so that the football crowds on Saturday go by another route . . . and so forth. By the year 2500 or 3000, *Homo sapiens* could end up as a race of uncomprehending parasites, living, like fleas on the backs of dogs, in the nooks and crannies of automated cities run by giant electronic nerve networks with their own inscrutable strategies and laws of action. Worse than that, we might become a superseded species, when the dogs ask of the fleas, "What have you done for us lately?" To prevent this happening, it is not just a matter of taste but of dire necessity that technology acquire a human face and style.

THE CHAOS SCENARIO

Turning to a less cataclysmic but more immediate set of problems, let us ponder the widespread economic stagnation, soaring unemployment, and crises of confidence that have been gripping the globe ever more tightly over recent years. The phenomena are real enough, but superficially they are distinctly odd. Consider first economic growth, or non-growth. The productive capital of industrial nations is not actually shrinking. It is, however, being steadily transformed by the continuing advance of technology. What is the nature of this steady transformation? Fixed capital is getting more productive. Workers in factories can produce far more in a day than they could thirty years ago. A man can mow more meadows than are needed to offset the rental of his mowing machine. Next comes the self-piloted mower.

Moreover, technology is not merely advancing at a constant rate. All reasonable scales of measurement show it to be accelerating. So why are we not much better off? Even allowing for the inevitable disturbance that is caused in sectors immediately affected while change is taking place, the human race as a whole should be receiving substantial benefit. Something must be in the works, clogging up the cornucopia that by now we would expect to be delivering abundance to us all.

Everyone is, it seems, united in a common sense of grievance about the matter. But people differ as to which component in the whole process should be in the pillory. To some it is evident that the union bosses of our land, possibly in league with tightly knit politically motivated subversives and wreckers worldwide, have worked the whole baleful trick. To others, the master culprits are to be found in the boardrooms of the giant corporations and finance houses, possibly in league with tightly knit politically motivated multinationals and cartels, topped up with a gnome or two of Zurich. There is a third school of thought, not inflammatory like the foregoing two, but twice as loony. This school puts the blame on technology itself. It is not unknown for a frustrated user to set out systematically to punish a nonvending vending machine, not satisfied until all future capability has been removed from it.

Perhaps, though, the anti-technology school is not entirely loony. At least we should consider the idea, since the analysis given here makes technology look uncommonly like a nonvending vending machine.

We have to take a long backward look over the sweep of our history and ask whether there has been any settled evolving pattern running through it. Such a pattern does stand out. The discovery of agriculture set it going. But through the dozen millennia since then our ancestors seem to have been unaware that a unidirectional process was in train until the last phase of acceleration during the nineteenth and twentieth centuries. The consistent pattern, step by painful step, with many falterings and setbacks, has been the augmentation of man's comprehension and control of his world.

How has it come about? Without doubt through technology, leavened in recent centuries by a pinch or two of science. "Technology" is here used in its broadest sense to include all the useful arts. So if science and technology give us comprehension and control and if their power and extent are growing faster and faster, does it not follow that so too must man's mastery of his environment, including the production of wealth?

If the environment stayed put, then well and good. But comprehension and control must be measured as a ratio. Specifically, we must relate the power of our instruments for comprehending and controlling to the *complexity* of the environment to which they are to be applied. A prime consequence of the rise of technology has been that man's environment is increasingly man-made, becoming, in the nature of the whole process, more and more complex.

So let us consider the comprehension/complexity ratio. So long as the numerator is growing faster than the denominator, we are winning. If it is the other way around, then sooner or later complexity begins to be spawned faster than our ability to understand and subdue it. The change-over point was reached by industrial man at some point during the past decade. Fewer and fewer people are employed to produce. More and more are employed in the effort to keep track of what is going on.

COMPLEXITY THE CULPRIT

Unfortunately, their efforts are not doing much good. It is becoming increasingly clear that it is this very administrative complexity that is in large part to blame for our economic stagnation. Production and trade entail action, and this is blocked by complexity and confusion. If we do not understand how to operate the system, we cannot expect to get much out of it. Complexity slows things down—surely *that* is the spanner that is lodged in the works.

Again the solution becomes clear: for us to escape from complexity pollution, we must reshape technology into a form designed specifically for comprehension. We may thus be able to turn the comprehension/complexity ratio on its head.

To get an idea of how it is possible to do this, let us consider again the commodity we have already shown to be crucial to any cognitive activity—namely, knowledge. The question is, how is knowledge represented in a machine? Traditionally, in a way totally different from the way humans represent it. This has occurred for reasons of economy, or simply because technology has not accepted comprehensibility as a primary goal. Either way, the result is that while the machine may do its job satisfactorily under normal conditions, if something untoward happens, the humans around the machine will be hard put to know what to do or even to be sure whether something has gone wrong at all. A striking example can be drawn from the field of computer chess.

Why chess? Readers acquainted with research into genetics and heredity will be aware of the significance of the fruit fly *Drosophila melanogaster*. This insect's small size, fecundity, and generation cycle of only eleven days allow scientists to observe the effects of their manipulative breeding on subsequent generations without having to wait long periods and commit large floor space and funds for feeding. Chess is a problem-solving task compact enough to be embodied to a workable extent in a computer but large enough to make industrial problems of scheduling seem almost trivial. Chess has been described as the *Drosophila* of machine intelligence.

THE STRANGE CASE OF THOMPSON'S TABLE

At the meeting in Toronto in 1977 of the International Federation for Information Processing, Kenneth Thompson of Bell Telephone Laboratories presented a computer program for playing the chess end game of king and queen against king and rook. He had done this by the ultimate in "hammer and tongs" methods: in the absence of a complete set of rules for playing the end game, he had previously programmed the machine to work out what to do in every single possible position—and there were four million of them. This was done backward, by taking every position and working out what the best-move predecessor would have been. All these moves were then loaded into a gigantic look-up table in the machine's memory, each entry in the table simply saying, "If the pieces are in *these* positions, move *this* piece *there*."

It is known from the theory of chess that given best play, this end game is an inevitable win for the queen's side, except for a few special starting positions. Chess masters can ordinarily guarantee to execute the win against any opponent. So when playing with the rook, Thompson's program merely made whatever move would stave off defeat for longest. Present at the conference were two International Masters, Hans Berliner, former World Correspondence Chess Champion, and Canadian champion Lawrence Day. Thompson invited them to demonstrate winning play for the queen's side against the machine. To their embarrassment, they found they could not win, in spite of many attempts. Yet every position they were confronted with in the entire course of play was a winning one for their side.

The machine repeatedly conducted the defense in ways that to them were so bizarre and counterintuitive that they were left grasping air, time and again missing the best continuation. For example, the cardinal rule chess players learn about this end game is, "Never separate king and rook." The assumption is that the rook needs the king to help protect it from the queen. Yet the super-table separated the king and the rook again and again, having found some path, however narrow and convoluted, through the problem space that maximally postponed its supposedly inevitable doom.

Naturally, Berliner and Day found the experience upsetting. They wanted to ask the program to explain its strategy, but this of course neither it nor its author could do. The answer in every case was, "It's in the table." Its knowledge was comprehensive, but there was no representation of the knowledge in terms of goals, opportunities, risks, themes, tactical ideas, and the rest of the rich conceptual structure in terms of which chess masters frame questions and receive answers. The machine was in no position to give answers like: "At this stage white must drive the enemy king onto the edge of the board." What it was lacking was a *conceptual interface* whereby the machine and the human could share knowledge in forms that humans could grasp—namely, concepts. It is the task of knowledge engineering to design and construct such conceptual interfaces to allow people (who are still much more intelligent than machines) and machines (which are already much cleverer than people) to understand each other.

HAZARDS OF THE SUPER-TABLE

It may be said that chess is just a game. But let the reader generalize a little. Thompson's super-table is not an unrealistic example. While the search for solutions to difficult problems struggles slowly ahead, electronic technology is galloping. This has been bringing the price and physical size of computer memory down at an unheard-of pace. Trillion-bit memories are already in existence, and Lawrence Livermore Radiation Laboratories has issued specifications that call for this to be pushed up by a factor of several thousand. Optical storage promises to exceed even these scales of capacity. Such changes will inevitably tempt people to set up in such memories huge data bases of questions and answers in a very wide range of subject areas, wherever problems need to be solved. While these might appear a boon to man, they actually pose a major social hazard.

At first sight the ability to hold in a crude fashion trillions of questions paired with their answers might seem not very useful, but in fact most practical knowledge can be expressed in this form:

"What is the square of 31?" . . . "961."

"What is the right thing to do when lost?" . . . "Ask a policeman."

"What is the freezing point of the seas?" . . . "$-2°C$."

"What is the truth-value of Fermat's Last Theorem?"
. . . "Unknown."

Computer technology seeks today to move into difficult problems of the sort computers now cannot solve, problems for which there is no straightforward procedure which in a feasible number of steps can find the answer directly from the question by calculation. But it often happens that although a problem is difficult, its *inverse* is not. For instance, calculating a square root is quite involved, but finding a square is easy. So a schoolchild might consider it more economical to work out the squares of every number he or she could conceivably be asked for, and fill a huge table with the answers (listing the answers, not the questions, in numerical order, perhaps with some interpolation to fill in gaps). Then whenever a square root is needed, it is looked up in the table. This is the "inverse function method," by which Ken Thompson's chess-playing program was built. But as we saw, this technique has one major drawback—the result is inscrutable to human users.

SOCRATES AGREES

One might say that a race of blind question-answerers such as this, which so debases (by dispensing with) human understanding and judgment, would be better uninvented. Interestingly enough, this argument was first raised over 2,300 years ago by Plato. In *Phaedrus*, he has Socrates tell a story about the Egyptian god Thoth, who goes to the god-king Thamus and says: "My Lord, I have invented this ingenious thing called writing, and it will improve both the wisdom and the memory of the Egyptians."[7]

Thamus replies that, on the contrary, writing is an inferior substitute for memory and understanding. "Those who acquire it will cease to exercise their memory and become forgetful; they will rely on writing to bring things to their remembrance by external signs instead of on their own internal resources." He cites Ammon against the fallacious view that "one can transmit or acquire clear and certain knowledge of an art through the medium of writing, or that written words can do more than remind the reader of what he already knows on any given subject." In other words, men will be led to think that wisdom resides in writings, whereas wisdom must be in the mind.

"You might suppose," Socrates adds, "that written words understand what they are saying; but if you ask them what they mean by anything they simply return the same answer over and over again."

In short, Socrates's complaint is that writing fails to pass Alan Turing's famous test (by which a machine can prove it is really intelligent if it can fool a questioner, over a telephone link, into thinking he is conversing with a human being[8]). So it does fail. If it could explain what it contained, we could say in a sense it "understood," and so was showing intelligence. As writing fails the Turing Test, so too will the trillion-bit question-answerers of the future. But like writing, they will assuredly survive and help to change our world. Will this be good or bad? Unless the substance of Socrates's complaint is seriously investigated in the new context, then these giant question-answer systems will be a mixed blessing and could on occasion get their users into trouble. Such data bases, remember, store only the basic elemental unvarnished *facts* of the given case and contain nothing corresponding to understanding, inference, judgment, classificatory concepts, and the like. Truly ". . . if you ask them what they mean by anything, they simply return the same answer over and over again."

So long as the contents of the electronic super-table remain purely factual in the ordinary sense, then nothing worse is likely to result than exasperation. Infallible answers obtainable on tap, over unimaginably vast domains of discourse, will be readily accepted. But the absence of any explanations to accompany the answers will be taken by the users in bad part. "*Why*," a chemist user will say, "does this pattern from the mass spectrometer indicate that the unknown compound is some particular poly-keto-androstane?"

Answer: "Because the trillion-bit dictionary says so!"

The chemist then asks, "How does it know? How did that answer get there in the first place?" If the super-table has been constructed by the inverse function method, then even telling him *exactly* how it got there will not make him much the wiser. He and his colleagues may be goaded into building new explanatory theories of what they find in their super-tables. If so, then this is to the good and presages new pathways of scientific advance.

THE LUNATIC BLACK BOX

On the other hand, a table of question-answer pairs is not restricted to encoding factual information of this kind. The format lends itself equally well to expressing *strategies*, with the table consisting of *situation-action* pairs. This is exactly what Ken Thompson's chess program consisted of, and we have seen the problems that led to. But what if the system were doing something of social importance, such as managing a complex control function in factory automation, transport, or defense? Two supervisors, let us imagine, have the responsibility of intervening manually in the event of malfunction. The system now does the equivalent in industrial or military terms of "separating its king and rook." "Is this a system malfunction?" the supervisors ask each other. They turn to the system for enlightenment. But it simply "returns the same answer over and over again."

The problem becomes of global importance when the system being operated is in air-traffic control, air defense, or nuclear power. It is not too difficult to decide that a human decision-maker, say a policeman directing the traffic at a crossroads, is drunk or mad. But U.S. plans for air-traffic control envisage ultra-powerful data base and scheduling computations encapsulated in giant "black boxes." What will the human supervisors do on the presumably rare occasions when East Coast flights are mysteriously rerouted to Dallas or inexplicable groundings of harmless carriers raise doubts as to the system's sanity? As control devices and their programs proliferate, their computations may more and more resemble Magical Mystery Tours. Most critical of all, if an air defense warning system suddenly says, "There are twenty Russian missiles heading this way," before the officer in charge pushes the Doomsday button, he *must* be able to ask, "What makes you think that?"

Any socially responsible design for a system must make sure that its decisions are not only scrutable but *refutable*. That way, the tyranny of machines can be avoided.

There is of course a totally different method of solving difficult problems, in contrast to the use of super-tables—namely, exhaustive searching through branching trees of possibilities: "look-ahead," as in working out the outcomes of possible chess moves and choosing the best. Tables—we could call them "look-up" systems—require vast amounts of data storage but little processing. In contrast, in order for a look-ahead search to be completed in a tolerable length of time, a great deal of processing power is needed but little memory. These two extremes are shown in Figure 15.

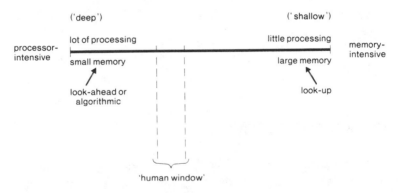

Figure 15. The spectrum of processing vs. memory

What happens when you get a pronouncement from a look-ahead system and you ask it, "Why?" Can it tell you anything? Most certainly! It can detail all the calculations it did in sequence. It can even disgorge the entire analysis tree. Could anyone wish for a more profound response?

On the contrary, no mortal mind could possibly digest so much information. The tree could contain a hundred million nodes! The Three Mile Island fiasco is to the point—the operators made *more* mistakes, not fewer, because they were deluged with alarm signals, meter readings, and computer printouts. While a look-up system is too *shallow* in that it gives too little information, a look-ahead system tends to be too *deep* in giving too much. This is a separate issue from the *power* of the system—how much it is capable of doing. This distinction is shown in Figure 16.

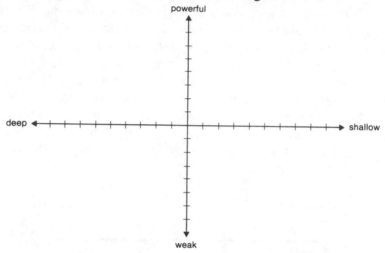

Figure 16. Two dimensions of a computer embodying an intellectual skill

THE HUMAN WINDOW

On the scale shown in Figure 15, "deep" systems are at the processor-intensive end, while "shallow" ones are at the memory-intensive end. Somewhere in between is a narrow band where both the processing capability and the scales of memory are equivalent to those possessed by humans. We call this the *human window*, and it is here that computers must operate in order to be comprehensible to us whom they are intended to serve. Both the reasoning power required and the way in which information is held must be on a human scale—elsewhere lies inscrutability.

A view we shall call *technomorphic* goes as follows: "The machine's way of going about chess or weather prediction or plant control or route scheduling is bound to be different and ought to be different. The relative costs and constraints associated with the various aspects of the problem-solving process are quite disparate for machines and brains. Strategies that optimize performance with respect to two such contrasted profiles are doomed to diverge. Whatever way is most efficient for the machine to do the problem, that's the way we want to go. If Karpov has not got the calculating speed and working memory to grow a mental look-ahead tree of a million board states or if our top meteorologists are not smart enough to be able to do partial differential equations in their heads, that is just too bad. Why should the programmer seek to copy their defects?''

From the point of view of optimizing the use of the machine, the technomorph is right. But in the light of the brain's woeful disabilities as regards storage and processing speeds, efficient machine programs are not workable as representations for people. Where the technomorph goes wrong is in supposing that there is no other criterion involved but machine efficiency.

Futurologists, in particular I. J. Good and Ed Fredkin, director of MIT's celebrated Project MAC, have speculated about the development of an ''ultraintelligent machine'' that would be able to ''reprogram itself within hours, constantly improve itself and rapidly become hundreds of times smarter than human intelligence.'' Some people are worried about this. But the real social danger, certainly the first we shall see becoming manifest, is not the ultraintelligent machine but the ultraclever machine. The dangerous system is the one tuned by economic pressures to perform its task with machine-efficient inscrutability. These machine-oriented criteria can be shown to be irreconcilable with easy communication of concepts between man and machine. So performance must be sacrificed for the sake of transparency. Is that an economically acceptable sacrifice? Surely it is. Machines continue to become cheaper; human beings on the other hand do not. Adding artificial intelligence to the machine can offer the needed humanizing bridge. But if machine optimality rather than human optimality remains the design criterion, we are ultimately headed toward a technological black hole.

SYNTACTIC SUGAR IS NOT ENOUGH

So how should we design our machines so that they fit the human window? The answer is not as straightforward as it may seem. Interactive diagnostics and trace routines, even when sprinkled with the very best syntactic sugar, do not necessarily suffice. Such things resemble orthopedic shoes built to correct a patient's rolling gait. They may help, but if his trouble stems from a congenital abnormality at the hip joints, then the patient also needs reconstructive surgery. Just as there are walkable and nonwalkable skeletal structures in human anatomy, so there are explainable and nonexplainable computations, and the differences can be traced to the respective program structures.

Putting it another way, the addition of a simple "user-friendly front end" when the subject area is very complex is like distributing powerful telescopes to inhabitants of Dover anxious to gaze upon the Eiffel Tower. To people ignorant of the curvature of the earth, it could seem like a good idea.

In order for any beings, human or machine, to talk to each other, they must share the same mental structures. People's mental structures cannot be changed, so we must change the machines'. We need to restructure the *entire way* problem-solving programs do their jobs, not just how they interact with the user. The way the program holds information—its problem representation—must be recognizable to a human as a *concept* with which he is familiar. Both Ken Thompson's table and the weather-forecasting differential equations are non-starters in this respect. Rule-based expert systems on the other hand are specifically designed to operate with human concepts, both accepting them from the domain specialist and displaying them to the user as explanations. These provide a start, but much research still needs to be done on the technology of the conceptual interface.

SOFTLY, SOFTLY AUTOMATION

The application of these ideas to factory equipment and other control systems we call "soft automation." This is increasingly needed for cleaning up the complexity pollution that hard automation tends to generate. The greatest social urgency attaches not to extending automatic processes but to *humanizing* them. Of course for tasks of low-to-middling complexity, opacity is not really a problem. We have lived with it for a long time without any ill effects. Suppose that a resource-allocation program schedules a job better than a human project director. How much desire does he feel to pry into its detailed workings or to argue with it, so long as it is doing what he wants? It can be as much of a "black box" as it chooses.

Man-machine understanding, however, acquires importance in certain applications for which an "open box" mode is mandatory. The fact that these latter are still few is a measure of the extent to which information processing has yet to penetrate into the more complex and responsible levels of human affairs. *Complex* and *responsible* correspond to separate reasons why we may insist that a program operate within the human window. Some problems are so difficult that a man-machine intellectual partnership is needed. Others involve life and death, or the manageability of the economy.

One computer program for diagnosing acute abdominal pain, entirely lacking in "explain" facilities, only continues to be used by the doctors involved through pressure from higher authority. Despite its potentially life-saving power, clinicians cannot feel confident using a black box. True expert systems such as Mycin, however, are capable of giving answers to the question "How did you work that out?"

With soft automation, systems are forced at the design stage into the human mental mold. Looking to the future when teams of cooperating robots are at work in our factories, we should ask,

"How should signals be passed between robots? Along wires, by infra-red beams, radio, or some other humanly inaccessible channel?" Synthesized voice would be better, so that human supervisors can keep an ear open for what is going on, as has been shown feasible by work at Edinburgh.

SEE THE RISING SUN

Whether or not these ideas are widely accepted in Europe and North America, they certainly are in Japan. The Japanese government has unveiled plans for a highly ambitious program to design and build a completely new range of computers for the 1990s—the Fifth Generation, as it is called.[9] These machines as projected will be able to understand natural language and speech, interpret the visual world, tap large knowledge bases, and solve problems by deductive and inductive inference. How exactly are they going to do these things? They have a few details to work out yet! However, it is clear from what the Japanese are saying that the notion of the conceptual interface is *central* to their ideas. Despite their lack of experience in intelligent knowledge-based systems up to now, they are determined to move substantially in this direction. They are even talking about the main programming of their machines being done in a "logic programming language," a technique originating from artificial intelligence work and differing radically from conventional computer languages, as we discuss in Chapter 8.

Edward Feigenbaum points out the interesting fact that the Japanese are not uncomfortable at all with the idea of intelligent machines. There are few debates in Japan agonizing over the social impact of this new technology. He suggests this is because a central part of Shintoism is reverence for objects, in which sentient beings are seen.

Be that as it may, the Japan Information Processing Development Center, as part of its exposition of the Fifth Generation program, has produced a widely circulated picture, which we reprint as Figure 17. While the diagram may seem confusing, it clearly

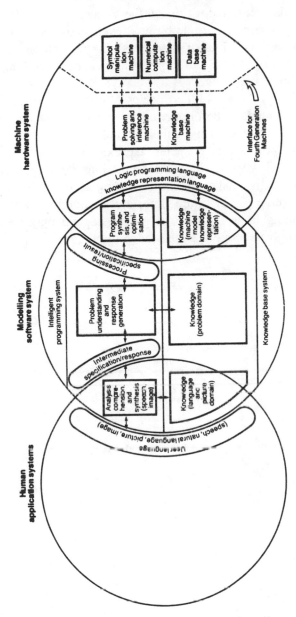

Figure 17. Conceptual diagram of the Fifth Generation Computer Systems *(After JIPDEC)*

shows the central position of the conceptual interface. Certainly the Japanese plans are ambitious, even grandiose, but in the light of that country's industrial success in other fields so far, it may be prudent for Europe and North America now to think hard about where they are going.

All over the world, certificates of humanoid mentality may one day be demanded before certain responsible tasks are entrusted to machines. Motorists have their vehicles certificated for road-worthiness. More recently, society has extended its interest beyond the question of whether the vehicle functions reliably, to the question "Does it also make an intolerable noise or emit clouds of poisonous fumes?" In future time, any computing system on whose functioning large numbers of people depend may be refused certification if its strategies are hidden in clouds of impenetrable complexity.

4

THINKING ABOUT THINKING

THE USE OF COMPUTERS to implement processes of thought has given rise to more nonsense than ever came from Bishop Wilberforce. In 1860 in Oxford, this worthy debated publicly with Thomas Henry Huxley the newly published evolutionary theories of Charles Darwin. The level of the debate can be judged from his question to Huxley as to whether he claimed descent from the monkeys through his father or his mother. Even today, children of the American Bible Belt are taught to sing:

> I ain't no kin to the monkey, no, no, no,
> And the monkey ain't no kin to me.
> I don't know much about his ancestors
> But mine didn't swing from a tree!

Regrettably, the Artificial Intelligentsia are to blame for contributing their share of nonsense. As an example, one can even find in textbooks the definition of AI referred to earlier that equates it with solution by computer of problems that would require intelligence if performed by humans. That is nonsense even now, when unintelligent computers are taking on tasks that require high orders of intelligence from human solvers. Ken Thompson's program Belle embodies little chess knowledge and no capacity at all for general reasoning, but by dint of growing a tree of several million possible future board states in its analysis of each move, it can without difficulty defeat 499 out of every 500 chess players in the world. Any one of these would surely have our sympathy were he to exclaim:

> I ain't no kin to the chess program, no, no, no,
> And the program ain't no kin to me.
> I don't know much about its thought processes
> But mine don't grow on a tree!

THE VAN DUSEN DELUSION

It is clear that the machines we build must think the way humans think. So how *do* humans think? That is a large question, but we can shed light on it by looking at some results of research into vision, speech, the way people with prodigious skills in memory and calculating seem to work, and the techniques all of us use to make sense of the world around us. Prodigies at mental arithmetic provide an interesting example. Some make a living as stage or fairground performers (or nowadays as television performers), while to others it is just a pastime. In the age of computers, human calculators are not of great economic value. The comparison with computers is apt, because most people imagine that these human prodigies have brains with the raw bit-handling capacity of at least an 80-million-instructions-per-second Cray 1 machine. This is the "van Dusen delusion," brought out by Julian Symons in reviewing the short stories of Jacques Futrelle, an American thriller writer of around the turn of the century. Futrelle's hero-detective is Professor Augustus S.F.X. van Dusen.

He is introduced to us when he refers contemptuously to chess, saying that a thorough knowledge of the rules of logic is all that is necessary to become a master of the game, and that he could "take a few hours of competent instruction and defeat a man who has devoted his life to it." A game is arranged between the Professor and the world champion, Tschaikowsky. After a morning spent with an American chess master in learning the moves, the Professor plays the game. At the fifth move Tschaikowsky stops smiling, and after the fourteenth, when van Dusen says, "Mate in fifteen moves," the world champion exclaims: "Mon Dieu!" (he is not one of those Russians who know no language but their own), and adds: "You are not a man, you are a brain—a machine—a thinking machine." [1]

To calculate a mate in fifteen moves *knowing nothing but the moves* would occupy the Cray 1 for something like 10^{30} years of continuous running, so it is hard not to feel sympathy with Tschaikowsky. Had he known more physics, Tschaikowsky would have realized that the great detective's performance was not just superhuman, but actually supernatural. Limitations of the speed of light and the atomic dimensions of matter decree that *no* machine could ever perform by brute force look-ahead calculation the feat he had witnessed, not even a "thinking machine"!

THE PUNY HUMAN BRAIN

In fact, real calculating prodigies are not particularly good at calculating. Their skill lies in the ability to assemble rapidly in their heads a calculating plan that trivializes the arithmetic needed. Their strategies are totally different from those of computers, which is hardly surprising considering that the human's calculating device is made of jelly rather than silicon. Let us take a look at some performance parameters of the brain, viewed as an information processing device. The calculating and memory capacities shown in Figure 18 are so low by present-day electronic standards as to be embarrassing.

Bearing this in mind, it must be that the virtuoso performance, whether of calculating prodigies or chess masters or any other giants of intellectual life, is built in another way, very different from the electronic—a way that compensates for man's tiny working memory and lumbering processor.

1. Rate of information transmission along any input or output channel	30 bits per second
2. Maximum amount of information explicitly storable by the age of 50	10^{10} bits
3. Number of mental discriminations per second during intellectual work	18
4. Number of addresses that can be held in short-term memory	7
5. Time to access an addressable "chunk" in long-term memory	2 seconds
6. Rate of transfer from long-term to short-term memory of successive elements of one "chunk"	3 elements per second

Figure 18. Some information processing parameters of the human brain.[2] Estimation errors can be taken to be around 50%. "Bits" refers to units of information measurement. Thus, thirty Yes-No decisions are sufficient to discriminate in a second one photographic portrait from an ensemble of a billion alternatives. The number of black-and-white dots scanned in the process is typically very much higher.

Consider, in particular, the upper limit to the quantity of information that can be acquired and stored in a lifetime. It could be argued that holding in memory a few economically coded facts and principles might suffice to generate much larger quantities of explicit information, by high-speed deduction from the initial compact form. But the fact that the brain's calculating speed amounts to a mere twenty binary discriminations per second eliminates that possibility. The rate at which we can mobilize information by calculation is of the same order as the rate at which we can take it into store directly from the outside world. It follows that our perceptions of the objects and events around us must be heavily eked out by reference to information previously taken in and stored. The meager flow of sensory data is in itself insufficient for perceptual interpretation.

SQUARES IN MEMORY

The form in which people store visual information is far from being simply a copy of the image from the retina. A great deal of analysis and coding is done. This has come out of some interesting studies made of children's drawings by Jean Piaget's school. In the course of a systematic follow-up,[3] Jean Hayes showed one 3½-year-old girl a square and asked her to copy it. What she produced is shown in Figure 19.

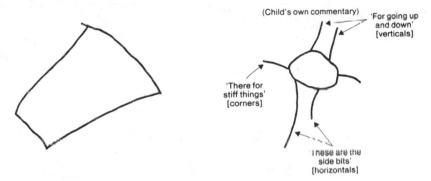

Figure 19. Copies of a square, drawn by a three-and-a-half-year-old girl

First she drew the picture on the left, which is unsurprising. But then she drew the beetlelike object on the right, which is totally unlike anything an adult would expect to represent a square. When asked to explain it, she pointed out three elements of the drawing: "Stiff things," things "going up and down," and "side bits." On further prompting she pointed these out on the original square, and it became clear that "stiff things" were the corners, things "going up and down" were the vertical sides, and "side bits" were the horizontal sides.

Why did she draw it like this? She had already shown she could make a "proper" adult-type copy, as on the left. The Piagetian explanation, which Hayes's work has confirmed, is intriguing. Presume for a moment that when we store squares in our memory, we retain not a two-dimensional image but a structural description. A semantic network of a square might be such a structure, as in Figure 20.

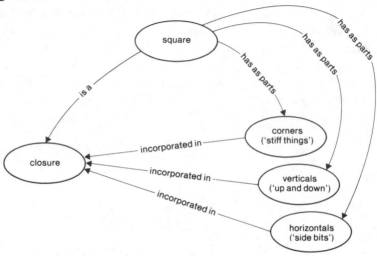

Figure 20. Semantic network of a square

The resemblance of this to the child's second drawing is distant but uncanny. It seems as though, as it were without noticing, she has for some reason on this occasion omitted the final reconstruction phase of the remembering process and is symbolizing in a graphical language the descriptive structure with which she represents squares in memory. What seems to emerge from this and other studies by psychologists is that the brain stores information according to pattern-based rules in a manner strikingly similar to the way expert systems hold their knowledge.

BOXES OF THE SPEAKING BRAIN

Certainly, the brain has special "boxes" for doing the different jobs required of it. These appear to be individually tailored for whatever function is involved, and even the most elementary forms of storage and retrieval are handled in this way. Investigators some years ago were confused by the clinical effects of brain injury on the ability to speak. This ability is lost as a result of damage anywhere in quite extensive regions of the cortex (outer layer) of the left half of the brain. It seemed that the function somehow had to be diffusely represented. More detailed analysis has refuted that conclusion. The clue is that there are many different subfunctions of speech production, from vocabulary management and sentence construction to articulatory movements of tongue, lips, palate, control of vocal chords and voice box, breathing control, and so forth. It is now established that injuries in different brain locations undermine speech production differently. So the design principle of "special boxes" is saved.

A form of "Broca's aphasia" results from highly localized injury. The patient talks like a telegram, omitting all the grammatical signposts like *the, a, up, down, by, to, in, this, of, when, is, are, will,* and so forth, and also the grammatical inflections that distinguish, say, *bite, bites, bit,* and *bitten.* Since these people seem to understand the speech of others, the condition was at first thought to be a disorder of speech production, leaving comprehension unaffected. This has now been disproved. These aphasics have their "grammar box" as totally inactivated or absent when listening as when speaking. But by inferring likely meaning from their knowledge of nouns, verbs, etc., they manage to perform plausibly on comprehension tests.

Normal brains employ different retrieval mechanisms according to whether they are handling words of the "signpost" or the substantive type. This provides us with an instance of "special boxes for special tricks." Patients with this aphasia, as expected, have only one word-retrieval mechanism and do not handle words of the first type at all—except to recognize that the words exist and belong to the language.

Color vision is another example of "special boxes for special tricks." While the color spectrum is physically no more than a continuous range of different wavelengths, it is convenient to break it down into segments for summarizing and classifying, and this is what the biological system does. We give colors names: red, yellow, green, blue, and so forth. From the point of view of a technologist building a robot with color vision, this is arbitrary, especially considering the fact that different cultures draw different boundaries between colors and that some languages have numerous color names and others have hardly any. The technologist might go ahead and design a system using color filters to break the spectrum down in a way that optimizes some parameter of engineering cost or convenience. Belatedly, he would hear of the neurophysiological discovery that the human retina has three types of color receptors, each tuned to respond to a different segment of the spectrum, corresponding broadly to "red," "green," and "purplish-blue." Ignorance of such "special boxes" may add to the technologist's difficulties when he wishes to provide for communication of color concepts between user and robot.

THE MEMORY MEN

Although the van Dusen delusion is at its most conspicuous in the matter of processing power, the onlooker tends to endow the expert's brain with equally impossible properties of storage. Just as calculating prodigies do not calculate any faster and chess masters do not analyze larger numbers of moves in the forward tree of possibilities, so the professional memory men impress large audiences without in fact having any better or worse memory than the next man. Somehow the audience convinces itself that the performer is actually storing and addressing each atomic item, just as though he had some vast trillion-bit random-access store inside his skull.

Harry Lorayne, in his *How to Develop a Super-Power Memory,* claims that anyone can acquire the same gift just by learning his mnemonic rules.[4] These center around the systematic formation of associations of pairwise linking of concepts, coupled with the use of imagined sequences of events, i.e., stories. This latter was regularly exploited by ancient Greek orators for learning speeches. The textbooks on rhetoric advised reading through the speech while perambulating accustomed terrain, for example one's house and courtyard. Each time the speech was conned, the same journey would be made, until each sentence was tagged by association with a familiar spot. When finally launched on the speech, the orator needed only to imagine himself sauntering over the route. As in his mind's eye he passed each familiar sight, the corresponding passage of text would be triggered from memory.

Ridiculous, weird, obscene, violent, and generally far-out images make the best associations. Suppose that your private mnemonic code for the first ten numbers is *"Nought* is for *sport; one* is a *bun; two* is a *shoe; three* is a *tree; four* is a *door; five* is a *hive; six* is *Weetabix; seven* is *heaven; eight* is a *date; nine* is for *wine."* Someone speaks fairly slowly the following number to you with the idea that you should recall it later: 803,735,204,381,692. The memory man's approach is to put together a rapid mental scenario as the digits are spoken, something like this: "I have a *date* with an all-in *wrestler,* but she gets up a *tree* thinking to make it to *heaven,* but falls out of the *tree* onto a bee*hive,* getting bees into her *shoe* which sting, so that she breaks the *high-jump* record through the *door* of a passing plane, which crashes on the *tree,* so I have my *date* again and start with a *bun* for the two of us with *Weetabix* and *wine,* which she pours into her *shoe* to drown the bees."

The fact that the extemporized story is violent, childish, grotesque, in bad taste, and otherwise embarrassing will prove to be its strength if some weeks from now a colleague should suddenly say, "What was that fifteen-digit number?"

"Would it have been 803,735,204,381,692?" you reply innocently as your inner eye follows the muscle-bound lady through her appalling antics.

Ed Seaman, the chief engineer of Newall Research Corporation in Saratoga, California, is inclined to ask guests on the spur of the moment to invite him to cube any number between 0 and 100. "Okay!" one will reply. "Try 73."

After a little knotting of his brows and silent mouthing Seaman comes back with "389,017."

"Well," says the guest guardedly, "I suppose that *might* be 73 cubed . . ." A calculator is eventually fetched and up comes 389,017. "How about 37 cubed?"

More screwing of the eyes and then "50,653." Ed explains, "I'm out of practice, so I'm pretty slow and probably have a few gaps. But you know the secret? It's really quite simple. I learned it from some book of magic tricks when I was in junior high school. It told about how you could memorize actually anything at all with the right mnemonics. This cube table was just one of the examples. Now I have one of God's most lousy memories, just lousy. Really. What you do, though, you have a code of sounds for each of the digits 1, 2, 3, and so on. Here, like this—" and he writes on a scrap of paper:

1 . . . T or D		6 . . . Ch or J or Sh
2 . . . N		7 . . . K or G
3 . . . M		8 . . . F or V
4 . . . R		9 . . . P or B
5 . . L		0 . . . S

"You make up words using any old vowels between these consonant sounds. Then forget the vowels. They don't matter: 37, see, can be written **S M O K** E, and that's how it was done in that old table. Never mind the leading zero, 0 3 7, right? Then we have 'Lose a chilly home,' like this:"

0 3 7 – 5 0 6 5 3
S M O K E – L O S E A C H I L L Y H O M E

The guest remarks, "But you still have to remember a hundred items, except that instead of numbers, you have all this garbage."

"Yes, but you remember the garbage. You just do . . . here, I'll show you the whole thing." Ed produces two yellow sheets from an old exercise book, written in pencil in a careful hand. Here is an excerpt:

21 hand	= punched	9 2 6 1
22 nun	= does share a vow	1 0 6 4 8
23 name	= a dandy joke	1 2 1 6 7
24 New Year	= with my fine rye	1 3 8 2 4

25 Nile	= a dull channel	1 5 6 2 5
26 wench	= took all cash	1 7 5 7 6
27 nag	= to buy each wife a home	1 9 6 8 3
28 knave	= naughty plan	2 1 9 5 2
29 knob	= no army fop	2 4 3 8 9

Entries like 30 and 40 are down simply as numbers, presumably because they give less trouble than finding phonetic equivalents.

To mention a few tricks of the trade is only to graze superficially the deeply worked territory of the memory men. But the principle is not in doubt. Their achievements, just as those of a grand master in remembering chess games of his own or others, are not attributable to the Creator's having allotted them some special hardware. Grand masters have an extraordinary power to recall briefly glimpsed chess positions, and this can seem to indicate the possession of special mental equipment. But try randomly shuffling the pieces on the board before the brief glimpse. As experiments on this have shown, when the grand master is robbed of the meaningful associations with which, for him, a chess position overflows, the gift deserts him. This is what overthrew Berliner and Day in their unsuccessful battle with Thompson's table. Their opponent's bizarre style bore no trace of the simplifying concepts that give shape to human play.

Studies by Binet and de Groot have revealed that the skills of chess masters lie in their powers of conceptualization, together with a vast accumulation of knowledge of past games and positions.[5] Nor do they look ahead more than ordinary players: according to de Groot, six or seven half moves tends to be the limit, with a total of perhaps thirty positions considered on the look-ahead tree. According to legend, the great Richard Reti dramatized the true pattern-based nature of grand-masterly skill when he was asked how many moves ahead he looked in tournament play. "One," he replied. "The right one!"

GRAND MASTER OF ARITHMETIC

So too with mental-arithmetic prodigies, the most celebrated of whom was Alexander Aitken, the senior professor of mathematics at Edinburgh University who died in 1967. His extraordinary powers were investigated by the psychologist Ian Hunter, who recalls Aitken's account of how he carried out a problem given to him by his children: multiply 987,654,321 by 123,456,789.

> I saw in a flash that 987,654,321 times 81 equals 80,000,000,001; and so I multiplied 123,456,789 by this, a simple matter, and divided the answer by 81. Answer: 121,932,631,112,635,269. The whole thing can hardly have taken more than half a minute.[6]

How on earth could he have seen these things "in a flash?" Hunter explains that Aitken's knowledge of and familiarity with the number system was simply very much larger than most people's. While the average person if shown the number 22 would be conscious of it being 2 times 11, Aitken, on the other hand, when coming across 1,961 immediately thought of it as 37 times 53, and 44 squared plus 5 squared, and 40 squared plus 19 squared. This power to apprehend attributes in a flash, reminiscent of a grand master's glimpse of a chess position, was the basis of what Hunter called the "first phase." Aitken's response to a problem was divided into two phases. During the first, he was occupied with rummaging around in his huge internal library of facts and useful tricks concerning the number system so as to put together a "calculative plan." During the second phase, he executed the plan by doing the specified calculations in sequence. But this he did no faster than anybody else would have done, as was apparent from how fast he spoke the digits of the solution. So calculation itself is not where the calculating prodigy's genius lies. Rather, it is knowledge. Program synthesis, not the program, is at the heart of the matter.

BELIEVING THE UNLIKELY

The White Queen admonished Alice to believe six impossible things every day before breakfast. It sounds difficult but actually is not. You just have to be careful to choose things that many other people already believe, such as that Brand X washes whiter than white. The hard thing to believe is not the impossible but the unfamiliar. This is the meaning of the story about the old lady at the zoo seeing a giraffe for the first time.

When she said, "I don't believe it!" she was obviously not complaining that the animal in front of her was *impossible.* Her difficulty lay in finding a way of fitting the apparition into her existing knowledge about the world. Even the addition of new information to memory is conditioned by what is already there. We all know of cases where someone is presented with an irrefutable fact, but he fails to grasp or even to remember it because it contradicts something he already presumes to be true. People say of such a case, "There are none so blind as those who will not see!" but they miss the point. Unless a compatible body of preexisting belief is already present to provide "hooks," so to speak, to which the new item can be attached, chances of assimilation are slim. Even with "seeing," unless large bodies of visual knowledge have already been amassed, a man in possession of healthy eyes will not "see" what is in front of him.

Partly, these problems of perception and belief are no more than the difficulty of filing things before you have established file categories for them. Partly they may be related to the fact that our species evolved in slow-changing environments that put a low premium on the ability to assimilate drastically new experience. It is not only belief and memory that are disabled if mental models are not appropriate. Comprehension itself, which should be the taproot of remembering and believing, can utterly fail, however simple the basic facts seem to be.

THE LURE OF SIMPLICITY

If the facts are *not* simple, however, a whole new game is joined. To make sense of a complex world, the mind needs to simplify. This is not an example of the perversity of human beings—the simplifications are essential for the mortal mind to handle complexity. The simplifying slogans produced are inevitably distortions of reality: they can range from minor distortions to downright lies, depending on the case. "When defending with king and rook against king and queen," says the chess master, "always keep king and rook together," and he does not err. Although not always necessary, this rule cannot do harm. But the assertion "With king and knight against king and rook, keep king and knight together," although widely believed, is sometimes wrong.

At no time are the mind's simplifications more active than when under stress or emotion. Some years ago at a crowded departmental seminar at Oxford, the audience sat thunderstruck as the reader in cytology, John Baker, attacked the seminar speaker, Dr. J. B. Rhine. The latter was founder and director of the Institute of Parapsychology at Duke University, North Carolina, later to be tarnished by the departure of its deputy director caught in a flagrant scientific fraud. But even at that early date Baker, a passionate scientific rationalist, felt that there was a rat to be smelled somewhere.

Gray-suited and manicured, Rhine sauvely parried each thrust, scattering a largess of cute remarks. So might one seek with parasol and peanuts to deflect the rhinoceros. John Baker, his voice a clarion, returned to the charge: "When Galileo dropped his balls from the Leaning Tower of Pisa—" It was enough. The audience had been stretched on the rack too long. With a shout of laughter the hall exploded. No one, least of all the normally meticulous Baker, noticed that he had it wrong anyway. Galileo did not drop his or anyone else's balls. He rolled cannonballs down an inclined plane. Baker had momentarily simplified by confusing this with a weight-dropping demonstration made earlier by the Dutch engineer Stevinus.

When simplifications reside in the phenomena themselves and can without cheating be conjured forth, there lies the gifted experimenter's greatness. Foucault's *coup de théâtre* in 1851 with a pendulum strung from the ceiling of the Paris Panthéon was of this kind. The demonstration can now be seen in most of the world's science museums. A brass ball, set swinging in a straight traverse, progressively knocks down a circle of sand on the floor. As the earth rotates beneath it, so the pendulum's swing by insensible shifts changes direction relative to the ground and in the course of a day or more, depending on latitude, moves through the complete 360°.

"Aha!" we say. "Of course!" and then "Beautiful!" Such is the lure of simplicity.

EPISTEMIC ILLUSIONS

But in pursuit of this lure our minds are prepared to tell us the most extraordinary lies. Some of the best known of these are the optical illusions, among which Richard Gregory has characterized a wealth of self-deception.[7] These are, however, merely a special case of a broader class of "epistemic illusions." These occur whenever we unconsciously falsify in order to understand. Faced with complex material—the history of science, for example—we tend, whatever the cost to accuracy, to file facts by stereotype. There is no better illustration than certain aspects of the Galileo story.

Galileo is remembered as a rational and honest mind standing courageously against church bigotry and the dark forces of the Inquisition. This scenario acts as a summarizing anecdote, a soothing mnemonic for overloaded minds. It is, after all, historical fact that the new astronomical physics encountered theological opposition. Rather than memorize such a dry abstraction, can we peg it to a good story?

In his marvelous book *The Sleepwalkers,* Arthur Koestler marshals the documents in the case. They tell quite a different tale, of an abrasive prima donna bent on provoking a mild and sophisticated Vatican intelligentsia into confrontations in which he could shine. How little these mature and cultivated men were concerned to muzzle the voice of reason may be judged from an excerpt from the correspondence of the Pope's leading theologian of the day. In a letter written in 1615, Cardinal Bellarmine, who was to issue against Galileo the admonition of 1616, stated:

> . . . for to say that the assumption that the Earth moves and the Sun stands still saves all the celestial appearances better than do eccentrics and epicycles [of the Ptolemaic system] is to speak with excellent good sense and to run no risk whatever. Such a manner of speaking suffices for a mathematician.[8]

And again:

> . . . if there were a real proof that . . . the Sun does not go round the Earth but the Earth round the Sun, then we should have to proceed with great circumspection in explaining passages of Scripture which appear to teach the contrary, and we should rather have to say that we did not understand them than declare an opinion to be false which is proved to be true. But I do not think there is any such proof since none has been shown to me . . .

As the Vatican astronomers were aware, Galileo had no proof.

In the short term he temporized by pretending that his critics would be too stupid anyway to understand his proofs. In the longer term his campaign culminated in the publication in 1632 of his *Dialogue on the Two Principal World Systems,* which finally precipitated his trial. In this work he pressed into the service of proof a wholly fallacious theory of the tides, pouring scorn at the same time on Kepler's view that they were to do with the moon. It is hard not to reverse the labels "reason" and "bigotry" that tradition has assigned to the two sides. Yet false tradition prevails because the truth so often has awkward corners. Why not make the jigsaw easier with a little sandpapering?

At least now there is no doubt about the scientific content of the Galileo story. Turning to a more recent and much more complicated issue, namely, the theory of relativity, we find that distortion is universal. Virtually every author who has tried to tackle the subject has got it wrong—and not just the history, but the substance as well. They write that in 1887 Michelson and Morley in an attempt to detect the "ether drift" obtained a null result, and this led Einstein to devise the Special Theory of Relativity. Michael Polanyi points out that in fact Michelson and Morley did *not* get a null result, and in any case Einstein had never heard of them when he first formulated his ideas.[9] Despite this, the legend continues.

It is "well known" that Abraham Lincoln was a dedicated crusader against slavery whose Emancipation Proclamation in 1863 freed the slaves. In fact, he was not and it did not.[10] Returning to our time, it is widely thought that advances in the technology of computers and data banks provide opportunities for the wholesale violation of the privacy of individuals which our existing structure of laws is powerless to combat, but which will succumb to a wholly new type of "data protection" legislation. They don't, it isn't, and it won't.[11] But still, this is a field that is so complicated as to present rather special obstacles to the task of dealing with it rationally.

MACHINES WILL HAVE TO LIE, TOO

While it is easy to scoff at the efforts of mortals to come to grips with complexity, one must realize that many simplifications are an essential part of dealing with life and that therefore cognitive science needs to understand them. When machines start to deal with very complex issues, they will have to lie for the same reason that humans do, namely, to make problems manageable and explainable. This is inevitable, but it also raises dangers in that lies can be harmful. Mechanisms will be needed to keep such "approximations'' within a reasonable distance of reality and generally watch over their consequences. We will need a mathematical theory of lying.

Suppose that we have a network of intelligent machines that have to cooperate with each other. Imagine a group of automation robots in a factory that are to some degree specialized—one does the paint-spraying, another welds, one rivets, and so forth. For each knowledge base that each robot has, there will be a part that for reasons of economy is common to all the robots. The common part might include facts about the workbench. Not all the robots will need exactly the same facts or the same emphasis. Obviously, if one robot works on top of the bench it may be easier for it if, like the ancients who believed that there was nothing on the other side of the world, it does not believe that there is any world beyond the bench top. That is a kind of myth, and there is no point whatsoever in the robot having in its knowledge base the information that it *is* a myth. The supervisory robot might as well let it believe the myth and save memory. The attempt to imagine control systems for cooperating intelligent devices, even at the mundane level of the assembly line, is brought up against something that we knew already but have not hitherto thought important. This is the fact that if we want to influence inanimate matter in a highly predictable way, then we have physics to tell us how to do it. But suppose that the object we want to influence is itself an information processing system, a human being. Then we may *either* seek to influence the system's actions like a military general by issuing imperatives, *or* we may make assertional statements, having a good enough model of the target system to know that these will have the same effect as the imperatives, but in some circumstances will act more quickly and cheaply.

Consider as an example the economy practiced by the British road-sign authorities. A typical sign at a traffic circle is shown in Figure 21 (the drive is on the left). Everybody instantly interprets the sign as saying: ''When you get onto the circle, go clockwise.'' But that is not actually what the picture says. It presents its viewer with an *assertion,* namely that there is a defect, a gap in the road, and this is a lie. Strictly speaking it is a joke lie, since there is no intent to deceive. But those who invented the sign have a good enough model of the motorist to know: first, that if he believes it, he will go around to the left; second, that if he does not believe it and knows it to be false, he will be subtle enough to perform an additional inference and realize that the *intention* is to give him an imperative.

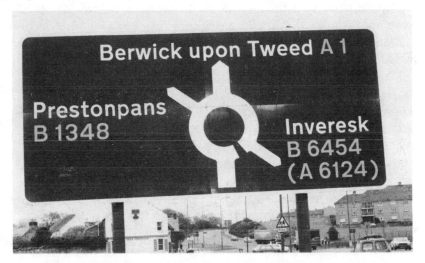

Figure 21. Scheme used in road signs to indicate required direction around a traffic circle. Strictly, the depicted defect in the road is a lie, but the motorist understands what is required of him. *(Photo: John Wilkie)*

The same phenomenon is exemplified when parents tell children absurd untruths, as politicians also do voters, on the hypothesis that this is the easiest way to get them to do something or not to do something: "It will make you sick!" meaning, "Don't eat it!" in the private knowledge that it will *not* make the child sick. Like the motorist, the child usually knows this too. But because time is too short either to have a clash of wills or alternatively to explain the real reasons, this shortcut is tried—and it is in assertional language.

Hence, we will be obliged to devise an economics of lying. Presumably, lying has arisen following regular economic laws of costs and benefits. Presumably, we shall be bound by the same laws to construct analogues in intelligent machines.

MYTHS FILL THE GAPS

Myths perform a function in society related to lies. Wherever there are complex systems, there will always be incomplete information. Computer programmers know this well, and their systems include default values for those items where information is essential but has not been specified by the user. So with society: religions offer mental "slot fillers," but there are also gaps in the religions' explanatory or predictive powers. Myths are made to plug these gaps. Cognition always confronts a dilemma. We feel that explanations and predictions should be rationally grounded. Yet—presumably for good evolutionary reasons—we cannot leave the matter alone. When we lack rational grounds to explain or predict, we fill in if necessary with irrational grounds. For example, in an agricultural community we ask: "When will it rain?" We feel better if we plug vacant slots with made up explanations. It will rain if the god becomes well disposed. At least we can then try to do something about it (by performing a rain dance perhaps). For some temperaments, this is the important consideration.

Much depends on the habitual mood of the given community—whether for example its tradition is of an effortful, goal-seeking type. At one end of a spectrum is the American work-oriented paradigm, anxious for achievement, anxious for explanation. At the opposite end lies a society like the Tikopia, a community living in the Pacific in idyllic circumstances.[12] When anthropological study began, there was no sign that this little community of two thousand people had changed in recorded time. Most of their interests centered around gossip, making love, dancing, preparing the midday meal—on which they spent hours—and sometimes a little exploration. Their life was healthy and, by our standards, we would say happy. It approximated more closely than one would think possible to Rousseau's idea of the Noble Savage.

But when members of such idyllic communities are asked *why* things happen—things that to us, who weave our mental lives very tightly out of causality, seem to require explanation—they tend to give fanciful reasons that can be caricatured as follows:

"Why does the sun go down in the sea every day?"
"It's a big red bird and it wants to go back to its nest."
"Ah! But if it is a big red bird seeking its nest, then why doesn't it stay there? It comes out of the sea the next morning from the other side!"

Having thus revealed an entirely wrong mental approach, the questioner may now be requited with something like, "The bird goes where he goes and knows what he knows!" or (ultrasophisticated), "Well, maybe the sun isn't a big red bird, then!" These are reasonable attitudes for happy men.

Robots will need myths for the same information-processing purposes that humans need them. We take a myth to be a belief that is treated as certain knowledge, and felt desirable that it should be, by some group of interacting information systems. It can sometimes be better to run along with a set of false hypotheses *as though* they were true, if they are quick and computationally cheap. The myth designer will say, "Kindly specify what tasks this machine must do and how far out of its depth, in terms of computational complexity, it has to operate." Empty belief-slots, in both robots and humans, must be plugged with default values.

Certainly the need for machines to operate with myths and lies will present problems to technologists and society alike. But at the same time it may be that computer extensions of human powers of thought and memory will lessen our own dependence on stereotypes for the sake of comprehensibility. Being able to handle more complex systems of information, we may learn to resist the lure of simplicity, the sandpapering of awkward corners. Fewer epistemic illusions, more command of detail: we may yet come to cherish the multifold corners of things as they are.

5

EXPERIENCE AND DISCOVERY

ONE OF THE STRANGE SOUNDS of the semiconductor age is the elder's lament for the death of arithmetic. Schoolchildren no longer know of the existence of certain sacred motions by which we, and our fathers' fathers, were taught to extract the square root. Instead, we see the touch of a button on a hand-held calculator. Just as passive gazing on pornography is believed by cautious souls to deprave and corrupt the senses, so, it is feared, may access to instant sums pervert the intelligence.

There is something that the elder may overlook. In his own world, whether he works on the shop floor, on the Queen's Bench, in the executive suite, in the computer room, or down on the farm, the delegation of detail invariably goes hand in hand with the expansion of powers. What prize-winning architect bothers to learn how to cast a concrete beam so long as he can recognize a badly cast one? When dealing with complexity, the lazy way is the best way. In trying to automate some complicated mechanical or intellectual task, the smartest thing of all is to make the outside world do the calculations for you.

An example comes from the Charles Stark Draper Laboratories in Massachusetts, a leading center for research into computer-controlled assembly. Like everyone who has looked at the problem, the engineers there are much exercised by close-fitting parts. The human worker slaps these into place with speed and abandon. An industrial robot attempting this runs into every kind of wedging and jamming. We can, of course, compute lots of little feedback loops. Instead, the project director, Jim Nevins, asked, "Is there any mechanism that can substitute for these and that can be sited in the external world, not in the computer?"

The answer seems by hindsight obvious. The human assembly worker, in addition to feedback adjustments computed in his nervous system, is also aided by mechanical compliance provided by the resistant softness of fingertips and the "give" of joints. Accordingly, Nevins wondered whether such compliance could be so extended as to substitute entirely for the need for feedback computations. He now has all parts mounted so as to "give" a little along two of the three spatial axes. Behold, in fractions of a second, square pegs slide smoothly into square holes, round into round, just as if millions of tiny feedback adjustments to a rigid system were being continuously computed.

TOP-DOWN VERSUS BOTTOM-UP

There have always been two ways of solving problems. One, which we shall call "top-down," is based on *theory*. It requires that we understand the fundamental principles by which something operates so that we can work out logically the consequences of any actions and so predict the future. The other method, "bottom-up," works without any grand explanatory schemes, possibly without any understanding at all, but rather with various compilations and catalogues of know-how. The bottom-up practitioner may well say, "I don't know why it works—I just know that it *will* work."

Both of these approaches have their uses. When launching a rocket to the moon, it is no good hoping that the astronauts will be able to navigate by trial and error. They only get one try. It is vital to know beforehand the orbital mechanics of the celestial bodies involved, and plan accordingly. On the other hand, a child learns to ride a bicycle without first studying Newtonian dynamics or modern control theory. How does he do this? He uses empirical *rules*, albeit in this case unconscious ones but rules nevertheless, working in conjunction with the outside world. The basic rule, held in his brain's sense-of-balance mechanism, is "If the bicycle is tipping to one side or the other, turn the handlebars in that direction." There is no mention of Newton—no explanation of why it works, but it does.

In contrast, if a computer using Newtonian theory were to ride a bicycle, then in a sense two bicycles would be in play, the real-world bicycle and a ghostly bicycle implicit in the detailed mathematical model used by the control algorithm. The human cyclist's philosophy is that one bicycle is enough and that sensory data can be used to extract from moment to moment the few relevant state-features needed for a simple and sufficient set of decision rules. Between successive rule-invocations the real bicycle computes the dynamics, and the rules, laid down in the form of reflex stimulus-response bonds, do the rest. Pity the computer, doing it the hard way. Indeed, a project was started at the Aeronautics and Astrophysics Laboratory at Stanford University to program a computer to control a bicycle by physical theory, and it was abandoned as too difficult.

As technology comes to deal with more and more complex problems, problems that are less and less understood from first principles, it is essential to be able to operate as the child does, without an explanatory theory. Even when one does have a theory, using it can run foul of the combinatorial explosion in trying to work out every possibility, as we have seen. Rule-based systems, on the other hand, offer an alternative of great potential. Indeed, these have already become established as fundamental to expert systems, as has been shown.

BUILDING A ROBOT OUTFIELDER

An illustrative fancy: we wish to design a robot baseball player. The device must stand in the outfield until the batter flies a ball in its general direction. The robot's task is then to plot and follow an appropriate interception course.

Solution 1: Take successive sightings of the ball on the fixed retina. Use geometry, trigonometry, and statistical curve-fitting to extract a trajectory, eked out by optical range-finding. Extrapolate to the expected point of descent. Move at top speed the calculated distance to this point. Halt. Await impact. *Verdict:* Much computation, little certainty of outcome owing to incomplete information and errors of measurement.

Solution 2: As above, but move to the expected impact point in a succession of springs, repeating the above computation from scratch at each halt. *Verdict:* Improved outcome, but even more work.

Solution 3: Take time off to watch a human outfielder.

According to the late Seville Chapman of Cornell Aeronautical Laboratory, the human uses a simple rule. He moves toward the ball, continuously adjusting speed and direction and moving the head at the same time, so that his line of sight to the ball is uniformly rising. For approximately parabolic trajectories, this rule suffices. The details of the trajectory, which in windy weather may be quite complicated, are left to the external physical system to work out, assisted, according to Peter Brancazio of Brooklyn College, by the brain's monitoring of the changing tilt of the head through signals from the organs of the inner ear. Solution 3 achieves exquisite accuracy for almost no computational work. The lucky robot is left with spare thinking capacity for the higher theory of baseball.

In the same vein, children who sensibly push the labors of school arithmetic into the electronic box have their energies freed for better things, like saving up for a hand-held programmable with which to do more interesting work. This is not to say that children should not learn their "times" tables. They should, and will continue to learn them regardless of the pocket calculator, if only to be able to judge whether an answer is in the right ballpark as a guard against keying errors. Although long multiplication and division will probably not drop from the syllabus, it must be conceded that skill in these procedures will decline. Children will spend more time on the new skill of programming. So the education process has to lose a little to gain a lot.

LEARNING BY EXPERIENCE

There is another notable aspect to the child's bicycle riding apart from the absence of theory, namely, the way he learned the skill. No one told him the rule "If the bike is tipping . . ." His learning was entirely by *experience*. We have seen how the major problem obstructing the growth of expert systems is the cumbersome work of acquiring the expertise—encoding the rules. What we need is for computers to be able to learn from experience too.

An example of how this is possible is a program developed at Edinburgh in the early days of machine intelligence, which taught itself how to balance a pole. This is a classic problem in the design of control systems. A small electric cart running on rails carries a pole hinged at the bottom (Figure 22). The cart has to move back and forth to keep the pole balanced, like a Scotsman in the first stage of tossing the caber. In addition, the cart must not run off the end of the track. First-year students of mechanical engineering build systems to do this with complex analogue circuitry. Computer programs using control theory can do it, but not very economically. In contrast, the Edinburgh program, called Boxes, worked entirely bottom-up, using 225 rules that were adjusted by the program in the light of experience. Data on four parameters was collected from the mechanism: position of cart, velocity of cart, angle of pole, and rate of change of angle. The ranges of these were divided up and laid out in a four-dimensional "state space," with each local region watched over by a separate rule (or "demon," to use the now-fashionable term coined by Oliver Selfridge in 1959) that accumulated its own private store of knowledge of what to do in those particular circumstances. The whole system worked on the "Committee of Experts" principle, with a Chairman (central control routine) inspecting each input state and calling on the appropriate rule (Figure 23).[1]

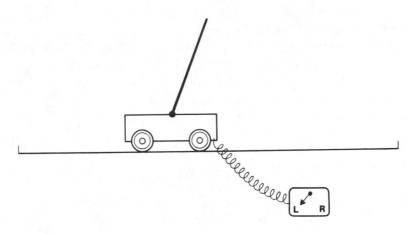

Figure 22. The pole-and-cart apparatus

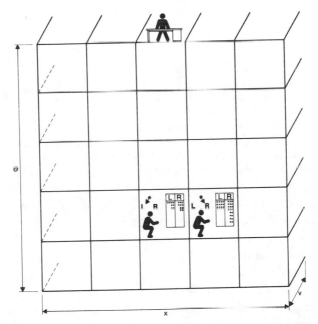

Figure 23. The state space of the pole-and-cart program (for clarity, omitting the fourth dimension) divided up into boxes, with a separate rule ("demon") in each box and a Chairman supervising

A situation might take such a form as "cart near left-hand end of track, cart moving to the right, pole moderately inclined to the right, pole swinging to the left." Once invoked, the rule would prescribe a burst of power from the motor either to the left or to the right, and a new input state would be generated. The collective expertise of all the rules put together determined the quality of the system's performance. At the start of a learning series, the "left" and "right" decisions were set at random over the total of 225. As the program went along, it modified the rules according to their success rates and, with accumulating experience, learned to perform as an expert pole-balancer (Figure 24).

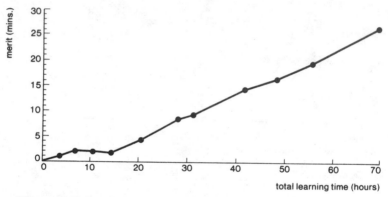

Figure 24. Progress of the pole-and-cart system in trial-and-error learning. "Merit" is the time-until-crash, plotted against total accumulated learning time, e.g., 27 minutes of balancing after 70 hours of learning.

In problems of this general category, some regions of the space exhibit markedly counterintuitive features, as when the cart wanders dangerously near the "precipice" at the end of the track. In a proportion of cases, according to the values of pole angle and angular velocity, the solution is to drive initially *toward* the precipice, so as to impart a swing of the pole away from it. Only then can it be safe to direct the motor away from the danger area, "chasing the pole" with proper control over its angle.

The rules could have been derived symbolically from a detailed mathematical model, although that would have required an exact and exhaustive specification of the system's physical parameters. In a real-life situation these might or might not be available. Instead, they were assembled piecemeal from the system's own operational experience. Similarly, the outfielder has extracted from experience the simple rule that keeping his line of sight to the ball moving upward at a constant rate will cause them both to arrive at the same place at the same time.

LEARNING BY EXAMPLE

Boxes acquired its rules in a slow and crude way. What is needed is a much more powerful, universally applicable system. We want to be able to show a computer examples of things, be they statements of fact, pictures, sample actions, or what have you, and have it by a process of logic discover rules that connect these—finding patterns amid apparent chaos. Only this way can the bottleneck of encoding rules for expert systems be overcome. Apart from facilitating the construction of expert systems, other benefits would accrue.

Working out rules from examples is the classical process in logic of *induction*—inferring from the particular to the general, as opposed to *deduction*, which is reasoning from the general to the particular. Traditionally, computing has been based around deduction, working through a process exactly specified beforehand, and it is a large step to turn to the messier, less theoretically complete process of induction. Is it possible for computers to induce? Experiments over the last few years have shown that indeed it is. We will describe some examples.

The rule-devising game is nicely conveyed by the following test, from a tutorial devised by Ryszard Michalski and James Larson.[2] Looking at Figure 25, find the best rule you can that accurately distinguishes the trains going east from the trains going west. (Presumably they have not yet left the depot, so we cannot just use a compass!) There is not necessarily a unique best solution, but highest marks go to the rules that are in some sense simplest.

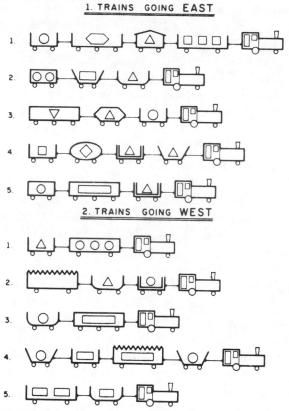

Figure 25. Find the simplest rule to distinguish "trains going east" from "trains going west." *(Copyright © 1980 IEEE)*

Michalski and Larson's Pascal program succeeded very well in finding rules to solve this puzzle. To start with, the program had to be given descriptions of all the trains in a language that it could handle. This was a simplified version of first-order predicate calculus, a symbolic representation of logic. It works rather like algebra. The calculus consists of variables, which stand for propositions that may be true, false, or sometimes unknown; connectives that link these, such as *and, or, not, implies,* etc.; a bracketing convention; and the quantifiers *for all* and *there exists.* Together, these comprise a tool of great power and generality: virtually any interpretation can be substituted for the variables.

The trains were described to the program in terms of eleven descriptors for the cars and their freights, such as:

infront   (this car is in front of what other car)
length   (car is long or short)
car-shape   (open rectangle, U-shaped, ellipse, jagged top, etc.)
cont-load   (car contains what load)
load-shape   (either: circle
                        triangle
                        rectangle   polygon)
                        hexagon
nrpts-load   (number of parts in car's load)
nrwheels   (number of wheels on car)

From these, the program was able to work out more selectors, such as the number of cars in a train and the positions of each car. It then proceeded to make up generalizations about the trains, using "metaselectors" built from the information given, some more promising than others. It would form the generalizations into a sequence of "partial stars" and work through these, weeding out inconsistencies until it came up with a complete rule. It could judge the simplicity of a rule by counting the number of elements in it. (The preference for simplicity is known in experimental science as "Occam's razor": the principle that given two theories of apparently equal merit, the simpler one is to be preferred.) Before seeing what rules the program induced, the reader could try developing one or two for himself.

The first rule the program produced looked like this:

$\exists \, car_1 \, [length(car_1) = short] \, [car\text{-}shape(car_1) = closed \, top]$
$::>[class = Eastbound]$

Translated out of the logical language, this means:

(1) *If a train contains a car that is short and has a closed top, then it is eastbound, else it is westbound.* *

*A more literal translation would be: *The truth of the statement "There exists a car_1 such that the length of car_1 equals short and the shape of car_1 equals closed top" implies the truth of the statement "The class of train is eastbound."*

Two more rules produced by the program:

(2) *If a train contains a car whose load is a triangle, and the load of the car behind is a polygon, then it is eastbound, else it is westbound.*

(3) *If there are two cars, or if there is a jagged-top car, then westbound, else eastbound.*

It is interesting to note that Michalski constructed the test with rules (2) and (3) in mind. The machine's rule (1), simpler than either of the others, came as a surprise to him.

A trial of this puzzle was run with human subjects, and out of a total of 72 attempts, 44 hit on rule (3) and six others offered a version of this rule based on counting axles rather than cars. Surprisingly, only three entries corresponded to rule (1), the simplest of all. A fourth entry could be scored as (1) except that the various kinds of short closed cars were separately listed instead of being given as a single description! No entries coincided with (2), but some were at least as terse, such as: *If there are more than two kinds of freight, then eastbound, else westbound,* produced by two subjects.

MACHINE VERSUS MAN

How do we compare the efficiency of the Pascal program running on a CDC Cyber 175 with the ponderings of human subjects? Computation time was around ten seconds. The Cyber can be credited with approximately 10 million instructions per second, making a total outlay of 100 million instruction-executions. According to J. M. Stroud, the number of binary discriminations per second that the human brain can manage at a sprint is about twenty.[3] Although Edsger Dijkstra was once clocked at fifty per second for a three-minute burst of program writing, for lesser mortals an average of ten per second can probably be assumed. Let us hazard that one instruction-execution of the Cyber 175 is worth at least ten binary discriminations. If this be so, then the Michalski-Larson program required a total of 10^9 binary discriminations, the equivalent of thinking continuously for one hundred million seconds—that is, three years of uninterrupted mental effort. So readers who polished off the problem in seconds or minutes are well ahead of the computer in their algorithms (whatever they may be) for inductive logic, although not in their ability to represent the processes explicitly.

Children have more difficulty in inventing rules. Even at age ten, the transition from judging everything by its concrete circumstances to an ability to cope with abstracts and hypotheticals has only just begun. Readers might like to try their children on their ability to understand the train problem.

An interesting feature of the first two rules is that a program knowing nothing about counting could still have gotten them. At the other extreme, one subject who was bitten by the counting bug found that the number of sides in the cargo (circle counts 1, triangle 3, etc.) is a divisor of 60 if and only if the train is going west!

We sometimes forget what an elaborate trick counting is. "At first thought," writes Levi Conant, "it seems quite inconceivable that any human being should be destitute of the power of counting beyond 2. But such is the case; and in a few instances languages have been found to be absolutely destitute of pure numeral words."[4] Counting is entirely an invention of relatively advanced civilizations—it is not intrinsic in man or beast. Interestingly enough, though, man and some birds and insects have a "number sense" that enables them to appreciate the size of a collection up to four or five *without counting*. Lichtenberg gave his nightingale three meal-worms a day, one at a time, and remarked that after the third it knew the meal was over. Crows have exhibited the ability to distinguish between three and four, but not between four and five, while wasps have an uncanny way of sensing the number of the grubs they are doling out to their young.[5] But Clever Hans, the counting horse, had no such ability, despite his owner's faith. The horse's art consisted in reading his master's involuntary signs when the preset number was reached.

ELEUSIS AND THE SEARCH FOR TRUTH

The Australian aborigine system of "One, Two, Many" works well for a variety of purposes. It certainly suffices for all normal situations in Robert Abbott's rule-guessing game of Eleusis. As a psychology student at the University of Colorado, Abbott became interested in the "Aha!" reaction—that flash of insight in which we grasp the underlying principle behind some messy-looking phenomenon. Eleusis is a card game for four or more players, one of whom is designated as God. The other players lay down cards on the table in turn. God has thought up a secret rule to govern the sequence in which cards should be laid, and as each card is played, he announces whether it is "right" or "wrong." The other players try to work out what the rule is by trial-and-error guesswork through the cards they put down.[6]

Correct cards are laid in a straight line across the table and incorrect ones on side lines. When a player thinks he knows the rule, he can declare himself to be a "prophet" and take over God's functions, judging the subsequent moves of other players. But woe betide false prophets! Examples of reasonable rules could be:

(1) *The number of a card must differ from the previous one by 1, 2, or 3.*

(2) *If the last legally played card was black, play a card of equal or higher value. If the last card was red, play a card of equal or lower value.*

Rules must deal only with the sequence of cards, not with anything external to them, such as the sex of the last player or whether God scratches his ear. The opening of a typical round is shown in Figure 26: the rule for this is at the bottom of the page.

Rule for the depicted sample round: *If the last legally played card was odd, play a black card. Otherwise play a red one.*

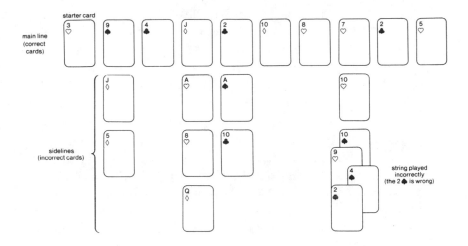

Figure 26. A typical round of Eleusis at an early stage *(After Scientific American)*

What the players are doing of course is induction. In 1977, Abbott himself described attempts to get a computer to play Eleusis as "doomed to failure." How wrong he was has been shown by James Larson, who developed a program for his master's thesis at the University of Illinois, and by Michael Berry, of I. P. Sharp Associates, who did the same as an exercise in the mathematical programming language APL. Berry's program plays alongside humans, so their moves need to be conveyed to it by typing them in on the keyboard, together with God's judgments on them and on the machine's moves.[7] The program looks for sequences and alternations in the attributes of the cards (suit, color, and number) and in sub-attributes (parity, primeness, divisibility by three, etc.). The standard patterns that all these fit make it relatively easy for the program to construct an English-language version of the rule when it has been found, a paraphrase, but a readily recognizable one, of the way God would put it. For instance, in the case of example (1), given above, it would say,

THERE IS ALWAYS A CHANGE OF NUMERIC VALUE. NO CARD
DIFFERS FROM ITS PREDECESSOR BY MORE THAN 3.

Martin Gardner has pointed out that Eleusis is an excellent
model of "a search for truth," and of induction, "the process at
the very heart of the scientific method." So success by computers
at playing it has implications far broader than the world of games.
To take an example from a serious academic discipline, we look at
discovery in pure mathematics.

EUCLID REDISCOVERED

At the Stanford Heuristic Programming Project, Douglas Lenat
was looking for a subject domain in which a computer could discover things in a very broad sense, not just looking for one rule, as
in Eleusis and most other problem solving, but working in an entirely open-ended way. He chose the theory of numbers, as a well-
contained and understood mathematical field, and developed the
program AM (originally Automated Mathematician). This started
with an extremely basic set of mathematical concepts and "wan-
dered around" the problem space looking for more. It constructed
on its own a number of well-known mathematical ideas and even
rediscovered important theorems, such as Euclid's Unique Factorization Theorem, which states that a composite number can be
factorized into primes in only one way. It formulated a curious
geometric interpretation of Goldbach's Conjecture to do with the
sums of primes and made one discovery concerning "maximally
divisible numbers" that was entirely original.[8]

The program started with 100 elementary concepts of finite set
theory: objects like sets, lists, bags (sets allowing replication of
elements), and truth-values; relations like membership and equal-
ity; operations like inversion, composition, and intersection. It also
had a number of *heuristics,* i.e., rules of thumb, providing advice
on what to do. One of these was: *"Coincidences are interesting."*
Thus, when AM discovered multiplication in four different ways,*

---

*As repeated addition, as an analogue to the Cartesian product of sets, as the cardinality of
the union of the powersets of two sets, and as the total number of symbols one gets by
replacing (in parallel) each element of bag X by a complete copy of bag Y.

it decided that if that many different procedures led to the same thing, it was interesting and probably important. Another heuristic was: *"If an operation is interesting, look at its inverse."* Thus from multiplication, division came to be explored. This led to the process of dividing up large collections of numbers into their factors. Yet another heuristic was: *"Look at extreme cases of things."* So AM examined the sets of numbers that had only one or two divisors, and behold, it had discovered the concept of prime numbers. It then explored the opposite extreme to that, namely, numbers with many divisors, a topic Lenat thought had never been studied before. He then found out that Srinivasa Ramanujan, G. H. Hardy's self-taught collaborator, had worked on maximally divisible numbers, but even he had not found one particular regularity discovered by AM.

If number theory seems obscure and inconsequential, remember that the Unique Factorization Theorem is the basis of the latest encryption procedures being developed by the U.S. government as a universally applied standard for the protection of privacy of computer data. AM was also the starting point for Lenat's current work, which is concerned with applications to practical problems, as we shortly describe.

NEW WAYS AND MEANS

Despite its successes, AM had one fundamental deficiency—it could develop new concepts but not new heuristics. As the concepts grew further and further away from the primitives AM started with, the heuristics turned out to be too general and too weak to guide effectively. To overcome this problem, Lenat has devised a new program, Eurisko.[9] This modifies its heuristics in small ways from time to time, sometimes randomly, sometimes in an effort to "specialize," as in replacing "Or" by "Most of." There are heuristics *about* heuristics, such as *"Avoid replacing 'And' with 'Or' because that can lead to explosions."* New heuristics are judged for usefulness and retained or put aside as the case may be. There were initial problems caused by the fact that the heuristics were held in chunks of Lisp code that were too large to be manipulated meaningfully; these were broken up into smaller pieces. Lenat also relates how a heuristic that had made a discovery would put its own name down in the list of heuristics of high worth and then take that realization that it had made a discovery as a discovery in itself. So the heuristic would award itself more points, then take *that* as yet another discovery worth still more points, and so on, in an infinite loop! Lenat had to stop the program changing its own goals in an uncontrolled fashion. After that, useful new heuristics were devised, mainly ones specific to particular subject domains.

It turned out that the heuristics from mathematics were often relevant to dealing with the real world. For example, if we take an issue such as employment, we see that it consists of a large number of relationships, of people being employed by other people. Looking at the extremes of this set of relationships as recommended by our third heuristic leads us to examine at one end people who are not employed at all (unemployment) and at the other end people who have several jobs (moonlighting), both important issues.

Eurisko has already made contributions to real-world problems, most notably in the design of three-dimensional electronic integrated circuits. As originally conceived by humans, these were just ordinary flat integrated circuits folded over in order to reduce the straight-line distance the electricity had to travel between elements—paring a few picoseconds off the circuit's response time. Instead of just accepting that, Eurisko asked, ''How could the elements interact?'' It would take a typical junction, as shown schematically in Figure 27a, and apply to it the heuristic *''If you have a valuable structure, try to make it more symmetric.''* The result was as shown in Figure 27b.

The extra bits added on allowed the structure to perform more than one function at a time, so that one unit could act as both a ''Not-And'' circuit and an ''Or'' circuit. It had not occurred to the human designers that this could be done, partly because the complexities of VLSI had compelled them to simplify the design space in their minds and rule out the possibility of an element acting as a gate and a channel simultaneously. Designers Jim Gibbons and

Lynn Conway are now using Eurisko, and the potential of VLSI could be greatly expanded as a result.

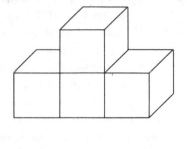

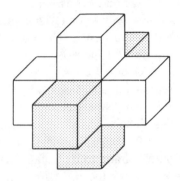

Figure 27a. Junction in an integrated circuit

Figure 27b. The same with bits added in all directions as suggested by Eurisko

I SEE NO SHIPS

Eurisko has also been notably successful, some say too successful, in taking part in an annual naval war game in the U.S. called the Trillion Credit Squadron Competition. Participants have to design a battle fleet within given constraints of cost and see how the fleet performs in a simulated action against all the others. Eurisko came up with some extraordinary designs, all perfectly feasible, including one consisting of a vast number of virtually impregnable ships, each one hardly bigger than a lifeboat. On being presented at the game, Eurisko's bizarre fleets caused much laughter among the other players, followed by consternation when they were seen to be winning. Lenat is not surprised that for two years running the rules have been changed with the effect of outlawing Eurisko's successive concoctions.

Turning to pure science, Lenat is devising ways of getting Eurisko to model biological mutations. The idea is that if somehow there were a way that information about previous states of a species could be retained after mutations, it might be that evolution proceeds not in an entirely random fashion as has been thought, but by heuristics in some way, just as Eurisko evolves its own concepts. Buried in the tortuous mechanisms of DNA, there may be things that act as heuristics, in effect telling nature, "Try mutation *this way*," or, "*That* sort of mutation has not turned out very well in the past." The possibility here is that an explanation may be found for the extraordinary effectiveness of evolution.

AM and Eurisko are fundamentally further along the road of creativity than Michalski's trains program, because instead of just finding links between existing concepts, they explore and find new ones. The trains program, for instance, could not invent the concept of "jagged-topness" by which some cars were described—it could not add to its vocabulary. AM and Eurisko can, and this is in many ways the most important part of creativity—the top "notation" layer of Aaron Sloman's model described in Chapter 1.

DOWN ON THE SOYBEAN FARM

An example of computer induction that is literally more down to earth comes from Illinois, where the soybean crops can be smitten with any one of twenty or so common diseases and correct diagnosis can make the difference between a ruinous harvest and riches. The state operates a network of agricultural extension offices, which farmers can phone for advice. Queries that cannot be dealt with on the spot are sent to university plant pathologists, who are greatly overburdened with requests. Large delays and backlogs develop, so an expert system would be useful. Michalski and his colleague Richard Chilausky proceeded to construct such a system and obtained a set of rules, by the usual laborious process, over 45 hours of consultation with the plant pathologist Barry Jacobsen. These rules covered 19 diseases, such as brown stem rot, downy mildew, bacterial blight, and diaporthe stem canker, and the diagnoses were based on 35 descriptors of the condition of the plants including leaf spots, holing, seed shriveling, and information on the time of year, rainfall, and the like. These descriptors were deliberately chosen to be easily visible so that observations could be accepted from non-experts in the field.

It was then decided to try an experiment with computer-induction of rules. Data on 307 diseased plants was collected on forms, specifying a value for each of the 35 descriptors. Every example was then given a diagnosis by a human expert (See Figure 28).

The data was fed to Michalski and Larson's inductive inference program, essentially the same as that used for the earlier "trains" example, which produced a completely different set of rules from those obtained from Jacobsen. Comparing the performance of the machine-generated rules with the human-generated ones on a new test set of 376 cases, the machine's rules got 374 of them right, while the rules obtained from Jacobsen scored only 83% right. The machine's rules are now the ones that are in use.[10]

Another expert system that has been extended to generate its own rules is Dendral at Stanford. A new program, Meta-dendral, was written to take mass-spectrometry data from molecules of known structure and infer rules connecting these. It has created rules for subfamilies of molecules for which none existed before.[11]

Many computing tasks come down to *classification*. This is what pattern recognition in computer vision and hearing is about, and rule-based inductive inference systems have shown their worth in tackling these problems. Michalski has been working on a program for automatically discovering the categories themselves into which objects are to be classified, going beyond the construction of rules for sorting objects into preestablished categories. This new technique, called conjunctive conceptual clustering, has been used at Illinois in a project to classify 100 Spanish songs.[12] At Carnegie-Mellon University, Hearsay-II is a speech-recognition system that uses a knowledge base rather as an expert system does. Repositories of knowledge are held for different levels of analysis—syllables, words, phrases, and so on—and these communicate with each other through a common work space called a "blackboard." Hypotheses are set up about the probable meaning of the sounds being deciphered, and these are tested as the analysis proceeds.[13]

Environmental descriptors
  Time of occurrence = July
  Plant stand = normal
  Precipitation = above normal
  Temperature = normal
  Occurrence of hail = no
  Number years crop repeated = 4
  Damaged area = whole fields

Plant global descriptors
  Severity = potentially severe
  Seed treatment = none
  Seed germination = less than 80%
  Plant height = normal

Plant local descriptors
  Condition of leaves = abnormal
    Leafspots–halos = without yellow halos
    Leafspots–margin = without watersoaked margin
    Leafspot size = greater than $\frac{1}{8}''$
    Leaf shredding or shot holding = present
    Leaf malformation = absent
    Leaf mildew growth = absent
  Condition of stem = abnormal
    Presence of lodging = no
    Stem cankers = above the second node
    Canker lesion color = brown
    Fruiting bodies on stem = present
    External decay = absent
    Mycelium on stem = absent
    Internal discoloration of stem = none
    Sclerotia–internal or external = absent
  Conditions of fruits–pods = normal
    Fruit spots = absent
  Condition of seed = normal
    Mould growth = absent
    Seed discoloration = absent
    Seed size = normal
    Seed shrivelling = absent
  Condition of roots = normal

Diagnosis:
  Diaporthe stem canker( ) *Charcoal rot*( ) *Rhizoctonia root rot*( ) *Phytophthora root rot*( ) *Brown stem root rot*( ) *Powdery mildew*( ) *Downy mildew*( ) *Brown spot*(×) *Bacterial blight*( ) *Bacterial pustule*( ) *Purpose seed stain*( ) *Anthracnose*( ) *Phyllosticta leaf spot*( ) *Alternaria leaf spot*( ) *Frog eye leaf spot*( )*

BACON'S IMPROPRIETY

Despite its obvious successes, induction is still looked on with suspicion. It lacks the one great attribute of deductive systems based on theory, namely, the ability to *explain* things, to give us that Aha! flash of insight when we understand a principle. Induction is by its very nature bottom-up, with all that implies in terms of lack of elegance and completeness. Top-down reasoning has the air of a formal science. Speaking at a conference in London, Manny Lehman, professor of Computing Science at Imperial College, commented disapprovingly on the lack of scientific theory in Artificial Intelligence at the present moment. "We don't want to rely on a bridge built only on experiment, not on science," he said. Of course, for centuries bridges were built in just that way, of necessity.

Occasionally, an empirically minded thinker like Francis Bacon offers an explanatory annotation on the bottom-up world, arguing that it too has its unifying principles. Bacon conceived in bold outline the entire possibility and structure of technological R&D as a world-transforming enterprise. But Baconian logic models too faithfully for public exhibition the actual cognitive style of *Homo sapiens,* just as certain physical functions of man, however life-giving in their effects, are thought best not publicly performed.

Top-down theories will continue to be centrally important, principally for the sake of understanding. But for mechanizing complex tasks they are often not usable at all. In these cases, for every computing device, whether electronic or protoplasmic, skill must be built as a bottom-up creation in which, as the philosopher Herbert Spencer put it, "The vital actions are severally decomposed into their component parts, and each of these parts has an agent to itself." [14]

Figure 28 (opposite). Completed questionnaire describing a diseased soybean plant, used as input to the inductive learning program AQ11. Below the line, "Brown spot" has been singled out from the range of possible diagnoses. (*International Journal of Policy Analysis and Information Systems*)

6
THE CREATION OF NEW KNOWLEDGE

COMPUTER PEOPLE ENGAGED in barking up the tree of knowledge were more than a little dumbfounded by the view taken of computer-stored information by three Appeal Court judges in January 1980 in the case of the Crown versus Pettigrew, accused of stealing banknotes. Three five-pound notes in his possession had serial numbers matching a list printed by the Bank of England computer. To be admissible, according to the Criminal Evidence Act 1965, a document must have been prepared by someone with knowledge of its contents. A computer cannot be regarded, so the Appeal Court ruled, as having "knowledge" in this sense.

Something is clearly wrong here, either in the state of the law or in received notions of what constitutes knowledge. Yet examining boards down the ages have made no bones about knowledge. If the candidate can mentally retrieve the requested information, then he is credited with knowledge of it and hence with knowledge of the contents of any document he prepared in his attempt to satisfy the examiners. Why the Bank of England computer's final printout should be flunked in the analogous case seems mysterious.

Knowledge is the capacity to give correct answers to questions. Of course there is sometimes disagreement over what constitutes a correct answer. The outraged husband, finding a nude man in his wife's bedroom closet, barks at the intruder: "What the hell are you doing in there?"

"Everyone," comes the reply, "has got to be somewhere." Does this answer rate 10 out of 10, or 0 out of 10? Any intermediate mark would seem to be wrong.

Still, there is no disputing that computers can answer questions and therefore can have knowledge. With all respect to their lordships of the Court of Appeal, this is well known. What is not well known is that computers cannot only possess knowledge, they can *create* it.

INFORMATION IS NOT KNOWLEDGE

At this point, readers with memories of long-past physics lessons may ask, "Surely the Second Law of Thermodynamics tells us that information cannot be created?" Indeed it does, but information and knowledge are not the same. Information on its own does not take you very far. Consider the number 4.38. It is useless unless you know *it is the time of the train to Birmingham.* Not only that— you need to know where Birmingham is in relation to where you are now and where you want to go.

Knowledge is a special form in which information can be packaged so that it can be stored, retrieved, and understood by the human brain. In a similar way, drinking water can be said to be a special form of H_2O. Creation of a chunk of knowledge from a mountain of information is thus like the creation of a cupful of water from a mountain of ice. In both cases, hard work is required for a small but possibly precious return.

We shall have more to say on this distinction between information and knowledge. But first, let us look at the physicist's quantified definition of *information,* formalized by Claude Shannon while working at the Bell Telephone Laboratories in the 1940s.[1] In some ways, the definition may seem foreign to our intuitive idea of information. In its simplest form, information content is just a measure of the number of bits needed to encode a message:

1001011010100011

is a message containing sixteen bits. There are 2^{16}, or 65,536, different messages that can be encoded in sixteen bits, and this is just one of them. But as a measure of true information content the bit count is misleading, because in reality there is another factor to be considered. Take a different sixteen-bit message:

0101010101010101

There is a clear pattern here that obviously allows the message to be rephrased as:

"01" eight times over

A long, regular message of this sort can naturally be condensed into far fewer bits than it contains in its full form. Messages on the other hand that are effectively random cannot be condensed.

Lack of randomness is a very common phenomenon, for example in natural language. In computers, the crudest and commonest way of encoding English text is to assign eight bits of memory to each letter, but this entails a great deal of waste because there is so much extra information, or "redundancy," in the language. Try leaving all the vowels out of a sentence:

W'R SRGNT PPPR'S LNLY HRTS CLB BND
W HP Y WLL NJY TH SHW.

This makes so little difference that ancient Hebrew in its early days was actually written all the time without vowels. There is another factor, and that is that some letters in English (E,T) are much more common than others (X,Z). So it makes sense to give the common letters shorter codes than the rare ones—this is exactly what Samuel Morse did with his original telegraph code. All this results in the true information content of English being closer to one bit per letter than eight bits.

Essentially, the information value of a message is its capacity to surprise the recipient. If you know what message or part of a message is coming, its arrival conveys no information to you. For example, in normal English the letter Q is always followed by U, so the U has no information content at all. It might as well not be there; in a technical sense, it is *redundant*. Shannon constructed his measure of information by considering the probabilities of each symbol occurring so that the more likely symbols are credited with less information content. Summing and averaging the "surprise-values" of the individual symbols constituting a given message gives a measure of the "surprise-value" of the whole message and hence of its total information content.

Of course, this has nothing to do with the *meaning* of a message or with how *interesting* it is. A message consisting of an entirely random jumble of characters contains plenty of information but is very boring. At the other extreme, a completely non-random message such as:

NNNNNNNNNNNNN . . .

is also boring. "Interestingness" at the superficial level comes from messages that are somewhere in between. At a deeper level, interestingness is a property of what the message *denotes*, i.e., its meaning. This aspect is not covered in the classical treatment.

LAYING DOWN THE SECOND LAW

We now return to thermodynamics, and the law referred to by C. P. Snow in his assertion that non-scientists should feel guilty about not understanding it. The Second Law of Thermodynamics tells us that as the energy of the stars gets radiated out into the vastness of space, the hot areas and cold areas of the universe gradually even out their energy until eventually there will be a uniform, lifeless distribution of bitter cold everywhere—the "heat-death of the universe." So the whole contrivance is slowly running down and everything is getting more and more disorganized. The physicist describes this as a continual increase of entropy (his measure of disorganization), while at the same time information, the opposite of entropy, decreases. The organization of the cosmos is lost in the universal jumble.

A consequence of this is that information cannot possibly increase, except on a local scale, and then only when information is lost somewhere else. So information cannot be created—not by man or machine or by anything.

A qualification must be added to this account to take care of possible interpretations at the cosmological and subatomic levels of analysis. Paul Davies of Newcastle University explains that physicists are beginning to wonder whether across the breadth of the entire universe, continually expanding as it is, gravity might actually be creating information at the expense of its own entropy. At the totally opposite extreme of scale, considering subatomic particles, it is true that Heisenberg's Uncertainty Principle tells us that by the very nature of atoms, it is impossible to predict how and when they will split apart in radioactive decay. Therefore, when an atom does split, it comes in a certain sense as a "surprise," so that information might be said to have been created. Nevertheless, the laws of statistics ensure that this can have no effect on the quantity of information affecting us on a human scale. Further, we can detect the decay of an atom and the information contained therein only by amplifying the effects with a particle counter, and this device, requiring power to drive it, uses up more information than it supplies to us.

So while information can in some theories be created on a cosmic and on a subatomic scale, it cannot be created on the scale of humans and their machines.

Still, intuitively, it may seem strange to think that information cannot be created. Take the sentence "The height of the new skyscraper is 1,150 feet." This is definitely a piece of information, which seems to have been recently created. It exists now—how could it exist before the building was there? Ah, but it did, from the point of view of the information theoretician. It existed in the mind of the architect, not consciously to start with, even before he decided to design the building and before that in the myriad things which influenced him. Saying this is nothing more than affirming the principle of cause and effect: the information describing every effect is wholly contained in the circumstances of the cause. It is there, but in a different form—assuredly very difficult to obtain, but there. The issue of obtainability is central to the notion of knowledge; the knowledge that the height of the new skyscraper is 1,150 feet is created at the instant that the corresponding information comes to be structured in brain-accessible form.

NEW KNOWLEDGE FOR OLD INFORMATION

So computers cannot create information. This has long been clear. What has only recently become clear is that there is *no such barrier to computers creating knowledge.* It is this discovery, with the consequences that it entails, that forms the central impetus of this book.

What is knowledge created from? Information. A computer can, through purely internal operations, add to its knowledge (and thence to the knowledge of the world at large), using a fixed amount of information. To explain this, we will start with a trivial example. Suppose we write a prime-factorization program that will tell us whether any number we give it up to ten million is prime or composite. Moreover, we endow the program with the habit of keeping in memory the results of its own past computations. This is a slow home computer, so when we try it with 1,005,973, it takes such a long time that we get bored and interrupt it before it has found the answer. Every exam has a time limit, so no marks in this case. Then we try 997 and after a while the program says "Prime" and stores this result in memory. So its "knowledge" extends at least to 997. What else does it know?

We input 999,997 and go out, leaving the program running. So far, no marks. Knowing that the program enters its computed results into a table before exit, we are not surprised when we return and again ask it 999,997 that it knows the answer straight away, replying "Composite" instantly by look-up. Moreover, it can now answer the question it failed with utterly before—giving 1,005,973 as "Composite" in a few seconds. The seeming miracle can be traced to its use, for speeding up the computation, of the newfound primeness of 997. Knowledge here is clearly being created and used. Yet information remains constant, being fully contained in the original program. What changes, then? Simply the size of that fraction of the total information that can be mobilized fast enough to satisfy the examiners.

STRUCTURES MAKE CONCEPTS

This example is in no way realistic, because the knowledge generated is hardly significant in human terms, but from this we can begin to see what is needed to make information become knowledge. The information must be in appropriate *structures*. When these information structures are recognizable to human beings, we call them *concepts*. Useful knowledge is information *in conceptualized form*.

Harking back to the example of the train times, a very basic information structure might be a timetable incorporating a map, identifying where the stations are and how they are interconnected. For an example of something more substantial, recall Doug Lenat's program AM in the last chapter. The whole idea of this is that it handles concepts, each of which is stored internally in the computer in a special structure. Figure 29 shows one of these, namely the concept of a *set*. Without worrying too much about the details, one can see from this how a computer program can take the elements of the structure and manipulate them, finding relationships with other concepts and filling in the empty slots in the structure.

The concept of a set was one of those given to AM to start with. But look now at Figure 30. This is the concept *prime number*. You will recall that AM was not given this concept—it *constructed it itself*. In the process, it created knowledge.

DISCOVERIES FROM EDINBURGH

Of course the knowledge in this case was not original, as the idea of a prime number has been around for a long time. (Note also that the name Prime Number that appears in the structure was not generated by the program—it was filled in later by Lenat.) A different story, though, comes from Edinburgh, where several researchers have been constructing expert systems for playing chess

NAME(s): Set, Non-proper Class, Collection, Finite set
DEFINITIONS:
    RECURSIVE: λ (S)[S = { } or Set . Definition
                (Remove(Any-member(S),S))]
    RECURSIVE QUICK: λ (S) [S = { } or Set . Definition (CDR(S))]
    QUICK: λ (S) [Match S with { . . . }]
SPECIALIZATIONS: Nonempty-set, Set-of-sets, Set-of-numbers
    BOUNDARY: Empty-set; Singleton, Doubleton, Tripleton
GENERALIZATIONS: Unordered-Structure, Collection,
    Structure-with-no-multiple-elements-allowed
IS-A: Kind-of-structure
EXAMPLES:
    TYPICAL: { { } }, {A}, {A,B}, {3}
    BARELY: { }, {A, B, {C, { { {A, C, (3,3,9),< 4,{B}, A} } } > } }
    NOT-QUITE: {A,A}, (), {B,A}
    FOIBLE: ⟨4,1,A,1⟩
CONJEC's: All unordered-structures are sets.
INTUITIONS: Geometric: Venn diagram.
ANALOGIES: {set, set operations} ≡ {list, list operations}
WORTH: 600 [on a scale of 0-1000]
VIEW:
    PREDICATE: λ (P) {x∈Domain(P) | P(x)}
    STRUCTURE: λ (S) Enclose-in-braces
                (Sort(Remove-multiple-elements(S)))
IN-DOMAIN-OF: Union, Intersection, Set-difference, Subset,
    Member, Cartesian-prod, Set-equality
IN-RANGE-OF: Union, Intersect, Set-difference, Satisfying

Figure 29. An information structure: how AM represents the concept of a Set[2]

NAME(s): Prime Numbers, Primes, Numbers-with-2-Divisors
DEFINITIONS:
  ORIGIN: Divisors-of(x) is-a Doubleton
  PRED.-CALCULUS: Prime(x) ≡ (∀z)(z|x → z = 1 XOR z = x)
  ITERATIVE: (for x > 1): For i from 2 to x − 1, ¬ (i|x)
EXAMPLES: 2, 3, 5, 7, 11, 13, 17
  BOUNDARY: 2, 3
BOUNDARY-FAILURES: 0, 1
  FAILURES: 12
GENERALIZATIONS: Numbers, Numbers with an even no. of divisors, Numbers with a prime no. of divisors
SPECIALIZATIONS: Prime pairs, Prime uniquely-addables
CONJECS: Unique factorization, Goldbach's conjecture
ANALOGIES: Maximally-divisible numbers are converse extremes of Divisors-of
INTEREST: Conjec's tying Primes to Times, to Divisors-of, and to other closely related operations
WORTH: 800

Figure 30. AM's concept of a Prime Number

---

end games. Early on in this work Ivan Bratko, himself a master-level player, developed a set of rules for king and rook against king and embedded them in a structure called an "advice table." The rules were fed into the machine to be correlated, cross-checked, revised, refined, and proved. When the expert system was working, Bratko translated the rules back into English, expecting to find something like the original textbook formulation. Instead, something startlingly different appeared. Bratko discovered that the six rules obtained were more complete, concise, and understandable by far than the chess-master formulations to be found in the books. In place of pages of diffuse text and diagrams was a set of rules so simple and clear-cut that anyone could grasp and even memorize them (Figure 31). A child could learn the rules and use them to play this end game as skillfully as a master.

1. In obeying the rules that follow, make sure that stalemate is not created or the rook left *en prise*.
2. Look for a way to mate opponent's king in two moves.
3. If the above is not possible, then look for a way to constrain further the area on the chess board to which the opponent's king is confined by our rook.
4. If the above is not possible, then look for a way to move our king closer to opponent's king.
5. If none of the above pieces of advice—2, 3, or 4—works, then look for a way of maintaining the present achievements in the sense of 3 and 4 (i.e., make a waiting move).
6. If none of 2, 3, 4, or 5 is attainable, then look for a way of obtaining a position in which our rook divides the two kings either vertically or horizontally.

Figure 31. Ivan Bratko's strategy for winning with king and rook against king—knowledge created with the assistance of a computer

Bratko had made the important discovery that a computer could enable a human to formulate new knowledge that he could not have done otherwise. The formulation was completely original, never having been seen before by any chess master or writer of textbooks. But still the knowledge was basically created by a man, not by a machine. This was the case until two other researchers at Edinburgh, Tim Niblett and Alen Shapiro, tackled the end game king-pawn-king. They took as their starting point a giant table for this end game that had been mechanically compiled by Michael Clarke for use in the same sort of "blind look-up" we described in Chapter 3. The table indicated for every position whether it was "drawn" or "lost" but provided no explanation of why, or any structure or comprehensible pattern that could make sense to a human. Niblett and Shapiro ran selected parts of the table through an induction program called ID3, and following a semi-automatic iterative process, they developed a set of decision trees a human could use to evaluate any position.[3] The master tree is shown in Figure 32. This together with its subtrees makes excellent sense to a chess expert. From totally indigestible information, ID3 had actually created new knowledge.

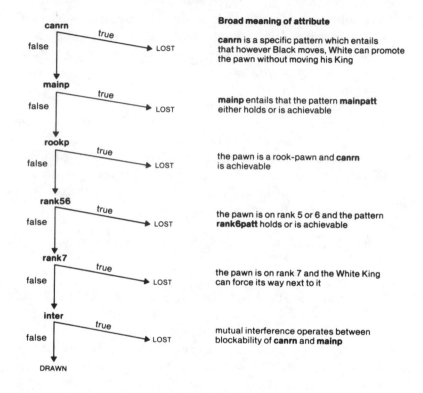

Figure 32. Knowledge created by computer in ID3's master tree for classifying king-pawn-king positions with black to move into LOST or DRAWN. For each of the six attributes, a similar tree was separately synthesized from a set of more primitive attributes.

Niblett and Shapiro had not only succeeded in getting a machine to create original knowledge; they had also engineered the exact opposite of the bafflement over Ken Thompson's table (Chapter 3). The information drawn from a computer was easily comprehensible and phrased entirely in human, not machine, concepts, so that it could be interpreted by machines and brains alike.

As it happens, the chess content of the last two examples is relatively simple in master terms. This was not the case, however, with Shapiro's next undertaking, which was the end game king and pawn against king and rook. This is of a level of complexity far beyond the power of the unaided chess master to codify adequately. Shapiro looked specifically at the situation where the pawn is on the next to last row, square A7. With the help of chess master Danny Kopec, he chose thirty-five primitive attributes describing the situation on the board, such as "the white king is on an edge," or "the black king can attack the white pawn." He then got Kopec to give examples of all of these, showing their consequences. These were fed into the program Interactive ID3 and used to generate a set of nine rules, arranged in a tree structure. The first of these (with a human-added description at the beginning) read:

> **PA7, Top-level rule.** This rule is used to decide if a KPa7KR position with white-to-move is won-for-white or not.
>
> KPa7KR is won for white (PA7,1) IF AND ONLY IF
>   the BR can be captured safely (rimmx)
>
> OR none of the following is true:
>
> there is a simple delay to white's queening the pawn (DQ,2.1)
> OR one or more black pieces control the queening square (bxqsq)
> OR there is a good delayed skewer threat (DS,2.2)

Each of the codes refers to the outcome of one of the lower rules. Again, useful knowledge had been created, expressed in terms comprehensible to humans, and this time from a highly complex domain.

What is also significant about these examples is that computers have created knowledge not just for their own use, but for the use of human beings in solving actual human problems. Of course, problems of how to classify chess end game positions are only of practical significance to end game experts, but a further achievement by Ivan Bratko has shown that knowledge synthesized by computer can make a contribution to the solution of important human problems, in this case, the diagnosis of heart disease.

LOOKING INTO THE HEART

The principal means doctors use to diagnose heart disease is by examining electrocardiograms, which are graphs of the electrical signals produced in the heart, drawn by an automatic pen recorder. The ECG of a normal heart looks something like Figure 33. Doctors describe the trace by how the main features P,Q,R,S, and T are grouped.

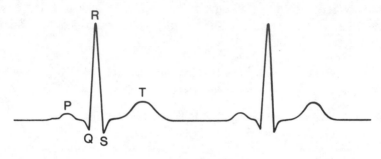

normal sinus rhythm

rhythm: regular,
frequency: between 60–100,
frequency P: between 60–100,
regular P: normal,

relation P–QRS: after P–QRS,
regular PR: normal,
regular QRS: normal

Figure 33. ECG diagram of a normal heart, with its qualitative description *(Ivan Bratko)*

Defects in the heart cause the timing and strengths of the pulses to be disrupted, producing ECG traces such as in Figure 34. Conditions such as this are known as arrhythmia. There are twenty-six different arrhythmias, each with its distinctive ECG pattern, and heart specialists learn to recognize these. The difficulty is that there is often more than one defect present at a time, leading on the face of it to over 100,000 conceivable multiple arrhythmias. The patterns for the separate arrhythmias combine in one ECG trace in ways that make it extremely difficult to decipher. It has not so far been found feasible, even with the aid of a computer, to identify multiple arrhythmias in a complex trace; by hand it is out of the question.

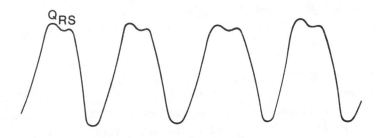

ventricular tachycardia

rhythm: regular,
frequency: between 100–250,
regular P: absent,
regular QRS: wide

Figure 34. ECG of a diseased heart, with qualitative description (*Ivan Bratko*)

To deal with this problem, Bratko and his colleagues at the Jozef Stefan Institute in Ljubljana decided to employ the inverse function method, as we described in Chapter 3, relying on the fact that while it may be very difficult to work out a function in one direction, it may be relatively easy in the other. Accordingly, the Yugoslavs got a computer to work out all the possible combinations of heart defects and what their resultant ECG traces would be. This was produced as a table in which a doctor could look up a particular trace to find the appropriate corresponding diagnosis.

Bratko's team did this by constructing, with the aid of cardiologists, a computer model of the workings of the heart's electrical system, involving four generators of impulses, two paths along which these propagate, and the rates of flow in the heart's chambers. The model consisted of sixty-two rules obtained with the help of the cardiologists, for example:

> IF there are ectopic impulses at the His bundle and in the supraventricles originating at the AV focus
> THEN this results in the following ECG features: either a short PR interval, or no P wave, or P wave after the QRS complex.

The rules described not only the origins of the ECG signals but also the fact that many combinations of arrhythmias are not physiologically possible, if for instance one depends on a particular factor in the heart being too high and another on it being too low. Other arrhythmias cannot occur alone. The ECGs were described in qualitative terms, as to how the features P, Q, and so on were grouped, rather than in numerical terms using frequencies. The rules were implemented in the computer language Prolog, and the system was then run to produce a list of all possible combinations of arrhythmias and their corresponding ECG traces. It turned out that there were 588 of these. A doctor could easily look up an ECG pattern in this table and find its corresponding diagnosis. Because the system in effect contains a complete qualitative description of the working of the heart's electrical system, an explanation of how a particular conclusion was reached could readily be obtained and also understood.

The table that the Bratko system produced is most definitely new knowledge, and knowledge that is of real human importance. The doctors at Ljubljana University Medical Center are already using the system for teaching purposes. For practical diagnosis, specialists are often able to get sufficient clues from other signs apart from the ECG. However, if a patient has been taking drugs, for example heart drugs prescribed as part of his medical regime, the situation becomes much more complicated and even the most experienced consultants have great difficulty in diagnosing correctly. The expectation is that an expanded version of Bratko's system, taking the action of drugs into account, could bring about a major step forward in the treatment of heart disease.

There is an interesting difference between the heart-disease system and earlier examples we gave of the creation of new knowledge by machine. While in the chess examples the new knowledge was condensed and compiled out of an expert's skill, here it was generated from the machine's own causal understanding of the mechanism of the heart. Thus in a way, the machine's contribution to new knowledge was greater in the second case.

Examples of the creation of new knowledge by computer have already been brought out in this book—namely, the discoveries of Doug Lenat's Eurisko (Chapter 5). This works on a different principle from the knowledge-based systems we have been discussing here, but its creations have been as original, and the technology of heuristics promises to be a growing source of new knowledge for the future.

SOLUTIONS FROM MACHINES

The discovery that it is possible for computers to generate strategies for the use of human beings is of incalculable significance. Let us look back to the question raised at the start of Chapter 2: can computers provide answers to such problems as "What is wrong with this patient?" "Would this be a good spot to drill a well?" . . . The technology of expert systems enables machines to deal with these problems using knowledge supplied by humans. The days are now in sight, however, when the required knowledge will originate not just from humans but also *from the machines themselves*. The potential impact of this is immense. The world is faced with a host of problems, great and small; among the great ones are overpopulation, poverty, disease, pollution, shortage of energy, international conflict, and economic stagnation. Can we see computers generating solutions to these? Most certainly. It is true that most of the problems that creative computers can tackle at the moment fall far short of these global issues, but it is early days. One would not expect a full-grown horse to be the first product of a laboratory seeking to synthesize life. Science always has to start small: in life, perhaps a virus; in problem-solving, a plan for an imaginary fleet, an analysis of a chess position, a design for an integrated circuit, or a scheme for diagnosing heart disease. It is true that someone could just conceivably have produced Bratko's arrhythmia table without using his techniques of knowledge engineering, but it is noteworthy that no one has done so. Certainly no chess master could have produced Shapiro's rule-base. The borderline of what is just not feasible by hand has now been reached. These achievements point clearly to where the technology is headed. Hardware is getting cheaper and cheaper, and it will not be long before it is worthwhile to set up computer-based "knowledge factories" dedicated to the accumulation and refinement by machine of bodies of knowledge geared to really significant solutions. People will have to decide whether the solutions *are* significant, but to a large extent so will the machines, in order not to bury their human controllers in the task of sifting wheat from chaff.

We envisage machine-based craft shops set up for the sole purpose of generating new knowledge, using as their raw material both the expertise of humans and the ruminations of huge computer models and look-ahead systems. Some of these operations would be tackling fairly narrow, self-contained problems, such as the diagnosis and treatment of particular diseases, while others would work on issues such as the world economy. A wide range of problems, large and small, will surely be susceptible to solving in this way.

MEASURES OF CREATIVITY

How much can we expect from computers in the way of creativity? This question brings us back to the point that a great deal of creativity in small ways goes on all the time—by people in their daily lives, for instance, puzzling out what is happening around them. Really substantial creativity on the other hand is rare. Bearing this in mind, we may expect to have to put a great deal of computing resources into a task in order to obtain a relatively small amount of new knowledge, but computing resources are becoming cheap, and the potential of the new machine induction methods remains largely untried.

In assessing how much new knowledge is being created, we need to be able to measure it. Clearly, quantity and quality are inextricably linked here. To get an idea of how this measuring might be done, we look back at expert systems. Complex problems abound that are beyond solution by knowledge-poor programs in feasible time. But when humans add advice to the programs in the form of heuristic rules, suddenly the machines can reach solutions after all. In a chess game, say, the machine with knowledge can make an immediate intelligent move instead of slogging through a look-ahead tree of millions of nodes. By measuring how much a program speeds up on receiving the advice, we can begin to quantify the knowledge contained in it.[4]

REFINING KNOWLEDGE

When expert systems were first devised, they were intended to act simply as substitute human experts. There was no thought that the knowledge fed in would ever be read out again. Instead, they have shown an unexpected bonus: they can actually help to codify and improve expert human knowledge, taking what was fragmentary, inconsistent, and error-infested and turning it into knowledge that is more precise, reliable, and comprehensive. This new process, with its enormous potential for the future, we call ''knowledge refining.''

One of the earliest examples of this was noted by Ed Feigenbaum, following the work at Stanford on chemical structure analysis by the expert system dendral. Chemists started writing to Stanford asking for copies not of the program, but of the rules it had assimilated. They found these rules useful because they were a much clearer codification of the subject than had existed before. Following that, the program's rule-generator Meta-dendral induced new rules for mono- and poly-keto-androstanes. The phenomenon of knowledge refining has been observed in several other areas of expert systems work, as we list in Figure 35.

Figure 35. Representative cases where knowledge-based programs have been used to improve previous codifications of human knowledge, a phenomenon termed *knowledge refining*

Domain	Previous codification
Chess: spotting mates "at a glance"	No non-trivial classifications published
Chess: how to mate with king and rook against king	Chess primers by Capablanca, Fine, etc.
Chess: how to classify king-pawn-king positions	Chess primers by Averbakh and others
Diagnosis of acute abdominal pain	Signs-and-symptoms checklist cards for general practitioners prepared by consulting surgeon
Internal medicine diagnosis and treatment	Medical texts
Chemical synthesis planning	Textbooks on synthesis
Planning robotic assembly sequences	Toy car assembly scheme for Edinburgh versatile assembly program
Plant pathology	Pathologist's diagnostic classification of soybean diseases
Mass spectral information on mono- and poly-keto-androstanes	No satisfactory preexisting explanation of spectroscopic behavior

Refining instrument	Desired end-product
PL1 tournament program "Master"	Reference text of mating patterns
AL1 "Advice Taker" program	Six sufficient rules, formally proved correct
Prolog and AL1 "Advice Taker" basis for ID3-mediated inductive learning	Micro-manual of pattern-based rules
Bayes's decision-rule program for relating symptom-pattern to one of a dozen common conditions	Improved checklists including numerical measures of relevance and reliability
"Internist" knowledge-based program	Improved medical texts
SECS program with database of chemical "transforms"	Improved source of synthesis-relevant knowledge for chemists
"Warplan" predicate-calculus-based program	Improved assembly sequence
"Aqval" program for inductive inference	Improved set of classificatory rules
Meta-dendral module of Dendral program	Substructures defining main cleavages, yielding prodictive theory for new keto-androstanes

Hitherto, expert systems have operated in two modes:

1. Feeding in the knowledge: user as teacher.

2. Getting answers to problems: user as client.

To these we now add a third mode:

3. Harvesting the knowledge base for use by humans: user as pupil.

Typically, the users in each of these modes are different people. For example, in the case of SRI's Prospector, the teacher would be an economic geologist hired or employed by a mining company to build, validate, and tune the system's base of useful knowledge. The user seeking solutions is likely to be a technical executive of the company. The pupil could be the original specialist or another geologist interested in picking up some of the first geologist's special knowledge in machine-refined form. For both the first and the last, the dialogue between machine and human must of necessity be conducted at the conceptual level to which the human specialist is accustomed. This means that for knowledge refining and all creation of new knowledge by computer, it is essential that the structures used to represent knowledge in the machine fit the human window, describing the subject domain in the same way the person does. Otherwise both teacher and learner mode become impossible.

There are a great number of specialist fields, each with its lore and texts and an ample degree of confusion and gappiness, which would make excellent raw material for knowledge refining. We can foresee a whole industry arising to tackle the job, based around a novel type of industrial plant, the "knowledge refinery," which would take in specialist knowledge in its existing form and debug it, pull it together, carry out creative gap-filling wherever the need becomes evident, and turn out knowledge that is precise, tested, and certified correct.

Looking further afield, there are large quantities of knowledge about at many different intellectual levels, most of it notably unrefined. Many man-centuries of mental work gather dust on library shelves—contradictory, disparate, and indigestible. Eventually it should be possible to set to work on reformulating and refining all this. The boon to mankind would be significant if even a fraction of the world's accumulated practical wisdom could be sifted, brought together, and turned into accurate usable knowledge in this way.

TURING'S VISION

Making all this happen will not be easy. There is much skepticism of the assertion that computers can actually create something new. People do not readily credit machines with creativity, partly because creativity has always been a thing of mystery, of essentially human quality, and they are offended to see it apparently brought down to the level of nuts and bolts. The cry is still heard: "You only get out what you put in." Many serious academics as well are bothered by the central role played by induction in computer creativity. The distinguished philosopher of science Sir Karl Popper denies that induction can be the source of new knowledge. Now, the evidence of concrete results is turning against the doubters. But we can also cite the vision of the man who in effect devised the whole theory of modern computing, years before electronic computers were technically feasible—the English mathematician Alan Turing, who died in 1954.

Turing's great achievement was to show, by a thought experiment in 1937, that a general-purpose computing machine was logically possible and would be capable of solving an unlimited variety of problems. He did this by conceiving a hypothetical device, since dubbed the Universal Turing Machine, that would wander up and down a tape on which was inscribed the data and a program, peering here, overwriting there, until an answer had been output onto the tape. As befits a person of such originality, Turing had an extraordinary turn of mind, and a carefree disregard of how the rest of the world behaved or thought. He used to cycle to work wearing a gas mask as a protection against pollen. While working at the top-secret code-breaking center at Bletchley Park during

World War II, he buried some silver in the woods nearby as a precaution against the liquidation of bank accounts in the event of a successful German invasion and later forgot where the hiding place was. He recruited a youthful Donald Michie after the war to help find it, with the aid of a gimcrack metal detector he put together himself, but to no avail.

Turing's own attempts at building machinery were inept, but his foresight about how others might do so was unsurpassed. He described before any real computers were operational a great deal about how these machines would be used, including many concepts that are now commonplace in data processing: loops, subroutines, bootstrapping, remote access. In a lecture to the London Mathematical Society in February 1947, he uttered some prophecies that strike a modern-day computer technologist (or user) as uncanny:

> Roughly speaking those who work in connection with the Automatic Computing Engine will be divided into its masters and its servants. Its masters will plan out instruction tables for it, thinking up deeper and deeper ways of using it. Its servants will feed it with cards as it calls for them. They will put right any parts that go wrong. They will assemble data that it requires. In fact the servants will take the place of limbs. As time goes on the calculator itself will take over the functions both of masters and of servants. The servants will be replaced by mechanical and electrical limbs and sense organs. One might for instance provide curve followers to enable data to be taken direct from curves instead of having girls read off values and punch them on cards. The masters are liable to get replaced because as soon as any technique becomes at all stereotyped it becomes possible to devise a system of instruction tables which will enable the electronic computer to do it for itself. It may happen however that the masters will refuse to do this. They may be unwilling to let their jobs be stolen from them in this way. In that case they would surround the whole of their work with mystery and make excuses, couched in well-chosen gibberish, whenever any dangerous suggestions were

made. I think that a reaction of this kind is a very real danger. This topic naturally leads to the question as to how far it is possible in principle for a computing machine to simulate human activities.[5]

EVOLVING THE TABLES

Turing describes in detail how the machine holds in its memory both data and "instruction tables" (the program). These tables would be worked out in detail in advance by mathematicians, but this mode of working would leave much to be desired. "What we want," Turing asserts, "is a machine that can learn from experience." He explains:

It has been said that computing machines can only carry out the processes that they are instructed to do. This is certainly true in the sense that if they do something other than what they were instructed then they have just made some mistake. It is also true that the intention in constructing these machines in the first instance is to treat them as slaves, giving them only jobs which have been thought out in detail, jobs such that the user of the machine fully understands in principle what is going on all the time. Up till the present, machines have only been used in this way. But is it necessary that they should always be used in such a manner? Let us suppose we have set up a machine with certain initial instruction tables, so constructed that these tables might on occasion, if good reason arose, modify those tables. One can imagine that after the machine had been operating for some time, the instructions would have been altered out of all recognition, but nevertheless still be such that one would have to admit that the machine was still doing very worthwhile calculations. Possibly it might still be getting results of the type desired when the machine was first set up, but in a much more efficient manner. In such a case one would have to admit that the progress of the machine had not been foreseen when its original instructions were put in. It would be like a pupil who had learnt much from his master, but had added much more by his own work. When this happens I feel that one is obliged to regard the machine as showing intelligence.

The technique of having a program change part of itself is already used to a certain extent with low-level languages. It is, however, frowned upon as untidy. Only one or two experimental AI languages have facilities for operating on code as data or executing data as code. Turing himself, though, knew where he stood, and characteristically it was not on the side of convention or tidiness. The closing passage of the 1947 lecture brings this home with eloquence and force, and a clear affirmation of the principle that machines should learn by inductive modification of their instructions in response to the behavior of humans:

> It might be argued that there is a fundamental contradiction in the idea of a machine with intelligence. It is certainly true that "acting like a machine" has become synonymous with lack of adaptibility. But the reason for this is obvious. Machines in the past have had very little storage, and there has been no question of the machine having any discretion. The argument might however be put into a more aggressive form. It has for instance been shown that with certain logical systems there can be no machine which will distinguish provable formulae of the system from unprovable, i.e., that there is no test that the machine can apply which will divide propositions with certainty into these two classes. Thus if a machine is made for this purpose it must in some cases fail to give an answer. On the other hand if a mathematician is confronted with such a problem he would search around [and] find new methods of proof, so that he ought eventually to be able to reach a decision about any given formula. This would be the argument. Against it I would say that fair play must be given to the machine. Instead of it sometimes giving no answer we could arrange that it gives occasional wrong answers. But the human mathematician would likewise make blunders when trying out new techniques. It is

easy for us to regard these blunders as not counting and give him another chance, but the machine would probably be allowed no mercy. In other words then, if a machine is expected to be infallible, it cannot also be intelligent. There are several mathematical theorems which say almost exactly that. But these theorems say nothing about how much intelligence may be displayed if a machine makes no pretense at infallibility.

To continue my plea for "fair play for the machines" when testing their I.Q.: a human mathematician has always undergone an extensive training. This training may be regarded as not unlike putting instruction tables into a machine. One must therefore not expect a machine to do a very great deal of building up of instruction tables on its own. No man adds very much to the body of knowledge; why should we expect more of a machine? Putting the same point differently, the machine must be allowed to have contact with human beings in order that it may adapt itself to their standards. The game of chess may perhaps be rather suitable for this purpose, as the moves of the machine's opponent will automatically provide this contact.

Now, three decades later, it is clear that the amount machines will eventually be able to add to the body of human knowledge may outreach even Turing's imagination.

7

A METAPHOR UPSIDE DOWN

IN THE PUBLIC MIND the notion of creativity is associated first and foremost with the arts. So when considering computer creativity, it is natural to ask, "Is it possible for computers to produce new works of art?" Of course in some ways art seems antithetical to modern technology. We still tend to think of the artist in his garret, too preoccupied with matters of the spirit to concern himself with nuts and bolts. But in fact, artists throughout history have embraced new technology whenever it has offered them tangible benefits: new colors, new alloys, new methods of printmaking, new musical instruments. On top of that, art is in its essence information, so we would expect the new information-handling technology to be relevant to it. Indeed since quite early in the history of computers, scattered individuals have braved the mutual suspicion of artists and technologists to explore how these machines could be used in such fields of aesthetic creativity as painting, sculpture, music, and poetry. The results have been uneven and surrounded by controversy. In what can only be a cursory review, we aim by citing some representative examples to give readers an idea of what is going on and of the issues involved.

PAINTING

Probably the field in which most work has been done, and in which the issues are most clear-cut, is painting and drawing. Here there are two distinct, indeed antagonistic, approaches to the use of computers. In one, the computer is being used simply as a tool—a very elaborate palette and canvas on which the artist "paints" by a variety of methods. In the other way of working, the artist supplies a program for the machine to follow, without himself necessarily having any idea what the end result will be. It is in this latter technique that we can begin to see the possibility of a computer actually creating art.

One follower of the "computer as tool" approach is the American David Em, who has the improbable job of artist-in-residence at the Jet Propulsion Laboratory in Pasadena, California. This is the control center for the U.S. unmanned space probes to Jupiter, Saturn, and beyond, and in the course of planning these probes the staff at JPL developed a very powerful computer graphics system for simulating what would be seen as the Voyager spacecraft flew past the giant planets in the outer reaches of the solar system. It was essential to make sure Voyager would get its pictures right the first time—there would be no chance of turning around and trying again.

Not only does the graphics system provide much higher color definition than is normally available on computers, but James Blinn's software can generate solid figures and surfaces in perspective and manipulate the image in sundry ways: enlarging, shrinking, moving it around, copying, reflecting, and so on. When he can find time on the machine in between scientific projects, David Em uses it to produce abstract "paintings" of startling originality and vividness, of a dreamlike, almost nightmarish, quality.

He starts by drawing lines with a stylus on an electronic tablet, directing the computer to convert these into a range of thick or thin lines or "sprays" in a choice of 256 colors, in the same way that a traditional artist chooses his paints and brushes. The results are shown on a very high-resolution color screen. He can then manipulate the pictures by various geometrical operations—transforming images, shifting them about, combining them with others, adding surface patterns and "textures," and experimenting with different types of "space." The whole process is one of trial and error. If the color or texture of one feature seems not quite right, it can be changed at the touch of a few buttons. A painting can be stored away and recalled later for further work.

The finished pictures are best viewed on the actual color screen, which gives brilliant, almost scintillating, images. Em describes himself as "fascinated by the nature of electronic light." For exhibitions where the computer equipment is not available, Em photographs the images from the screen and makes 30-inch by 40-inch color prints. He has also made some into lithographs, and is aiming to produce prints ten feet long.

Figure 36. David Em: *Persepol*. Software by James Blinn at Jet Propulsion Laboratory.

Em's visions are literally fantastic. Some have a flavor of science fiction, no doubt stimulated by his environment. As he says himself, "They are imagery that could not exist in reality." People often tell him that the pictures remind them of things they have seen in their dreams, and this seems to stem from the curious mixture of purely abstract and vaguely natural forms they contain. Architectural features, valleys, and rudimentary landscapes seem to be visible in many of the paintings, as Em himself points out. In some surprise he tells us, "It is forms found in nature that the computer likes to deal with on its own most of all." Although the picture is entirely under Em's control, he is certain that the end results are quite different from what he would be producing in a conventional medium. "The computer leads me into trains of thought that would never have occurred to me without it," he asserts. In a way, the medium does tell him what to do, and it is possible for him not to know at the beginning of a painting where it will end up. But that was true of classical painters too, he reminds us. The trail-and-error process has turned painting into a kind of exploration: Em can move about in the structures he has created and find out what is there, something painters have never been able to do before. "It's a different mental process," he says.

One thing of which he is certain is that he could never exhaust the possibilities of his new medium. "I feel I have an infinite machine here," he says. He is carrying on working with it to find new visions, new relationships between colors, new spaces. "The medium is only at the Neanderthal stage," he declares. It need not be confined to use with abstract art, he points out—others have used it to produce highly naturalistic, almost photo-realistic, pictures.

It was at a California plastics factory that Em was first lured away from conventional art by the aesthetic potential of technology. The firm's owner was interested in art and had the idea that his molding machines could be used for creative ends. Em was hired as artist-in-residence and spent some time producing room-sized plastic sculptures. This got him into an environment totally foreign to him as a solitary artist—he had to learn to organize helpers to operate the machines with him, and he had to learn to deal with management. These continue to be sizable preoccupations at JPL.

Outside the studio, or rather computer room, Em has a passionate interest in theater. Scattered around Hollywood are a host of ambitious small playhouses that provide a creative outlet for talented people in the film industry who have to spend their working days producing pap. For these Em writes and directs extraordinary multi-media performances, using projections of his own paintings as scenery, as well as lasers, synthetic music, and bizarre insect-like costumes likewise designed by him. As yet the computer cannot control the projections directly, but this is the next logical step. An on-line video projector would open up the fascinating possibility of varying the visual effects in accordance with the action on the stage, as it happens.

For other events Em has generated huge moving displays, ten feet high and eighty feet long, using more conventional analogue electronics and projectors. "Scale makes a lot of difference psychologically," he says. "The effect of that display was overwhelming."

How do people react to his work? "The public for this sort of thing is still very small," Em says, "and people tend to spend a lot of time wondering how it is done rather than looking at the pictures." He also has few peers to share his ideas with. Other artists he meets tend to be suspicious of technology, finding it cold and hostile, and he often finds more sympathy among scientists. Paul Brown, late of the Slade School of Art in London, has had similar experiences. He once showed some drawings to a supposedly learned critic, who was very excited by them and praised them profusely. He asked Brown how they were drawn, and on hearing that a computer was involved, immediately changed his mind about the pictures. "I thought there was something cold and calculated about them," he commented. Brown adds that while technologists may not be prejudiced in that way, they are often disinclined to regard art as a serious activity.

DRAWING BY EXPERT SYSTEM

Quite the opposite approach to Em's is taken by Harold Cohen, an English artist based at the University of California at San Diego. While working as a conventional painter in the late 1960s, Cohen became interested in seeing whether computers could be used to shed some light on the nature of visual experience—why it was that he could make some marks on paper and someone else would say, "That's a face." Friends, notably Ed Feigenbaum, taught him programming, and the outcome of this was a system called Aaron, which produced drawings under the control of a PDP-11/34 minicomputer. The actual drawing was done by a little electric cart, about four inches long and carrying a pen, which trundled around a large sheet of paper stretched out on the floor. The computer kept track of where the cart was by means of sonar.[1]

The machine drew entirely on its own and Cohen took no part in the process. The program consisted of about 300 rules worked out in advance by Cohen, which gave the system an understanding of such concepts as lines, closures, and shading. As the drawing proceeded, the program would make choices about what to do at various points by in effect "rolling a die"—that is, it would activate a special routine that generated random (or almost random) numbers in a given range. As the picture filled up, the program would be more and more constrained in what it could do, by what was already on the paper interacting with the rules.

Rules would specify what kinds of features would be desirable, such as "If there is such-and-such a feature here, don't put another feature close to it," or "If you are drawing a form and you run up against another form, lift the pen to let the earlier form overlap the new one." Objects the program handled fell into a strict hierarchy:

pictures
  groups
    figures
      "systems" (parts of figures)
        lines (curved)
          straight line segments

Particularly important concepts that the program was given included the difference between open and closed forms, and occlusion.

Figure 37. Harold Cohen: *Drawing by Aaron*

Figure 38. Harold Cohen: *Drawing by Aaron2*

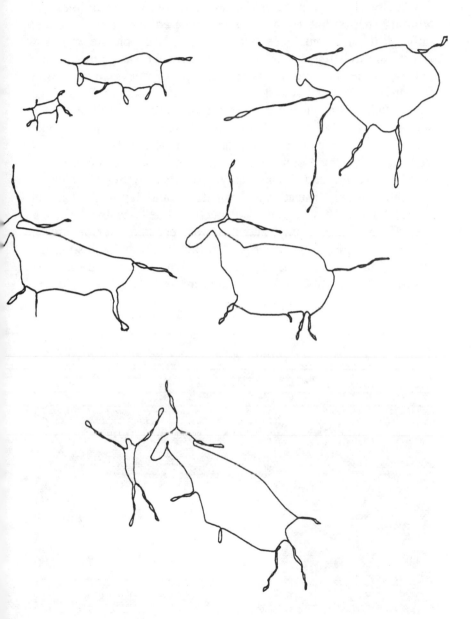

Figure 39. Harold Cohen: *Drawings by Anims*

The results were pictures containing plenty of zigzag lines and arbitrary shapes, but also what often appeared to be rocks, clouds, birds, fish, and sometimes lines of hills. Each picture was different, and Cohen had no way of knowing what was going to come out each time. In building his program out of rules, Cohen had in fact produced an expert system, albeit an unusual one. The human expert and the knowledge engineer in this case were the same person—himself. Cohen had also made a deliberate attempt to model the process by which a human artist draws, not as one smooth movement, but by a series of short strokes with continuous feedback. Hence the cart did not move directly to point (x,y) like a computer plotter. Instead, the computer would say to the cart, in effect, "Turn the wheels by so much and tell me by the sonar where it has taken you," and this was repeated over and over. There was slippage of the wheels on the paper, and adjusting the length of the axle and the rate and sensitivity of the feedback system would give considerable variation in the "style" of the drawings.

Figure 40. Aaron in action

Out of Aaron, Cohen has now developed Aaron2 which, apart from having greater knowledge, is intended to be much further down the road to genuine intelligence by being able to learn from experience.[2] Cohen sees it as dealing with *representations* rather than images, which were what Aaron worked with. An image, Cohen explains, is "a collection of marks implying ordering," while a representation is "a collection of marks implying intention with respect to the outside world." Again, the program's concepts are held in hierarchies: for example the set "representations of solid objects" is included in the set "closed forms." Aaron2 is designed to give much more of an illusion of three dimensions than its predecessor. Cohen has also dispensed with the drawing cart because it was too difficult to keep the sonar working properly and because the drawings were unmanageably large and slow to produce. He now uses a conventional computer plotter, in which a pen is moved around on paper by a mechanical arm.

Even in its infancy Aaron2's drawings show a distinct "maturity" compared to those of its progenitor. It remembers previous drawings, so it can relate its current work to them, and eventually it is intended to be self-modifying, so, like a human artist, it can learn from its experience. That will require, as Cohen says, some means of giving it criteria by which to judge its own performance. We will then have the first expert-system art critic.

Looking further into the nature of representations, Cohen at one point devised another program called Anims, which produced figures with random variations around the basic structure of body, head, and four legs. This was prompted by the work of David Marr into the question of how humans "package" information in their brains, much the same concern as that behind the Piagetian work we describe in Chapter 4. It transpired that remarkably little information has to be stored away in order for it to be possible to reconstruct images with a very real appearance. The figures from the program turned out to be surprisingly similar to prehistoric cave drawings of animals. However, Cohen felt this work was too limited to be viewed as art making and so has not taken it any further.[3]

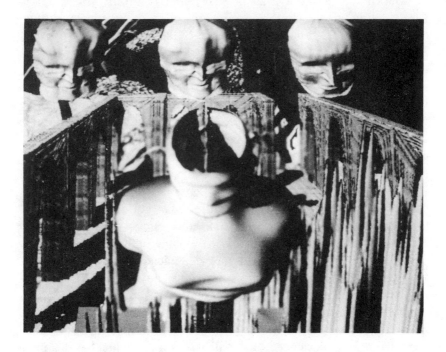

Figure 41. Hervé Huitric and Monique Nahas: *Venusberg*. The artists, who work at the Universities of Paris 7 and 8, use no graphics tablet in their work—the curves are all constructed mathematically from parameters they feed in, using a technique known as "B-splines" and others. Objects such as the heads come from real solid models that are digitized and fed into the computer as numbers, there to be manipulated by the machine.

THROWING AWAY THE DICE

Other computer artists tend to follow one or the other of the two approaches we have described, usually producing their work on an ordinary computer pen plotter. Sometimes they take the pen out and substitute a paint brush. In contrast to the "dice-throwing" technique of Cohen, it is possible to construct a drawing program in which there is no random element but in which the rules and the process they lead to are so complicated that the artist still has no way of knowing what the finished picture will look like. Chris Briscoe, while working at the Slade School in London, did this by letting a series of points in arbitrary starting positions move as if they were objects attracted to each other by gravity. The computer worked out the tracks and plotted them to make the picture.

The Canadian Chris Crabtree in his "story pieces" allows the computer to produce a linear sequence of images that look very much like people, flowers, and the like, giving the impression of a narrative.[4]

Another Canadian, Theo Goldberg, is interested in the connection between painting and music and has devised a graphics system and a music synthesizer that both work from initial sets of numeric data. He feeds the same data into both systems and from one gets pictures with large areas of soft colors overlaid with geometrical patterns of lines, and from the other gets electronic music in a modern cacophonous style. The music is played from tape while slides of the pictures are projected, and the viewer is invited by the artist to see how the picture represents the music and vice versa, as different manifestations of the same thing.

SHARPENING THE PALETTE KNIVES

The two approaches to computer art have led to a schism in the field every bit as vehement as the rivalry between painters and sculptors in Titian's day. The "tool" approach, as exemplified by David Em, tends to be dismissed by those in the other camp as trivial—as "painting by numbers"—its products scorned as banal. Harold Cohen was presented some years ago with the idea for an "electronic paintbox" and responded thus:

[The] image of the artist of the future painting with a paintless brush on a television tube with one hand—because it is after all an artist's touch that counts—while twiddling knobs with the other: dressed, presumably, in smock and beret, and cracking walnuts with his left foot: this image is as silly as misguided.[5]

Cohen's work in its turn is described by some of his opponents as "chicken scratchings." Analyzing the principles at issue, the English artist Dominic Boreham maintains that the way a computer enables him to paint by an iterative process, trying out something, judging, changing what is not quite right, is entirely valid as art and produces pieces that could not possibly be made without a computer. The judgments he makes in accepting or adjusting aspects of a picture could not be embodied in rules, yet rules are

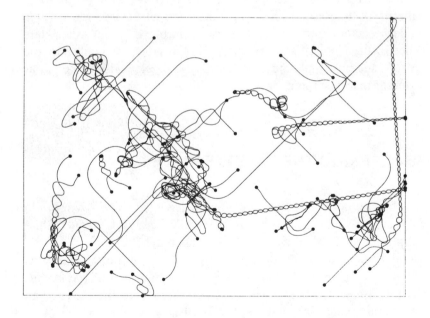

Figure 42. Chris Briscoe: Untitled

Figure 43. The creatures in Chris Crabtree's *Story Pieces* move about, eat, grow, fight, and reproduce in a manner reminiscent of John Conway's celebrated simulation of biological growth and competition, the Life Game.

what Cohen's system consists of in its entirety. "You can't produce art with an algorithm," Boreham declares.

The schism in David Em's case is accentuated by his determination not to learn the engineering skills involved in his art, but rather to rely on the experts around him. Otherwise, he feels, it is all too easy to dissipate all one's energy in just getting the equipment to work. Too many artists he knows have learned programming and now spend all their time writing software and never producing any art. Cohen in contrast is heavily involved in the technology, down to the smallest detail. He even builds all his circuit boards and plotting mechanisms himself. Artists are "enabled," he insists, by the technology they use:

> Devices are what we seem to use: but the truth is that, unless we have a clear view of what they are, unless we are sensitive to their functions within the economic hierarchy which generated them, *they* will almost certainly end up using *us*. Technologies constrain their users. The more powerfully a technology serves its designed-in purpose, the more the individual is constrained by its use: not simply in the sense that an etching will always look like an etching and not like a watercolor: but that the individual is constrained intellectually from conceiving of any possibility other than what is given him by the technology. . . .
>
> Just as the artist finds himself offered a whole toyshop full of new toys, he finds that a century of preparation has gone into ensuring that he asks no questions about what they are and how they work. They do what they do, and they are designed to require no participation of him more intellectually challenging than button-pushing.
>
> It must surely be the case that technological resources which do not challenge the artist's intelligence will not *enable* his intelligence, and through it the production of powerful and original work. . . .
>
> We know already that no one makes art by finding some tame programmer to write a few graphic subroutines. In the years that that game has been going on, not one single artwork

of major importance has resulted from it. When you consider that the parallel case in printmaking would be that of a printer who has no idea what art is, working for an artist who knows nothing about printing technology and doesn't want to have to find out, there is absolutely no reason to assume that one will.[6]

Brian Reffin Smith of the Royal College of Art suggests there is a third category of use of computers in art, in which the machine helps the artist to develop his concepts and perceptions:

It arises out of the observation that (certainly at the Computer Studio of the Royal College of Art) one of the most frequent modes of interaction between artists and computers is as follows. A person comes in, with a problem that they might normally try to solve using pen and paper, paint, film or any other medium. They then use the computer to "worry at" their problem, using graphics on the computer screen, or other, more conceptual representations of the problem. The person then, as often as not, goes away and carries on using the old materials—but their *perception* of the problem has changed. It has been externalized between the person and the computer screen a few inches away.[7]

Artists are constantly being influenced by the work of other artists, by the plays and films they see and so on, and experience with a computer can be just as valid, in Smith's view. This could be taken even further, with highly elaborate computer techniques of exploring art and perception. For example, one of the most important things computers can do for makers of animated films is "in-betweening"—taking two drawings of a figure in different positions provided by the artist and working out all the intermediate frames to give the illusion of smooth motion in the finished film. What would happen Smith asks, if you tried to "in-between" a Rembrandt and a Jackson Pollock? Many other fascinating insights into art are waiting to be found through the use of computers, Smith is convinced.

ANIMATION

In addition to taking over in-betweening and many of the other tedious processes of hand animation, computers open up substantial new possibilities in this medium. They can generate surface textures, shadows, reflections, and shines all automatically, giving a realism and an illusion of three dimensions that are quite impractical in hand animation. Figure 41 looks like a photograph of a model, but in fact it is a still from *The Works,* a forthcoming animated science fiction film being made at New York Institute of Technology. The principal problem involved is the computing power needed: each frame of a high-definition film can take up to one or two hours of processor time to produce because it contains so much detail.

As is the way with techniques of this sort, the first people in the outside world to take up computer animation enthusiastically have been television advertisers. Disney's feature film *Tron* combines a plot of extreme banality with uninspired computer graphics. *The Works,* with its articulated 3-D figures, promises to be much more stimulating, although there is a worry that the project was really too ambitious for NYIT's resources.

Most of the objects depicted in films of this genre are artificial—space ships and the like—and so can be generated as an assemblage of regular geometric shapes such as spheres and cylinders, as in Figure 41. The computer can handle these quite easily. On the other hand, if the film maker wants to include natural elements such as landscapes, he has a problem in that to seem realistic the scene has to be irregular and contain large amounts of detail. A picture of a lawn, for instance, must comprise many thousands of blades of grass, but they cannot all be the same. If one image of a blade were repeated over and over in the usual computer technique, the lawn would look utterly unreal. Each

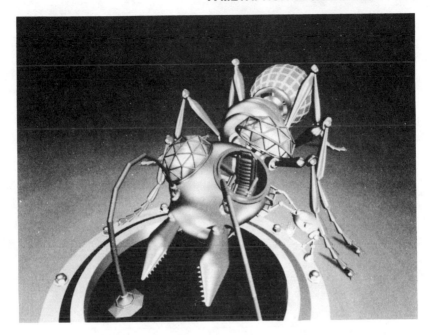

Figure 44. This still from *The Works*, New York Institute of Technology's animated science fiction film in preparation, looks like a photograph of a model, but in fact the pictures are "drawn" entirely by computer, resulting in realism unknown in conventional hand animation. *(Dick Lundin, NYIT)*

blade needs to be slightly different, but for an artist to specify every one separately would be a colossal task. On top of that, the vast amount of information thus compiled would have to be held in a large data base, unmanageable and costly. To overcome this problem, Benoît Mandelbrot of IBM and others following on from his work have devised the technique of *fractals,* whereby the irregularity of natural objects is simulated by the computer adding random variations to features supplied by the artist, making smooth lines crooked and so on (Figure 42). Using this method, surprisingly realistic mountains, rock-strewn valleys, coastlines, and star clusters can be generated, with the artist only having to specify a few points.[8] Indeed, fractals are now being used to produce still paintings and sculptures as well as animation (Figure 43). This raises the interesting question of whether fractal landscapes should be judged on the same criteria as the works of conventional landscape painters. Paul Brown thinks that up to a point they should, but other artists disagree strongly.

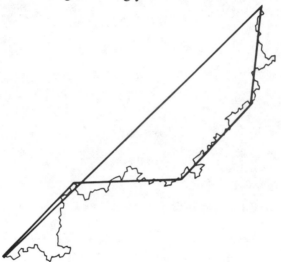

Figure 45. ". . . And the straight shall be made crooked . . ." Irregular curve obtained from four straight-line segments through the technique of fractals.

SCULPTURE

Some work has been done in producing sculpture by computer, with the processor connected to a machine tool that carves a block of metal or other material. However, the principal interest computers have aroused in this field is to do with kinetic sculpture. An early example of this was Seek, put together in 1970 by Nicholas Negroponte and his colleagues at MIT. This consisted of a model overhead crane driven by a minicomputer, which would stack up five hundred two-inch cubes in a random arrangement with plenty of nooks and crannies, remembering where all the cubes were. Into this "environment" would be released a colony of gerbils, who would run around knocking the cubes every which way, and the computer would try and put them back into some semblance of order.[9] What started as a demonstration of a computer observably dealing with unpredictable events turned into a metaphor of interaction between an animate and an inanimate world. Opportunities for misinterpretation by the public (at the Jewish Museum in New York, where Seek was on show) were endless. Negroponte comments:

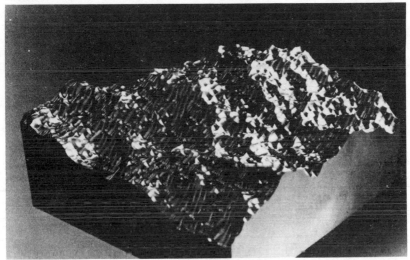

Figure 46. ". . . and the plain places rough." Sculpture of a mountain range produced by Benoît Mandelbrot using fractals and a computer-driven machine tool. *(Photograph: IBM)*

Reviews of the show failed to keep Seek intact, to see its animate and inanimate aspects as equally purposeful. *The New York Times* (September 18, 1970) reported that ". . . a mechanical grappler rearranges them [the blocks] to wall the furry creatures in"; *Art News* (December 1970, in a snide editorial entitled "Gerbil ex Machina") wrote, "The gerbils could use their blocks to achieve positive, socially meaningful ends, but not just mess around with them"; and *The Wall Street Journal* simply found it and computer art in general ideologically "kinky."[10]

Many of the gerbils died; legend has it that this was from frustration.

Edward Ihnatowicz is a Polish-born sculptor living in England whose interest in the kinetic stems from his conviction that the behavior of something tells us far more about it than its appearance. This led him to build The Senster, one of the most influential kinetic sculptures ever made (Figure 47). It consisted of a fifteen-foot-long steel frame articulated in six different places, with the joints all powered by hydraulics, the whole vaguely reminiscent of a giraffe made of tubular lattice. On The Senster's "head" were carried an array of microphones and a Doppler radar system. The Honeywell minicomputer controlling the mechanism was programmed to make it react to three things: moderate and low sounds, loud sounds, and fast motion. Moderate sounds the head would move toward, loud sounds it would pull back from, and fast motion it would track. The result was an uncanny resemblance to a living thing, and the crowds at the Evoluon in Eindhoven, Holland, where it was on show, reacted with enormous excitement. Children would shout and wave at it, call it names, and even throw things. Ihnatowicz explains that its movements seemed to stem from situations that people recognized.

In the quiet of the early morning the machine would be found with its head down, listening to the faint noise of its own hydraulic pumps. Then if a girl walked by, the head would follow her, looking at her legs. Ihnatowicz describes his own first stomach-turning experience of the machine, when he had just got it working: he unconsciously cleared his throat, and the head came right up to him as if to ask, "Are you all right?" He also noticed a curious aspect of the effect The Senster had on people. When he was testing it he gave it various random patterns of motion to go through. Children who saw it operating in this mode found it very frightening, but no one was ever frightened when it was working in the museum with its proper software, responding to sounds and movement.

Figure 47. Edward Ihnatowicz: *The Senster,* on show at the Evoluon exhibition in the Netherlands. The computer is at the right rear.

Although The Senster was dismantled some years ago, many people who saw it still remember vividly what a strong impression it made on them. Ihnatowicz has various ideas for further developments, including an investigation of how motion and perception are interdependent, an important topic for Artificial Intelligence. Unfortunately, the mechanisms are necessarily expensive and the resources to build them are not easy to come by.[11]

MUSIC

There are some instances of computers being used as tools in the composing of music. Peter Zinovieff has spent much of his working life building electronic synthesizers, but he is also interested in seeing how quite different sounds, some for instance from the real world, could be incorporated in music. An example could be the noise made by rapping with the knuckles on a door. He uses a computer to analyze these sounds and see how they could be captured and included in music.

At the same time computers have been widely used actually to compose music, typically employing conventional notes produced by a synthesizer under program control. It is quite easy to connect a loudspeaker to the output of a computer, and unlimited sounds can be made according to a pattern specified by the programmer, which may or may not include a random element.

Chance has, of course, long been used in what is known as aleatory music, in which the performers are given occasional choices as to what to play. In the eighteenth century quite a number of pieces of "dice music" were published, some attributed to Mozart and Haydn. A sixteen-bar piece might, for instance, give eleven different choices for each bar, written out in a rectangular array of sixteen columns of eleven bars each, and the player would make a choice at each bar by rolling dice. (Presumably, he rolled the dice sixteen times beforehand so he did not have to stop playing between each bar.) This was described on one score as "an easy method for composing an infinite number of minuet-and-trios." "Infinite," of course, is a bit of an exaggeration—the actual number is 11^{16}, or forty-six quadrillion, but in any case it enlarges the musicologists' corpus of Mozart's music more than somewhat.[12]

Each bar was carefully worked out to fit in musically with every other bar in adjoining columns so that the effect would be reasonably acceptable to eighteenth-century ears. Randomness in modern music tends to be much more obviously random. One of the best-known figures in British computer music is Alan Sutcliffe, whose early pieces he describes as "based on randomness but in a controlled way." Choices were made according to pseudo-random numbers generated by the program. Peter Zinovieff, working with Sutcliffe, had earlier used a real-random number generator in the form of a tiny radioactive source with a Geiger counter attached. Sutcliffe relates: "The unrepeatability of this device could be a nuisance. If you hadn't made a recording of the output, there was no question of 'Play it again, Sam,' as it was a genuine case of the lost chord."[13] The central routine of the program would generate pseudo-random patterns, which were fed back into the same routine to generate more patterns, and so on several times around the loop until a final set of patterns was punched out on paper tape and fed into a sound synthesizer.

Each movement of a work would have a number of control values, specifying whether notes were to be mainly long, mainly short, or of mixed duration; mainly high or low or with few in the middle, and so on. The result of this was that each movement had a noticeably different character: some were melodic, some were mainly chords, others had the flavor of counterpoint. There were plenty of boring passages but also some memorable parts, Sutcliffe attests.

His work more recently has been aimed at getting rid of the random element altogether, so that the music is produced entirely by algorithm. The process is the key. There are two distinct approaches to art, as Sutcliffe sees it—one in which the artist conceives of an effect he wishes to achieve and then tries to devise a means of achieving it, and the other in which he conceives of a process and then stands back to see what comes out of it. It is the latter that interests Sutcliffe: the artist having to keep his distance and resist the temptation to interfere and say, "I think it's going to be like this." The result is that the artist can be as pleasantly surprised as anyone by what comes out.

Very simple programs can generate an amazingly rich diversity of patterns, Sutcliffe asserts. In reply to the claim that you cannot make art by an algorithm, he remarks, "My hope is to produce things as interesting as trees or pebbles or old bits of wood. Those were produced by algorithms, together with some effects from the environment." Certainly the DNA in the seed of a tree can be seen as a program—why, Sutcliffe reasons, could not a human-devised program likewise yield something fascinating? On the lack of the human element in the process, he declares, "I abhor the view that art is to do with self-expression—with expressing emotions. Composers don't only write fast movements when they are happy and slow movements when they are sad." What is important, he says, is not the emotion of the producer of the art, but the emotion evoked in the receiver.

POETRY

Getting a computer to write poetry requires no elaborate output devices other than the printer, with the result that this has long been a popular form of machine art. The computer is normally given two things: a vocabulary of words or phrases to choose from and a framework in which to put these by some process, random or otherwise. The framework can be a "closed form" or an "open form." Robin Shirley explains:

> A closed form is one in which the elements (variable words or phrases) are slotted into predetermined holes in a fixed framework, whereas in an open form there is no fixed part and the poem is composed by assembling the elements together in a chain of indeterminate length.
>
> As Chomsky has pointed out, it is open forms which characterize natural languages, and despite their greater difficulty I think that the future development of computer poetry lies mainly in this field. Closed forms are very easy to devise and program, but seem to bear very little repetition before their artificial and limited character shows through.[14]

It is quite easy, as Shirley points out, to provide forms with slots, each labeled with the part of speech it is to contain. It is very much harder to give a program a sense of the enormous variety of sentence structures that human writers can employ. Various constraints are imposed on the poem-writing process as it goes along, such as a control over repetition of words or expressions. Repetition would not be prevented altogether—it would simply be made more or less likely according to the whim of the programmer.

Robin Shirley is an English crystallographer who has been writing poetry both with and without computers for over twenty years. He is especially interested in the effect that the medium has on an artist's work. "All art is shaped in part by the response of the artist to the character of his tools," he says. Computers have great potential for exploring this issue, he feels; for example, a human sculptor produces something quite different according to whether he is carving marble, or wood, or ice cream, but a computer-controlled machine tool would come up with exactly the same shape in all those cases.

Shirley brings up the concept of the indirect medium, in which something outside the control of the originator is interposed between him and the audience. In music it is the performers; in cinema, the whole production crew. It is a totally new experience for poetry to find itself in the position of an indirect medium, but that is what computers make possible. The poet can supply the computer with various ideas and then stand back and feel either pleased or disappointed with the results. "If you don't have control over the way things are arranged, you place yourself in the hands of fortune," he explains. "Skill is the art of being lucky."

Shirley is also interested in getting away from the traditional Western view of poetry as an entirely individual activity. He wants to make the medium open to collaboration, so he performs his work with a group of others, accompanied by (human-composed) music. An early work was "The Sunflower Suite," a collection of computer-assisted poems on the theme of transience. They were written using his program Bard, which he describes as "an element selector and arranger, to which a limited critical faculty has been added." Here is the opening poem, preceded by Shirley's introduction:

★   I want you to imagine a time in the distant future
     perhaps millennia from now, when (if it survives)
     the human race will be scattered over the vast wastes of the
        galaxy,
     where distances are measured in lifetimes.

★   I want you to imagine our descendants,
     travelling from generation to generation,
     seeking worlds that will give a foothold for existence.

★   This poem is dedicated to children born on such a journey,
    in the great voids between the stars,
    to whom the cities and forests of Earth are only a legend.

PAVAN FOR THE CHILDREN OF DEEP SPACE

Ice worlds,
Haunted by the legend of planets. Ice worlds—
Arcturus Andromeda Vega—orbiting,
Lost among stardust through aeons of crystal.

Your seed has dispersed, lit by the jewels of infinity,
Lost in the empty ocean;
In time with the measured dance of the universe
        orbiting . . . orbiting . . .

I am a child of eternity:
        down is a lifetime in every direction.
Through aeons of crystal your seed has dispersed
on a journey to no destination.
        sunburst starburst
        Mars Venus Jupiter Saturn . . .
Down is a lifetime in every direction

Born out of darkness:
Lost in the palaces of eternity;
Lit by the jewels of infinity
        of the land of nowhere,
Your seed has dispersed in the dark light-years.
        (Sunburst starburst)

I am a child of eternity;
I travel with comets . . .
        born of some other, lost among stardust.
Lit by the jewels of infinity
        down is a lifetime in every direction.

Mars Venus Jupiter Saturn: lost
    in the empty ocean.
Orbiting: on a journey to no destination.
    . . . Procyon Eridanus Rigel . . .

Lit by the jewels of infinity,
I travel with comets.

*   *   *

I TRAVEL WITH COMETS, I TRAVEL WITH COMETS

. . . through aeons of crystal . . .
    . . . of this island universe.

I am a child of eternity (Mars Venus Jupiter Saturn)
I am a child of eternity
    on a journey to no destination.

Lost in the palaces of eternity (Procyon Eridanus Rigel)
I weep no tears.
    I prophesy the beginning.

Born out of darkness on a journey to no destination.
Born of some other, your seed has dispersed . . .
    between the galaxies (born out of darkness)
    between the galaxies—of the land of nowhere.

*   *   *

Down is a lifetime in every direction;
Orbiting . . . dreaming of havens . . .
    (sunburst starburst, lost among stardust)
Lost, in the empty ocean between the galaxies.
I prophesy the beginning, dreaming of havens
    (Mercury Earth Uranus Pluto), lost
    among stardust.

*   *   *

I travel with comets; I weep no tears.
    sunburst starburst . . .
        . . . spindrift stardrift . . .
I prophesy:
    the beginning.

The punctuation and underlining is added by Shirley afterward, but otherwise, if the computer produces a good poem, he is reluctant to change it. "That would be spitting in the eye of the gods," he says. The poems employ an open form on which "an overall shape and design has been imposed." Indeed, Shirley specifies rather more and leaves rather less to chance than do many other computer poets. Nonetheless, he is convinced that his poems would be entirely different without the collaboration of the machine. He is not really interested in the usual questions "What is the place of the computer in the process?"; "Is the program intelligent?" He wants his poems to be judged on the same terms as any others.

FICTION

Poetry writing by computer is considerably easier than prose, not least because readers are used to the idea of poetry seeming to some extent incoherent and disjointed. A story-writing program needs a mechanism for constructing sentences that make sense and are elaborate enough to seem adult, and also a means of devising a plot by manipulating themes such as conflict, revenge, atonement, and so on. G. E. Hughes and some colleagues at the Jagiellonian University of Cracow produced by computer a complete short novel called *Bagabone, Hem 'I Die Now* (the title is pidgin English, from the story's Polynesian setting). It reads like an ordinary book, but was constructed, as Hughes describes it, like a giant game of Consequences. There was also some attempt to devise a literary style through analysis of Joyce, D. H. Lawrence, and various twentieth-century women writers.[15]

I KNOW WHAT I LIKE

All this can seem puzzling to the outsider. We think of the art that impresses us most and recall the enormous mental effort and anguish that went into its creation. What can be the value of art that is produced without a clear idea of a desired end result on the part of the artist? Intuitively, we think of art as negative entropy, and as a general rule the better the art, the more negative the entropy, with every single detail contributing to the overall effect. The process of laboriously selecting the attributes of each detail so that they will contribute to the overall effect is the very reverse of entropy. Surely anything that is random or unpredictable will almost never turn out to contribute in this way, to have any value? After all Stravinsky, no reactionary himself, said: "I hold that music is given to us to create order."[16]

In reply, some computer artists put forward the view that what goes on in the human creative process is no different in kind from what happens in their machines. An artist has an algorithm in his head just as much as a computer does. They go on to dismiss free will as an illusion, no different from random choice, so the chance element in their programs should complete the equivalence of human and computer artistic creation.[17]

The central question then is, what are the algorithms humans use? It is the search for an answer to this question that is the main preoccupation of many computer artists. Harold Cohen sets out deliberately to model human creative behavior, to externalize the process that would otherwise be going on inside him. Lawrence Mazlack at the University of Cincinnati is trying "to develop an aesthetic perception in a computer" in order "to investigate the codification and specification of aesthetic judgment."[18] This leads inevitably to the question, What is art? Some artists insist that art is nothing more than the process of asking, What is art? This has prompted Marshall McLuhan to comment, "Art is anything you can get away with."[19] Other artists are more positive. Edward

Ihnatowicz asserts that art is the process of "modifying the environment so that some aspect of nature, otherwise not discernible, can be revealed—to attract people's attention to an aspect of reality." Robin Shirley suggests that basically "art involves the human faculty of discerning order," and that the essential interaction is with the perceiver, not the creator. In its most general sense, art is the process of making metaphors, Negroponte maintains in a passage wryly headed, "A metaphor cannot be hung upside down."[20]

Throughout all this we see continuing the argument between classicism and romanticism that has been going on in art for hundreds of years, with classicists trying to find order in nature while romanticists prefer to take nature as it is. Earlier in this century the dispute took the form of Determinism *versus* Indeterminism, with its obvious pertinence to the use of randomness in computer art. Perhaps this art is not as revolutionary as it seems.

THIS IS JUST LIKE ART

So how successful have these artists been in their metaphor-making with machines? It is widely agreed that, taken as a whole, art with computers has not lived up to its potential. Negroponte is blunt about this: "Rarely have two disciplines joined forces seemingly to bring out the worst in each other as have computers and art."[21] Those who entered the field early have been disappointed at the low level of interest that has developed. Certainly this is due in part to the bad reputation computer art has acquired, deterring people with talent who might have contributed to raising the standard. Brian Reffin Smith puts forward his explanation of this:

> Traditionally the computer has been used to produce what you might call "pretty pictures." In a sense it's a kind of chocolate box art of information technology, which in some ways has given computing in art a bad name, because people have produced random number squiggles and spirals and so on—maybe they have been mathematicians or computer scientists. They've

said, "Hey! This is just like art!" and put it on their walls and so on. This drives artists and designers mad because if you had done it with a pencil or with string on nails or whatever, people wouldn't look at it twice. Certainly they wouldn't consider it worthy of having an exhibition.[22]

Harold Cohen sees the failure of computer art thus:

For an artist proposing to make images with a computer, the body of knowledge we should be considering is that which binds the nature of a program to the nature of an image, not simply programming skills, even though he can't do without them. "Computer art" has never accomplished that binding, because it has always accepted the characteristic 20th century definition of the computer as a transformation device. To get an image out you have to put an image in. The binding of program to image is impossible, since a transformation process is indifferent to what is being transformed.

To use the computer as a transformation device is to use it on a trivial level. It is a completely general symbol-manipulating device, and allows the writer of a program essentially to define what the machine is any way he or she chooses. That generality gives the computer a very special significance as the first modern device which allows itself to be used as a sort of do-it-yourself design kit, rather than as a single fixed-function tool.[23]

The problem as far as the layman is concerned is that most computer art is highly abstract, and abstract art is hard enough for him to appreciate and judge, superficially or deeply, even when there is no computer involved. Then the aspect of computer creativity is introduced to complicate matters yet further. It is often pointed out that the pictures produced by Harold Cohen's program look very much like the ones he used to paint himself. What then is the point of going to all that trouble with the computer? Cohen remarks that, "The art-sceptic's three-year-old daughter really cannot do as well as Picasso,"[24] and we agree, but can she do as well as Aaron? The exercise may be interesting intellectually but artistically. . . ? Many people watch with fascination as Aaron draws its pictures in the museum and happily buy the finished pieces, but it is hard to know how much of this is aesthetic appreciation and how much is novelty value.

Then there is the issue of randomness. Presumably, the bemused onlooker concludes, if Jackson Pollock could throw paint at his canvases, the computer might as well too, but the rhyme or reason can seem elusive. Then Cohen puts forward his view of randomness: "Primarily, I believe its function is to produce proliferation of the decision space without requiring the artist to 'invent' constantly."[25] But surely the whole business of an artist is to invent! He should hardly regard this as a chore to be evaded! It is easy to reach the conclusion, as Negroponte puts it, that the technology is the whole point: like a burlesque of Marshall McLuhan's ideas, the medium is the message.

Alan Sutcliffe enters the fray at this juncture and insists that computer art has not yet been given a fair chance to prove itself. All art involves the production of a great deal of mediocre work before anything exceptional comes along, and computer art simply needs a longer trial. The public also has a lot of learning to do before it can really appreciate these new media, because the ideas involved are strange and new.

THE SUNDAY PAINTER

Negroponte sees computer art developing in two particular ways. One is an extension of kinetic art, of which The Senster was a notable example:

> Imagine more moody pieces. Simple extrapolations of interactive art can embellish the behavioral model to include inputs from the weather, time of day, Dow-Jones Average, and the results of sports events, elections, or film ratings. In some sense, this could be the art form of off-track betting. Or, with more fantasy, we can imagine a future of the visual arts popu-

lated with patronizing pieces of sculpture and caustic canvases that recognize the viewer to be male or female, rich or poor, bewildered or blasé, you or me. In this fiction, the artist runs a kennel for cuddly art forms that get to know their future owners, who in turn get to know and love them.[26]

Even before Negroponte had written that, Edward Ihnatowicz had built a sculpture with an arm that the viewer pulled, as on a one-armed bandit, while the machine tried to make inferences about the puller's sex and temperament.[27] He must beware who prophesies in jest.

The other development Negroponte foresees is in the direction of personal, as opposed to public, art. He points to all the metaphors we treasure as individuals, but which are of no interest to anyone else: a drawing by one of our children, a stone brought back from an idyllic holiday years ago. Computers provide a whole new set of opportunities for self-expression.

Think of our Sunday painter reincarnated with an easel of electronics and a palette of computer graphics. His work is as invigorating as a game of tennis, his challenge is that of chess, his product is as ephemeral as a child's drawing. In this fantasy lies the potential for the major impact of computers on the visual arts of the future.[28]

Not everyone is happy with this vision. Harold Cohen relates a visit to Xerox's Palo Alto Research Center:

There was also a music program at Xerox, which, I was told, would enable people to compose music even if they didn't know anything about music. Didn't I think that was marvellous, I was asked? No, I said, I thought it was appalling. Why would anyone want to compose music without knowing anything about music? And why—as if I didn't have my suspicions already—would Xerox's well-meaning technologists want to encourage that particular form of lunacy? Well, they said, it was a beginning: I would surely have to admit it was a step in the right direction. No, I said, I was quite sure it was a step in the *wrong* direction.[29]

In the last analysis, if computers produce works of art that are original and interesting, by whatever process, then we have every reason to rejoice and accept the exercise as worthwhile. The problem must be fundamentally that art that says much to us is nearly always based on a great deal of knowledge about the world. The significant artist needs, above all, experience, both of his trade and of life. Up to now, computer art programs have incorporated little knowledge, except perhaps for Harold Cohen's Aarons. Cohen even refers to the work of his Anims program as "Drawings of a know-nothing, almost," although it is surprising how much knowledge of animals these pictures appear to contain. There is, as Robin Shirley puts it, "an immense problem of putting a useful model of the world into a computer, and the task has only just started." As we have said, Harold Cohen has embarked on the process of using the techniques of knowledge-based systems to make pictures, and other artists are certain to follow suit.

A really serious contribution by computers to the arts is still a long way off. Whether computers will ever create great works of art autonomously is hard to say. Negroponte declares that for that to happen, the machine would have to *want* to create the work of art—and that raises any number of philosophical questions. But even if computers only provide a useful augmentation of the human artist's mind, they will have added in an important way to creativity.

8
COMING TO MODEL HEAVEN

Hereafter, when they come to model Heaven
And calculate the stars, how they will wield
The mighty frame, how build, unbuild, contrive
To save appearances, how gird the sphere
With centric and eccentric scribbled o'er,
Cycle and epicycle, orb in orb.

—*Paradise Lost* VIII 79

THE HOUSE OF THOSE who work with their brains has always had two levels. Upstairs live the patricians of theory, whose role is to conserve, propagate, and improve society's treasures of descriptive truth and descriptive style. Here are tended the great explanatory theories that proceed top-down from the highest level of abstraction and show with great conciseness how particular consequences can be derived.

Downstairs live the practitioners: lawyers, doctors, architects, engineers, economic geologists. Not quite so far down we encounter applied mathematicians of various kinds—statisticians, operations analysts, software technologists, aerodesigners, and others. Humbler representatives are mechanics, welders, boat-builders, dressmakers, cooks. The lower levels are expected to keep themselves to themselves, except when called to serve some particular need—to make or mend a chair, to cook a meal, to run an errand. Very occasionally some servant-scholar arises—an Aristotle, a Bacon, or a Spencer—and argues that there are unifying principles in the bottom-up trade. Upstairs people usually smile indulgently at such quaintness. But they are not averse to descending the back stairs when it profits them. Thus a biologist can draw pay from a medical school. A social philosopher can earn a penny helping to school budding lawyers. Behind the engineer stands the physicist; behind the space pilot, the astronomer.

To Upstairs Man, true knowledge is constituted solely of the theorems and facts that define The Way Things Are, immutable. The rest is for tradesmen and troglodytes. Practical men on the other hand, especially in computing, tend to feel that the technology is everything and the theory nothing, that theory is an excuse for woolly-minded academics to stand on the toes of the real men who are grappling with the real issues. Is a chess master, they ask, strengthened by a course in game theory, or a racing cyclist by studying Newton's dynamics? So it has always been, a deadlock. But now the deadlock matters.

Computing is struggling to come to grips with problems for which no explanatory theories exist as yet, or for which using established theories entails impossibly large amounts of processing. So knowledge engineers are developing rule-based systems that use heuristics instead of theory. But in doing this, the engineers may fail to see the brick wall ahead. What happens when a rule-based system encounters a situation for which it has no rules? It has run out of know-how. What it needs is the ability to work out a way of patching the gap. But Mycin has no theoretical knowledge of meningitis with which to do this. Prospector understands nothing of scientific geology. It is becoming imperative that Upstairs and Downstairs should begin to fraternize.

UPSTAIRS MODELS, DOWNSTAIRS MODELS

The social divide looms largest when the time comes to build models for our problem-solving. A model is simply a description of the structure of a complex world, a representation small enough to be portable and manageable by a simple brain, yet large enough to incorporate all the relevant features of the system being modeled. We use models all the time, to help us predict the behavior of systems. They enable us to answer "What if?" questions. For instance, a map is a model that helps us solve the problem of how to get somewhere. It allows you to experiment quickly and painlessly—to find a route by trial and error. You say, "If I go that way and then that way—no, I need to go *that* way . . ." All of our dealings with the world involve mental models of one form or another that describe how we think the world works. It can be shown in psychological experiments that animals too use cognitive models, when a dog realizes that the only way he can catch a rabbit is by an indirect approach, by going around a screen which blocks the straight path. For computers to solve problems, they also need models, but of what kind? There lies the difficulty. There is a choice, corresponding to the two levels in the house of knowledge: heuristic models, based on rules and accumulated know-how, and causal models, based on theories of how the world actually works.

To illustrate the difference, here is a toy example. Figure 48 is a heuristic model—written out here as a couple of decision tables—which tells you when to open your umbrella. It also caricatures in miniature the whole tribe of Mycins, Sacons, Prospectors, Puffs, and Ritas. Each and every one of these is like a green-fingered gardener who knows nothing of botany.

Quite apart from the problem of what to do in situations not covered by the rules (falling ash from a volcanic eruption?), this heuristic model possesses only a glimmer of one of the most important features of expert systems—that is, the ability to provide explanations of its pronouncements when required. "Explanation" is only in the superficial sense of Mycin's explanations, via retrace of the contexts and rules invoked in the course of arriving at a decision.

UMBRELLA TABLE

Condition	Action
user soaked	do-not-open
user outdoors	go-to WEATHER TABLE
else	do-not-open

WEATHER TABLE

Condition	Action
very windy	do-not-open
raining	open
hailing	open
snowing	open
sleeting	open
else	do-not-open

Figure 48. Heuristic tables of when to open an umbrella. Rules are processed in strict order, until a match with the condition part fires some rule's action part.

For something more helpful than simply a regurgitation of rules, we need a causal model. What might it look like in this case? It would have to capture all the workaday physics of three-dimensional space and water, and gravity, fabric, and permeability, not to mention social and biological truths about houses and human likes and dislikes. These would need to be linked and structured in machine memory in relational representations convenient for checking the validity of heuristic theories, convenient also for explaining them and for generating new modules for such theories. Above all, the causal model would be very much bigger than its heuristic counterpart, the two tables. Of course in a nursery example such as this, "deep" explanations of system decisions might not be altogether welcome. Most of us have in our acquaintance some overintellectual person whose readiness to dive back in great detail into first principles is viewed as a mixed blessing by his friends. To such a one you say "Why?" at your peril. We can foresee ramifying sessions with the ultraintelligent umbrella-opener:

MACHINE: Please indicate state of affairs.

USER: Outdoors, user soaked. Umbrella closed. Weather raining.

MACHINE: Advice: "Don't open."

USER: Why?

MACHINE: Rule 003: If user soaked, then "Don't open."

USER: Why?

MACHINE: Necessary precondition of "open" is that user is not soaked. If precondition of an action not satisfied, then advice is "don't do it."

USER: Why?

MACHINE: In this case precondition is related to goal. If some condition implies non-achievability of a goal by an action, then the negation of the condition is incorporated in the precondition. The goal of the action "open" is a state in which the user is not soaked. If the user is soaked, then the goal is not achievable by the action "open."

USER: Why?

MACHINE: Drying action categories are: blowing, vacuuming, blotting, heating, freezing. "Open" is not in any of these categories.

USER: Why?

And so on, with the machine plunging deeper into the physics of evaporation, capillary action, and the rest—endless thorough patience for the endless repetition of "Why?" What a splendid interactive companion such a system would make for certain small children!

A graphic example of a heuristic model in action is Fischer or Karpov playing lightning chess. They can only use heuristic rules—there is no time for anything else—yet they can still hold their own against an ordinary master, who is allowed all the time in the world for search and reasoning. In contrast, an engineer who is fault-finding a machine he has just built is using an entirely causal model, based on his design of how it is intended to work. There should be nothing about the machine he does not understand. The equipment has not been in existence long enough for any heuristics to have been collected about its behavior.

DIFFERENT WAYS OF BUILDING

Quite separate from the type of model is the question of how it is derived. An almanac, for instance, is a model of the solar system that could be constructed either bottom-up, from observations of the movements of the planets, or top-down, using Newton's laws of motion and gravity. (Newton's laws were of course derived in turn from planetary observations.) Fischer's heuristics for lightning chess are built bottom-up from examples. In principle, they could be worked out top-down from the rules of chess, but this would be impracticable: cf. the van Dusen delusion. Primitive man has various models of the physical world, for example to do with the weather. "Red sky at night, shepherd's delight," is an entirely heuristic rule, incorporating no explanation at all, and it is derived bottom-up from observation. But "The reason why there is no fair wind for Troy is that the gods are angry," is a *causal* explanation using a model which, with the aid of analogy, was also derived bottom-up. So causal models can be constructed from empirical generalizations, and indeed this is what most of mythology has consisted of since prehistory.

In many practical domains it is possible to get by, sometimes with flying colors, on heuristic models alone. A cook ignorant of chemistry, a politician ignorant of sociology, a cabinet-maker ignorant of geometry, a weather forecaster ignorant of fluid dynamics—all these are cases in point. Another case is the ability to do arithmetic, which most readers probably brought to concert pitch for one or another school examination before their teens. But how many of us have any deep knowledge of arithmetic, any organized theory from which the reasons why these tricks actually work could be derived? How many could write out Peano's axioms or prove any major theorems of arithmetic?

The discovery that a domain specialist's top-of-the-head skill can be mimicked by relatively simple and uniform computational structures, based on pattern-derived situation-action heuristics, is what has led to the recent rapid development of expert systems. In the present state of the art, constructing causal models tends to be difficult and costly. We are reaching the stage, however, where heuristic models are no longer enough. An expert system needs to be able to follow heuristic rules most of the time, responding quickly and using little in the way of computing resources. Then when a situation arises to which none of the rules applies, it should be able to bring into play a causal model of the domain, which will be slow and expensive but capable of reaching a solution. This way of combining the two types of model in one system is shown in Figure 49.

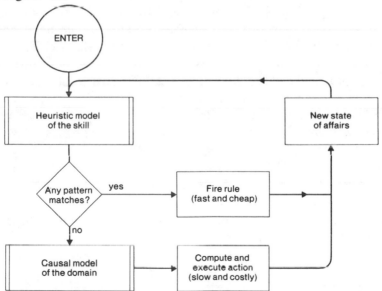

Figure 49. Respective roles of heuristic and causal models in a combined system

As yet, few knowledge engineers have taken this course, but there have been two notable successes. A team at Case Western Reserve University have constructed a system to control an electrical power distribution network. This includes both a heuristic model with 800 rules in an associative store and a causal model incorporating a description of the distribution network together with the quantitative physical laws governing the behavior of electricity.[1] At the University of Illinois, W. B. Rouse and R. M. Hunt produced a fault-diagnosis system for electro-mechanical equipment, based on a mapping from symptomatic patterns to decisions, and also a logical and physical description of the machinery.[2] As the technology moves in this direction, we will be able to have more and more expert systems that are insightful rather than merely skillful. Outlines of this deeper kind of expertise can be glimpsed in the diagnosis system for internal medicine under construction by Harry Pople and Jack Myers at the University of Pittsburgh Medical School.

There is a widespread notion that problem-solving representations built from causal models are necessarily error-free, proved so by their implementers, and thus in some important sense "sound," while heuristic models are by their nature tainted with unbounded and unquantifiable error. In actuality, formal proofs of correctness are no less obtainable for heuristic models than for those of other kinds, provided that the domain is such as to sustain precise mathematical reasoning at all. Someone says, "I need to build an expert problem-solver, but I don't buy heuristic production-rule models. How do I know they are correct, or with proved error bounds?"

He could equally say: "I need to make an omelet, but I don't buy eggs. How do I know that they are not addled?"

The answer can only be: "Get your eggs certificated, or at the very least buy from a reliable farm. If you don't want to do that, then you'll have to lay them yourself."

COMMUNICATING WITH ALIEN MENTALITIES

All models are in some way or other caricatures of the real world. To what degree reality has to be squashed to make it portable depends critically on what device the model is held in: a human brain, say, or a large computer. Different mentalities use different models—the problem arises when they need to communicate. They may be quite unable to describe what it is they are talking about in terms the other can understand. Consider communication with dolphins. Analysis of the high-bandwidth chat exchanged among dolphins is being carried out with the aid of computer signal-processing techniques. The sponsor is the U.S. Navy, which is training these intelligent sea mammals for salvage and retrieval work on the ocean bed.

At San Diego's Sea World, dolphins and their killer-whale relations outperform the trained seals, apes, dogs, and horses of the circus. Rewards for successful tricks include food, pats on the head, and sometimes just permission to show off, which takes the form of prancing around the pool in an unbroken sequence of spectacular high leaps. The dolphin's brain is anatomically more impressive than man's both in size and surface convolution, so it is interesting to note that Sea World's chief trainer places the dolphin as not substantially smarter than the chimpanzee, with which he has had extensive experience.

What then is the huge brain for? One remarkable trick of the dolphins is to be able to distinguish at a distance between two metal spheres suspended in the water, identical in all respects except that one is hollow at the center and the other solid. At first, some people thought this mysterious ability indicated that dolphins were blessed with extrasensory perception! Then it was realized that they use very high-channel-capacity sonar, with time resolution of the order of microseconds. They can detect the difference between the echoes from the two spheres. Two dolphins can also, as it were, mutually "lock on" their autopilots. As part of Sea

World's daily show, two dolphins swim at high speed in formation to transport to safety the relatively fragile form of a girl who simulates an accidental fall into the pool. Carrying her between their flanks, they are able to maintain a pressure that neither crushes her nor lets her slip.

Perhaps the capacious brain is for processing the sonar, so that information about other dolphins and the surrounding world can be cross-correlated with the simultaneous flow of visual data. The Navy research workers broadly agree with this. Part, however, of the high-speed traffic of weird noises seems interpretable as expression of mood and general sociability. A dolphin can teach a complicated new trick to another dolphin, but what part in this is played by linguistic instruction, as opposed to demonstration and imitation, is not yet clear.

The main obstacle to man-dolphin communication may lie in the disparity between the cognitive worlds of the two life forms. The fact that dolphins live in a marine world, remarks Michael Arbib of the University of Massachusetts, "must greatly condition what intelligence they have. If indeed they do have a language, the words they use will be different from ours. What may seem an obvious concept to them may be a very complicated concept to us."[3] Much of Arbib's discussion concentrates on problems of communications with inhabitants of other planetary systems. What sorts of messages should we send? Will the intelligence we talk to be natural or artificial? Should we send pictures, and if so, how will the recipients know which way up the pictures should be viewed? What are the linguistic and cognitive constants that might be expected to characterize all sufficiently intelligent beings, regardless of their perceptual and cultural milieus? On a more immediate level, the lack of cognitive compatibility between humans and machines presents a major obstacle to the builders of models in computers.

BEYOND THE BOUNDS OF MIND

The essential requirement of a model is that it be graspable. It is assumed by a good many workers in the knowledge-engineering field that all they need do to make their systems understandable to humans is to base them on rules. This is very far from the case. It is easy for rules to be based on a model that is outside the user's grasp, whether for reasons of structure or of scale. Take a primitive man living in tribal Africa who has never traveled more than a few miles from his home. We could tell him about New York and the fact that it is many thousands of miles away, and he might well set off to walk there just the same. The idea that there are places that are too far away to walk to may be beyond his comprehension. Today we know that the speed of light is 186,000 miles per second, but in Aristotle's time the idea that something could move from horizon to horizon too fast for the eye to perceive its motion was unthinkable. He concluded from the apparent instantaneity with which the rays of the rising sun illuminate prominences on the western horizon that light is not something propagated through space at a definite speed. How wrong can a scientist be? In Aristotle's case, by about four orders of magnitude. Apparent instantaneity would presumably disappear if the rising sun's light streaked across the sky at only 18.6 miles per second.

It is often thought that opposition to Copernicus's heliocentric model of the solar system was based solely on religious dogma. In fact reasonable people, including the great astronomer Tycho Brahe, pointed out that if the earth were circling the sun, the stars would appear to move back and forth across the sky over the period of a year—stellar parallax, as it is called (Figure 50). No such movement could be detected. They worked out how far away the stars would have to be in order for the parallax to be immeasurably small and decided *nothing* could be that far away! By Newton's time, other arguments had prevailed, but it was not until 1832 that astronomers' instruments were accurate enough to show parallax. The nearest star, Alpha Centauri, turned out to be 25,300,000,000,000 miles distant, with a parallax of only three-quarters of a second of arc.

Figure 50. Stellar parallax, greatly exaggerated. The angles are so small that no technology could measure them until the nineteenth century.

The vastness of the universe that science has revealed to us has widened enormously the scales on which we are prepared to think about space and time. We no longer object to being told that the speed of light is 186,000 miles a second. When Einstein was young, astronomers had not begun to conceive the idea that there could be other galaxies than our own. Yet so profusely do galaxies stretch in every direction of space that the small sample easily visible by telescope from the Northern Hemisphere amounts to one million. A computer compilation of these has been published as a poster image on a square yard of glossy black.[4] The distance to the farthest galaxies in this map is about a billion light-years. That is not all. By present optical telescopy, the number of galaxies we can see is about a thousand times the number selected for the star map as the million brightest. From observatories in space, we will be able to see a larger number still.

Be that as it may, no matter how much our minds have been stretched, they will always be finite, and model-builders must remember that if the end points of their description-graphs are strung out so far as to be out of sight, no human user will be able to comprehend them.

LANGUAGE AND THOUGHT

Researchers in AI are starting to make progress in a series of areas they have identified as crucial for the long-term goal of developing really useful intelligent machines. The question of how to build models is one of these. Another has to do with the nature of knowledge, and the languages in which it is embodied.

The question of whether thought is the mother of language or whether it is the other way around has received attention over the past hundred years from talents as diverse as Lewis Carroll, Ludwig Wittgenstein, Jean Piaget, and Josef Stalin. Benjamin Lee Whorf underlined the role of vocabulary in simultaneously reflecting and guiding perception, this in turn being conditioned by cultural and economic experience. Even in Scotland there is only one word for "snow," two if one counts "slush." The Eskimo has a dozen, so vital is it for him to distinguish between the various forms. The life of the Hopi tribe is such that no need arises in their language for a noun for "time," nor for a tense system of past, present, and future for the verbs. Whorf believed that language acts as a mold for thought, forcing it into preformed linguistic categories. The machine intelligence scientist must also adopt a position, for he has to decide on his research strategy for building intelligent agents in software. Is he to make the mechanization of knowledge-based reasoning the main thrust, only secondarily clothing the system, where he can, with linguistic trimmings? Or should he go bald-headed for computational linguistics as the heart of the matter?

Teachers of logic frequently introduce the notion of rule-based (and hence mechanizable) reasoning with the old chestnut:

Premise 1: All men are mortal.
Premise 2: Socrates is a man.
Conclusion: Socrates is mortal.

Christopher Longuet-Higgins has constructed the linguistic trap:

Premise 1: Men are numerous.
Premise 2: Socrates is a man.
Conclusion: Socrates is numerous.

Bertrand Russell gave as another trap the statements:

"George IV wondered whether the author of the Waverley novels was Walter Scott."

and

"Walter Scott is the author of the Waverley novels."

from which we do *not* want a computer to deduce:

"George IV wondered whether Walter Scott was Walter Scott."[5]

On such rocks as these has foundered much linguistic philosophy of the past. Today it is accepted that reasoning by formal manipulation requires prior reduction of the language text to some more logic-oriented symbolism. For example, using predicate calculus in the Socrates puzzle, we have:

CASE A
Premise 1: **for all** x, member (x, men) **implies** mortal (x);
Premise 2: member (Socrates, men);
Conclusion: mortal (Socrates).

CASE B
Premise 1: numerous (men);
Premise 2: member (Socrates, men);
Conclusion: ?

In Case A, the conclusion follows by substituting "Socrates" for *x*. In Case B, nothing can be concluded. So once the statements are reexpressed in a suitable formal language, the conclusions of logic are reunited with those of common sense.

IN THE POOL OF ANXIOUS DISCOURSE

The issue of language first *versus* reasoning first is assuming practical importance now that expert systems and computer information services are requiring frontends for dealing with users in something approaching natural language. Some of the endless streams of citizens' queries to the offices of bureaucracy may one day be redirected to automated systems able to advise with endless patience on, say, pension entitlements. But more than patience, alas, and more than linguistics, will be needed for a system that has to fish in the pool of anxious discourse for the inquirer's true meaning and desires. The following small sample is taken from letters reputedly received some years ago by the Ministry of Pensions.

> I cannot get eternity benefit in spite of the fact that I saw the insistence officer. I have eight children, what can I do about it.

> I should have more pension since my son is in charge of a spittoon. I get a separate money when he listened. You want to know what part he is wounded in. If it's all the same to you he was wounded in the Dardy Nolls.

> In accordance with your instructions I have given birth to twins in the enclosed envelope.

> I want money badly as quick as you can send it. I have been in bed with the doctor for a week and he doesn't seem to be doing any good.

One false step, one prolonged hesitancy of interpretation, and heaven knows what may ensue:

I am glad to state that my husband died yesterday. I will be glad if you will get a pension. If you don't hurry up with it I will have to get public resistance.

System responses might be quick enough, but on occasion they could be embarrassingly misplaced.

Re your dental inquiry. The teeth at the top are alright but the ones in my bottom are hurting terribly.

It is easy to mock present-day computerized natural-language processing for failing to handle instances such as these, but crude as existing systems are, they are already usable in commercial applications, and computational linguistics has penetrated laws of language obscure to theoreticians of the pre-machine era. But irrespective of the progress of natural-language processing, programming intelligent systems requires special logic languages, not only for dealing with the Socrates problem and its kind (for which conventional programming languages are really not adequate), but also for building systems that can *reason about what other systems know*.

KNOWING ABOUT KNOWING

What sort of systems might have such a requirement? Consider a program to assist a travel agent in planning routes and schedules. So long as the program's only source of knowledge is the contents of the airline timetables, there is no problem—except that it will be caught out by new information (concerning air-traffic control strikes, hurricanes, civil wars, compulsory groundings, hijacks, revisions or even misprints in the timetables) that "everybody knows about" but that has not yet reached the agent's desk of its own accord. So we would like a program able actively to assist in the search for knowledge, for example by calling somebody up. Then it must know what knowledge is and how to reason about it.

Suppose a system called Travelaid is being run for the benefit of a commercial travel agency. Pat is a travel agent who wants details on flights from Hong Kong to Ulan Bator for a client. Mary is a Thomas Cook agent who has special information on these flights. Mike is Mary's immediate supervisor at Cook's, whom Pat recently telephoned about another matter. What Pat does not know is that Mary and Mike share the same phone.

Pat asks Travelaid to get Mary's phone number for her and dial it. The machine does not have Mary's number in its data base, but it does have the following three facts:

Fact 1: Pat knows Mike's telephone number.
Fact 2: Pat just dialed Mike's telephone number.
Fact 3: Mary's telephone number = Mike's telephone number.

The program puts these facts together and infers (by substituting equals for equals) that Pat knows Mary's telephone number, so it asks her for the number, the very question she has just asked it! Moreover, when she protests, Travelaid types, "You just dialed Mary's telephone number!" Although for once Travelaid is telling the truth, Pat has no knowledge of having done any such thing and ends a beautiful contract by ripping Travelaid's cord out of the wall. What happened? The program put 2 and 3 together to infer (correctly) that Pat dialed Mary's telephone number. Of course Pat could not recognize the correctness of the inference, not knowing Fact 3. So why was the other inference wrong, proceeding as it seems according to identically the same scheme?

The short answer is that first, as noted above, this is what tends to happen if one tries to perform deductions directly on natural language statements, and second, even when translated into logic, statements about "knowing" are slippery. We need to understand how a machine can know that you know that it knows that she knows what it knows. John McCarthy of Stanford University has shown that this can be handled satisfactorily within first-order predicate logic.[6] Using his method, there would be little trouble in equipping Travelaid for deductions about knowing telephone numbers or knowing anything else—including "knowing that" and "knowing whether."

McCarthy leaves first-order logic unchanged and treats concepts simply as one kind of object, so that constants, variables, and terms can all have concepts as their values. By a notational convention he distinguishes between "concept constants," such as *Pat* and *Mike,* and the corresponding "person constants" *pat* and *mike. Pat* represents the concept of *pat.* Likewise, the concept-variable *Horse* represents the thing-variable *horse,* and *Telephone (Mike)* evaluates to the concept of *mike's* telephone number. McCarthy's key move is to introduce a function *Know* whose arguments must be concept-valued and which produces a concept as a result. The clarifying restriction is that only concepts can be known, just as only liquids can be drunk.

Fundamentally, what is needed is a sound and well-quantified theory of knowledge, giving the field the same sort of scientific foundation that Carnot provided for steam engineering and Shannon did for communications. We shall then have a calculus for reasoning about knowledge and other mental phenomena, and this is indeed what McCarthy has concerned himself with.

THE DRILL-SERGEANT'S WITHDRAWAL

As a high priority, Artificial Intelligence needs a language that will deal with logic directly, rather than through imperatives in the manner of Cobol, Fortran, Basic, and others of their breed. Do computers ever get bored with the interminable streams of commands—"Do this, do this, do this . . ."? The helpless indignity of their situation recalls that of the recruits marching toward the edge of a precipice-lined barrack square: "For God's sake say something, Sergeant, even if it's only good-bye!" For such of the world's teeming machines as may be afflicted with *ennui* or despair, there is news. They too may one day have to think for themselves. Tomorrow's programmers will one day indolently disburden themselves of the drill-sergeant chore. How relaxing to be able to bark out ". . . left, right, left, right . . . about-face . . . left, right . . . now get home using your own damn common sense!" and then withdraw to the mess hall.

This has to do with what Ed Feigenbaum calls the "What-to-How spectrum." Instead of telling the computer *how* to do something, we would like to be able to tell it *what* we want it to do and leave it to work out how. Feigenbaum sees this as the ultimate aim of all AI research.[7] The idea behind what is known as logic programming is that you should equip the computer with a basic reasoning engine and thereafter tell it nothing but facts, on the understanding that it will do its best with them. As you build its stock of knowledge with just the right set of relevant assertions about what is or is not the case in the world of sorting, merging, data control, queuing, scheduling, game playing, or other computing task, so the system builds its own capability to sort, merge, control data, manipulate matrices, etc., simply through its own efforts to prove that any goal statements fed to it really can be deduced logically from its accumulated store of facts.

As early as 1971, Robert Kowalski, then at Edinburgh, was already in effect saying: "Whatever you want the system to know, tell it the facts in first-order predicate logic. The result will have an obvious declarative semantics—it is quite unambiguous in what it says about its problem world. If, moreover, the system is equipped with a theorem prover behind the scenes, capable in principle of deducing anything deducible from the starting facts, then the logical statements can be given a procedural semantics. So we can forget the years of drill-sergeant programming, and use as a programming language a vehicle that has been there all the time, much studied and well understood by mathematicians—namely, first-order predicate logic."

WAITING FOR A MIRACLE

Kowalski showed in detail how a theorem prover based on J. A. Robinson's "resolution principle" could be made into an interpreter for such a language. But his hearers did not like this. Some felt that he was right but mad, others that he was wrong if only they could think exactly how. The majority took the pragmatic view, tried and tested on prophets in all times and ages—that you might as well ignore the whole thing until you are shown a miracle or two.

Miracles take time and sweat and ingenuity and doggedness and flair. Kowalski's disciples in Edinburgh, Marseilles, Western Ontario, and Hungary have deployed these qualities in good measure over the intervening years. The name of the result is Prolog, a programming system faithful in its fashion to the sweep and simplicity of the original concept, but running on commercial machines including microcomputers with efficiencies fully comparable with, for example, Stanford's highly optimized pure Lisp system.[8]

Prolog works with objects and their relationships, specified by the programmer as rules. Relationships might be:

John likes Mary
Philip father-of Charles
Charles father-of William
Mary likes John

New relationships can be defined:

x friends-with y if x likes y and
y likes x
and questions can be asked, such as, Is John friends with Mary?

In Prolog: Does (John friends-with Mary)
Answer: YES

A system of relationships has to be quite large before the computer can be seen to be providing real benefit, but at any serious level of complexity, a computing problem normally involves sorting out relationships between things—membership of sets and so on—and thus solutions can be represented as series of logical inferences.

Those in charge of the Japanese Fifth Generation Computer program are sufficiently convinced of the benefits of logic programming to have placed it as a central plank in their plans. Now that Prolog is becoming widely available, it will be possible to assess its effectiveness on a large scale and to see what further developments are necessary. Some observers are skeptical about the usefulness for real-world tasks of the basic operators provided in systems for mechanizing reasoning, wryly suggesting that in addition to "Implies" there should be "*Sometimes* implies" and "*Ought* to imply." Certainly "fuzzy" and "modal" operators are being studied as a possible extension of these techniques. Logic programming could turn out to be as fundamental to AI as the infinitesimal calculus was to mechanics.

THE SHAKY FOUNDATIONS OF EUCLID

It is not just our dealings with language that urgently need to be formalized. Reasoning about the physical world can also lead us into serious difficulties. In trying to build causal models, it would be nice to be able to derive them from our established formalisms of mathematics, logic, and physics. But when we set out to do this we find that the existing formalisms are not adequate.

Take Euclidean geometry, which we all have encountered in one form or another at school. Some of us were charmed by its elegance, certainty, and precision; others were frustrated by its insistence on proving the obvious and its obsession with exactness in a world in which all measurements are necessarily inexact. Certainly the techniques of exact reasoning are acquiring new importance now with the spread of digital processing and communications. There are, however, serious holes in the foundations of Euclid's geometry and the assumptions it makes. To illustrate, let us draw a triangle, any triangle at all (Figure 51). The dotted line dissects the angle BAC into two components, BAD and DAC. If the line AD is produced indefinitely as indicated by the dotted arrow, must it necessarily intersect the line BC?

Of course it must! But can you get out your geometry books and prove it? No you cannot. Lewis Carroll used this fact to devise an ingenious proof that all triangles are isosceles.[9] The problem, as

Peter Hilton of Case Western Reserve University explains, is to do with the idea of a "closure" (a line around which a bug could run forever). The notion that a closure partitions the plane into just two sets of points—"inside" and "outside"—and that passage from one partition into the other cannot be achieved without crossing the boundary is not embedded even implicitly in Euclid's axioms, although it is in elementary set theory. But set theory is a more remote branch of mathematics than geometry, and many people have never encountered it at all.

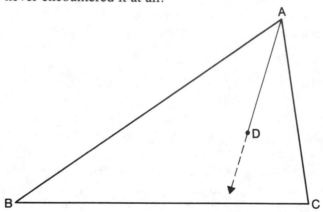

Figure 51. Must the dotted line intersect line BC? Could Euclid prove it?

At least with Euclid, when answers can be derived from the axioms and data, they come quite quickly. There is no fear of having to drop the whole project on finding the required chain of calculation and inference to be too long to execute in practice. With physics, once we leave cooked-up classroom problems for the real world, the matter stands differently. If some physicist disagrees, let him write a program to control a robot unicyclist. He will find the physics textbook model totally inadequate for dealing with such a complex real task. As with the problem we cited in Chapter 1 of how to get a robot to go down the street and buy a pack of cigarettes, the central difficulty is our lack of any formal representation of the nature of cause and effect.

CAUSATION AND THE DESERT TRAVELER

Most people think they understand causation perfectly well. When challenged, some will say that causation can be handled just like implication, which we certainly can mechanize. Actually, it is not like that at all.

First. A corollary of "A implies B" is IF not-B THEN not-A, but a corollary of "A causes B" is IF not-A THEN not-B.

Second. In contrast to implication, the accepted basis of causation is probabilistic.

Third. In the probabilistic model, transitivity does not hold. By contrast, if A implies B, and B implies C, then A implies C.

Fourth. No one objects if a chain of implication forms a loop: looping of causation statements is frowned upon.

There is a conundrum in causality concerning a traveler who dismounted from a transdesert bus to complete his journey on foot. This man had two enemies, each bent on causing his death. The first had surreptitiously put cyanide into the traveler's water bottle while still on the bus. The second, not knowing this, stalked the traveler for hours before he found a chance to pierce the bottle with a well-aimed bullet. The bottle's contents leaked away, and the traveler died a lingering death from thirst.

Both men were in due course arraigned, and both were found guilty of attempted murder. On the charge of murder, however, the court found itself in perplexity. Enemy No. 1 pointed out that all possible consequences of his action had been nullified by the escape of the bottle's contents. Enemy No. 2 pointed out that his action, far from causing death, had prolonged his intended victim's life. The court eventually felt obliged in logic to accept both these arguments. But at the request of the jury, a rider was entered to the effect that there seemed to be something wrong somewhere.

The Stanford logician Pat Suppes has been devising a technique for analyzing causation that might supply the juridical weapon the court was lacking. Simplifying somewhat, we start with the idea that A is a *prima facie* cause of B if and only if (1) A precedes B in time; (2) A has a non-zero probability of occurrence; (3) B's probability *given that A has occurred* is greater than B's probability otherwise.

Note that so far this is only *prima facie* causation, according to which, for example, a fall in the barometer reading is a cause of rain (*prima facie* it is). We now get rid of such spurious causes by finding some event C, earlier in time than A, such that (4) B's probability *given C and A* is equal to B's probability *given just C*. This shows that A is not the true cause of B. In the barometer example, C could be lowered atmospheric pressure (as opposed to barometric reading, which is A).

Back to the desert courtroom, Suppes-style. Enemy No. 1, it seems, takes the rap. Enemy No. 2 is acquitted of murder. Is this justice? It is hard to say. Perhaps our received ideas of justice do not correspond to a strict logic of causation. No. 1's deliberate action certainly doomed his victim to die. To that extent at least, the Suppes calculus seems to give a fairer result than the court's troubled verdict.

PHYSICS FAILS THE MONKEY

Returning to physics, we find that this science which is so often sold as a calculational cure-all for those who want to predict things was in fact developed for another purpose: to help physicists clarify their minds. While physics includes important concepts such as mass, force, and energy, there are many more just as important that it does not: for example the ideas of closure, containment, support, contact, obstacles, ways through. Without these, and without an explicit formulation of cause and effect, physics is incapable of dealing with the real world.

There is a classic problem in cognitive science to do with a monkey in a room: the monkey wants to get hold of a bunch of bananas hanging from the ceiling on a string, out of his reach. In the corner stands a pair of garden shears with long handles, long enough for the monkey to be able to reach the string with the blades (Figure 52). How does the monkey work out how to get the bananas? Imagine the monkey is instead a robot called Monkey, and the bananas are a toolkit it has been ordered to retrieve. How do we give it the necessary knowledge? By feeding it the contents of a physics textbook? While the robot will be able to derive from this all kinds of information it does not need to know, such as the tension in the string and the terminal velocity with which the toolkit would hit the floor were it to fall, Monkey will find nothing about how to make the kit fall in the first place—nothing about situations, actions, and causal laws. As a complete and workable description of how the physical world behaves, the physics textbook reveals itself as a fraud.

Figure 52. How does the monkey work out how to get the bananas?

Among those AI researchers seeking to remedy this is Patrick Hayes, who studies a subject he calls Naïve Physics. His aim is to generate a representation of the world that includes such notions as containment, connection, adjacency, and barriers that we mentioned.[10] Just as some ancient Greek, aware of the gappiness and small scope of Euclid, might have put out an exploratory probe into the then unknown calculus of sets, so today the first approaches are being tried to tomorrow's calculus of causality. The ghosts of the geometers waited more than two thousand years. Industrial robot technology, if nothing else, is this time ensuring a faster pace.

9

THE CAT THAT ISN'T THERE

A theologian and a philosopher were having an argument.
"You're just like all philosophers," the theologian
scoffed, and quoted: "You're a blind man in a dark room,
looking for a black cat that isn't there."
"Ah!" replied the philosopher, "but *you* would *find* it!"

—*attributed to William James*

THE SCIENTIST STARTING WORK on AI finds himself trying to deal with matters such as knowledge, belief, reality, truth, perception, causality, and creativity. These are vaguer terms than those he is used to dealing with. He might be inclined to turn to philosophy for enlightenment. Indeed, AI is sometimes described as the application of philosophy to technology, or alternatively of technology to philosophy.

At the same time, the public at large, on seeing this kind of work going on, tends to raise questions also of a philosophical nature. Can computers think? Are they conscious? Do they have feelings? Sadly, the answers that come back from philosophers are usually far from satisfactory. Still, the philosophical issues will continue to arise, but interesting as they are, they may confuse our commitment to exploit these new technologies as quickly as possible for the benefit of humanity.

It is no surprise that many are worried by the notions of computer intelligence and creativity. They have not only philosophical but emotional associations. People have always reacted with consternation whenever machines have acquired characteristics previously thought to be the exclusive property of human beings. If life is sacred, then ostensibly attributes that are essential parts of that life acquire sacredness: these might include the ability to move about, to reason, to act autonomously, to converse, to reproduce. Machines are gaining these abilities, or apparent abilities, in turn. Reproduction is not yet here, but it is certainly in the minds of some research workers, including Bernard de Neumann at GEC Marconi Laboratories, a distant cousin of the great John von Neumann.[1] The biggest source of concern, though, is probably the apparent encroachment by machines on man's free intellectual powers.

ALIENATING MYSTIFICATIONS

If it is impious to think that computers can be creative, further unease can arise as, through developments in AI, human properties become describable in terms of mechanisms. This can seriously affect the way we think of ourselves, raising the old question of whether we are nothing more than machines. As Margaret Boden puts it:

> In many humanists' opinion, the literature of artificial intelligence inevitably encourages the alienating mystification that there is no essential difference between people and machines, and thus subtly supports those social systems that effectually treat people as though they were machines.[2]

Thus, it is only to be expected that discussion of these issues can get emotional and discourteous, just as did consideration of Darwin's ideas in the last century. Consternation can easily turn to scorn, and in the same way as T. H. Huxley was made a figure of fun, so can mention of Artificial Intelligence provoke laughter. Thomas Watson, the founder of IBM, used actively to discourage talk about AI as bad for the company's image.

Efforts to reestablish the self-esteem of man from the damage it has supposedly received have led to much muddled thinking. Several philosophers have seized upon Gödel's Incompleteness Theorem as proof of man's superiority over machine. Kurt Gödel, an American mathematician born in Austria, showed conclusively in 1931 that in any sufficiently powerful mathematical system (such as arithmetic) there will always be propositions that cannot be proved within the system—they simply have to be assumed. Therefore, it is reasoned, science can never answer all the questions; therefore what a wonderful thing is man. What is overlooked in this argument is the fact that Gödel's Theorem applies just as much to human beings as to machines, so there will always be things human beings do not know for certain either. A deep understanding of what machines can and cannot do is the best reassurance of the continuing value of man.

PLATO'S INDIGNATION

Those outside the scientific community need feel no diffidence about their instinctive aversion to machines acquiring human mental properties. Such a reaction can come from the inside as well. Alarm has been aroused by every historical advance in the supporting technology of thought and knowledge, even, as we described in Chapter 3, in the case of the invention of writing! Of course, Plato's implied disdain did not inhibit him from writing himself, but then, things are always different when we do them ourselves, for then we can make sure they are done right. However, one development that Plato could not accept at any price was the construction by two mathematical colleagues of a device for machine-aided theorem proving. The story is related to us by Plutarch in the *Life of Marcellus*:

Eudoxus and Archytas had been the first originators of this far-famed and highly prized art of mechanics, which they employed as an elegant illustration of geometrical truths, and as a means of sustaining experimentally, to the satisfaction of the senses, conclusions too intricate for proof by words and diagrams . . . But what with Plato's indignation at it, and his invectives against it as the mere corruption and annihilation of the one good of geometry,—which was thus shamefully turning its back upon the unembodied objects of pure intelligence to recur to sensation, and to ask help . . . from matter; so it was that mechanics came to be separated from geometry, and, repudiated and neglected by philosophers, took its place as a military art.[3]

One might suppose that such snobbery had disappeared by the twentieth century, certainly within the realms of technology itself, but far from it. Edsger Dijkstra, one of the greatest computer scientists of our age and a spiritual descendant of Plato, has claimed that the development of the microprocessor has put computing back twenty-five years. His assertion is based on the view that the easy availablity of computing power to people with no systematic training in good programming will lead to the wholesale abandonment of the standards and techniques painstakingly developed over the years by him and his colleagues; all the old mistakes will be repeated. Dijkstra expounds:

The most common argument in favour of microcomputers that I hear is their low price. Now let me give you a general advice for "deconfusing" an otherwise confusing presentation. The advice is to remember that when anyone is talking in terms of money, it is highly improbable that he knows what he is talking about, for "money" is a vague and elusive notion when you come to think about it. For some people, their dollar or their pound, their guilder or their yen, is not just their currency unit, but has become their unit of thought. Love of perfection is then driven out by love of cheapness, and eventually they find themselves surrounded by junk . . .

The paradoxical fact is that we are back where we were twenty-five years ago. Again the arithmetic is too slow or the store is too small; again we have machines with chaotic, unsystematic order codes, the design of which has been influenced more by consideration of hardware technology than by the question whether a wise programmer would care to use them. Recently someone showed me an issue of one of the monthly magazines for the microprocessor hobbyist, and I tell you, it was a severe shock to see a revival of all our old mistakes. It was frightening, it was depressing, it was sickening, and I hope never to see such magazines again.[4]

One is left with the uneasy conclusion that the young discipline of computer science is already constructing a new conservatism to rival that of its older-established academic cousins—the aversion of Upstairs Man to whatever comes from the servants' quarters.

THE FOUR-COLOR PROBLEM SUCCUMBS

One can see how mathematicians might feel that to mechanize is to bedaub the mathematical subculture's precious tapestry with squirtings from an engineer's oilcan. After all, has computing ever helped real mathematics? Had not Plato, perhaps, a point? Until recently, perhaps he had. But in 1976 Ken Appel and Wolfgang Haken produced by computer a proof of the celebrated Four-Color Theorem in topology that had resisted mathematicians for over a century. A map-maker wants to color his maps in such a way that adjoining countries will always be of different colors, so that the boundaries can be clearly seen. What is the maximum number of colors that will be required for all possible maps? No map had ever been found that needed more than four colors, but all attempts to prove that four would *always* be sufficient had failed.

By an exhaustive computing process, Appel and Haken showed that all possible maps would have to contain at least one of around 1,800 submaps, which were individually listed by machine. They then proved that every one of these submaps had the property that it could not possibly form a part of a map that required more than four colors. Hence, no such map could exist.[5] Such a technique of exhaustive enumeration is offensive to many mathematicians, just as physicists tend to despise representations of the world that are not concise. But in the case of the Four-Color Problem, it seems that despite the simplicity of the initial question, the proof may be intrinsically "bitty" and that no elegant Platonic solution is possible. More and more mathematical problems are now fitting into this category. In the end, mathematicians may have to swallow their pride.

CONSIDERING CONSCIOUSNESS

Proof of a different kind becomes pertinent when considering consciousness. Futurologists speculate about when computers will be built that have consciousness and self-awareness. To answer this, we first need to be clear about terms. Freud in one of his later lectures wrote: "What is meant by 'conscious' we need not discuss; it is beyond all doubt."[6] All eminent men are wrong occasionally, but seldom as spectacularly as that. Consciousness is one of the most elusive concepts; we all know it, but no one can say what it is. Moreover, it is the most precious possession that any individual has. If he is permanently robbed of it, what is left to him? So it has for us an aura of sacredness. We are not readily going to credit a machine with this mysterious gift.

A dog is another matter. Dog owners will tell you that their pet is so empathic that it is aware not only of its own thoughts but of its master's. But how do we decide whether a computer is conscious? The question may acquire more than intellectual interest. Robots will one day be built that can move about and converse much as humans do. They will be turned out on assembly lines like motor cars are now and will become as ubiquitous and as much of a social nuisance. There could even be a stray-robot problem. Their humanoid characteristics will predispose people to take the same attitude toward them as toward animals. To be able to operate on their own, robots will have to be programmed with what would be in effect a sense of pain, to warn of physical harm, and an instinct for self-preservation, to tell them to withdraw from danger. Otherwise they would not last long through the mishaps of everyday life. The sight of a robot desperately trying to save itself when attacked could appeal to the kind of people who would have relished bear-baiting. Robot-baiting and Hunt-the-Robot could become pastimes.

Would it then be cruelty to torture a robot? If it is not conscious, presumably not. But how would a robot prove to us it was conscious? How, for that matter, would a human? An obvious answer might be, by telling us about himself. John Locke described consciousness as "the perception of what passes in a Man's own mind."[7] However, we must not be misled into the view that consciousness and knowledge of self are the same thing, despite the fact that in humans they go together. Conventional computer programs with good diagnostic and trace facilities can tell the user a great deal about their own internal states and processes, yet they can hardly be regarded as conscious. One might take the view, "Ah, well, if someone can*not* tell us about himself, then he is *not* conscious." But even that does not work. The drug curare can totally paralyze a patient so that though fully awake, he cannot so much as twitch an eyelid. A surgeon could operate on him without anesthetic, and the patient would suffer agonies and yet be unable to indicate the fact by the slightest movement. Another drug could be used to eradicate his subsequent recollection of the torment. So on the question-answering test of consciousness, it might be thought reasonable to operate, yet everyone would agree that to do so would be monstrous. Moreover, such procedures are prohibited in the case of laboratory animals.

Since it is not effectively possible to prove or disprove one's own consciousness, such proof cannot be required in order to determine an organism's rights. This has long been accepted in the case of animals, and laws against cruelty to them have been passed without first solving the problem of whether animals are conscious or have souls. Presumably, these laws exist not just out of feelings of kindness but because of the implications for humanity of inhuman treatment of anything. After all, no one tortures rocks; it is simply the humanlike response of an animal in pain that gratifies the torturer. For the same reason, therefore, laws will probably be enacted to protect robots. This could be out of simple self-interest on man's part. The habit of brushing aside the rights of minorities can be two-edged. Think what might happen if one day robots started asking themselves, "Are humans really conscious?"

KILLING AN EXPERT SYSTEM

Of course, animals often have to be "put down" for practical reasons, and so will robots, but an interesting question arises concerning expert systems. One of these constructed with the cooperation of a particular human expert can capture his skills in such faithful detail that colleagues and friends interacting with the system may recognize his personal style of thought. Long after he is dead, they could respond to the foibles and fancies of the intellectual companion they knew. This would be for him a kind of immortality, more vivid and direct than authorship of books, or passive relics such as photographs and tape recordings, since it would include fragments of responsive behavior. How should we regard the wiping out of such a system irretrievably? It would surely be reprehensible, in the same way as was the burning of the great library of Alexandria.

THE SOCIAL ACCOUNTABILITY OF STORED KNOWLEDGE

The knowledge stored in computers can raise moral questions of another kind. Take a statement from a book to be found in schoolrooms: "They are lazy individuals, apparently devoid of morals, and always prepared to lie, cheat, and steal." Whose conversation are we overhearing? Perhaps it is a data processing manager commenting on the maintenance staff. Or is it a board member of General Motors about the workforce? Yet it could just as plausibly be one of the shop stewards on the subject of the board! Maybe it was overheard in some social retreat of senior bureaucracy and the target was the new ministers of the Crown? And yet it sounds not unlike the late Richard Crossman writing about senior civil servants. Or in the groves of academe: "Tell me, young person, what are the professors like around here?" or "You were saying, Dean, about the students . . ."

The statement is from a New South Wales textbook, referring to the Aborigines.[8] Textbooks are purportedly sources of knowledge. This fact starts a train of uneasy thought. The knowledge base in, for instance, Prospector contains information about the geology of uranium. As it happens, considerable political tension has arisen over the discovery of uranium deposits lying beneath the Aborigines' traditional habitats. Son of Prospector or Grandson of Prospector might include information about non-geological factors that could affect decisions to drill, such as legal data on Aborigines and land rights. Beyond even that, the proprietors of automated systems might wish to add to the knowledge base more than dry technical and legal facts and to include looser generalizations about relevant human groups. Questions of the social accountability of stored "knowledge" will certainly then arise.

The data used by robots will be sensitive in the same way. Ask Super-Rob, a twenty-first century robot foreman, the question "What is lazy, apparently devoid of morals and always prepared to lie, cheat, and steal?"

You might get the answer: *"Homo sapiens."*

WHAT IS YOUR ROBOT FOR?

The question "What is your robot for?" is a particularly delicate one now. The social problem of galloping unemployment makes many people suspicious of any technology that reduces the need for human labor. We need to remind ourselves that there is no logical reason why knowledge about how to do things more efficiently should be a bad thing. Fundamentally, what robots must be for is the same as any other technology: to raise the quality of life. They can do this by increasing the sum total that society can produce, both goods and services. Despite our current shortage of *jobs*, there is no shortage of *work* waiting to be done: renovating our housing, rebuilding our rapidly deteriorating heritage of Victorian engineering works, looking after the sick, the aged, and the infirm, providing continuing education for everybody, to say nothing of feeding the starving millions in the third world. As Tom Stonier of the Bradford School of Science and Society has put it, health and education are "an infinite sink for employment."[9] The problem is getting it organized to happen.

Naturally, when it does happen, it will entail a great deal of change, and many people will have to change what they do, like it or not. If society no longer needs what you produce, you have to produce something else. Expectations will have to change—but not expectations about material standards of living—rather, expectations about what is a respectable way of spending one's time. By that we do not primarily mean leisure: those traditionally averse to providing services as opposed to making objects will have to change their views.

The change can only be managed by a judicious mixture of public and private enterprise, perhaps quite unlike anything we have had before. Education and retraining will have to be on a massive scale. Some people say this will have to be a job for government, others that only small private enterprises can react quickly enough. However it happens, the main thing that will be required is imagination.

THE LIFE OF A HARLOT

Despite the continuing accumulation of work to be done, technical developments have always been reducing working hours, and automation will certainly carry on this trend. It is only to be welcomed if we can spend less time doing what we have to do and more time doing what we want to do. Some years ago a former lord provost of Edinburgh was so moved by this thought that in his retirement speech he misspoke himself to immortal effect. "I'll be away now to the far highlands," he informed the solemnly assembled company, "where I plan to live the life of a harlot!"

Historians of the occasion now believe that the intended word was *hermit*. Yet as Freud was the first to emphasize, these slips can reveal hidden attitudes. Doubtless in a Scottish lord provost's secret mind doing quietly what one wants to do is not filed, as it would be in the mind of a Roman Catholic or a Buddhist, under "RETREAT, SAINTLY" but rather under "IDLENESS"—with all the depravities into which that devilish state may plunge even the best Presbyterian! It is a particular obsession of our age and few others that the only path to spiritual fulfillment is through work.

We are in no danger of having everything done for us by robots in any sort of future that can be foreseen, nor is the computer a risk to the high flights of human creativity. It is a mistake to take up too much time asking, "Can computers think?" "Can they be *really* creative?" For all practical purposes they can. The best course for us is to leave the philosophers in their dark room and get on with using the creative computer to the full.

10
INVENTING FOR ALL MANKIND

> There are thousands of them at present in England as well
> as I believe elsewhere; the offspring of the march of
> intellect. Their object is money; which, please God, they
> shall not get from the Publick Treasury.
>
> —THE DUKE OF WELLINGTON,
> *on Inventors (1830)[1]*

THE JAPANESE CHALLENGE in information technology has provoked many government spokesmen in Europe and the U.S.A. to assert that despite an abundance of talent, there is a shortage of innovative projects. Clearly, there is a shortage of *something*. Is it really a shortage of innovation?

No one certainly is claiming that innovation is in itself an automatic boon. The call is for midwives, to deliver the inventor to the investor. If, however, neither the invention's true mother nor the financial foster-mother can afford to take the baby on, what then?

There is an almost religious veneration for the newborn. Babies are crooned over, tweaked, tickled, treated as holy. But let the admirer be asked to act as nursemaid for the little creature, and how his ardor cools! So with innovation. Reverential hogwash about creative genius flows today from all responsible spokespersons. What are their real feelings? In some earlier times, at least, it was safer to be a baby than a clever inventor. The eighth-century Arabian traveler Ibn Fadlan found an interesting custom among the Volga Bulgars:

> When they observe a man who excels through quick-wittedness and knowledge, they say: "For this one it is more befitting to serve our Lord." They seize him, put a rope round his neck and hang him on a tree, where he is left until he rots away . . .[2]

Arthur Koestler quotes the Turkish commentator Zeki Validi Togan:

> There is nothing mysterious about the cruel treatment meted out by the Bulgars to people who are overly clever. It was based on the simple, sober reasoning of the average citizens who wanted only to lead what they considered to be a normal life, and to avoid any risk or adventure into which the "genius" might lead them.[3]

It is easy to suspect that this is the basic philosophy at the root of government reluctance to stimulate investment. That the philosophy is older than the Bulgars is evident from this ancient Chinese fragment:

> Returning to one's destiny is known as the constant:
> Knowledge of the constant is known as discernment.
> Woe to him who wilfully innovates
> While ignorant of the constant . . .

The author was doubtless head of a civil service department.

As long ago as 1887, T. H. Huxley was urging a radical change in the relationship between science and industry. In a memorable letter to *The Times* in January of that year, he wrote:

I do not think I am far wrong in assuming that we are entering, indeed have already entered, upon the most serious struggle for existence to which this country has ever been committed. The latter years of the century promise to see us embarked in an industrial war of far more serious import than the military wars of its opening years. On the East, the most systematically instructed and best informed people in Europe are our competitors; on the West, an energetic offshoot of our own stock, grown bigger than its parent, enters upon the struggle possessed of natural resources to which we can make no pretension and with every prospect of soon possessing that cheap labour by which they may be effectually utilized.[4]

The remedy Huxley pressed for was "a public and ceremonial marriage of science and industry"; industry had to call to its aid "every possible help which was to be gathered from science."[5] Almost a century later, neither the European nor the American situation is ideal. In the rolling state of Ohio, a local dust-storm involved an obscure robot and a famous politician, leaving the robot on its six legs, but Democratic Senator William Proxmire from Wisconsin standing inelegantly on one.

THE SIX-LEGGED ROBOT OF THE PRAIRIE

The senator specializes in withering and hilarious assaults on federally financed research projects. He regularly presents a "Golden Fleece Award" to the projects he feels have been the most ridiculous waste of taxpayers' money. Past winners have included a study on why people fall in love, an experiment on how long it takes to cook breakfast, a study of relationships in a Peruvian brothel, and the abortive development of a $2-million prototype police car so gadget-laden as to "make James Bond green with envy." On this occasion Proxmire laid into Robert McGhee, professor of electrical engineering at Ohio State University, whose development of a six-legged walking robot had been funded in part by a $400,000 grant from the U.S. National Science Foundation.

In presenting the machine with the Golden Fleece Award, Proxmire suggested that the "Bionic Bug" would be of more use as an adjunct to the university's football team. In reply, McGhee pointed out that the Veterans Administration was already launching tests of an artificial kneejoint for humans, developed from his technology, and that NASA had expressed interest in connection with the Mars Rover project. The senator had not sought McGhee's own comments before releasing his outburst. In the end, the chief staff member of Proxmire's committee accepted blame.

Figure 53. Design model of a new development of Robert McGhee's walking machine, the ASV-84. With six legs, there are always three on the ground at any one time, ensuring stability. *(Ohio State University)*

Ironically, thirteen years earlier Ivan Sutherland had been inquiring in Britain whether any academic laboratories would be interested in bidding for a contract to investigate automated walking. He was then on secondment to the U.S. Defense Department and in charge of its Advanced Research Projects Agency's R & D spending on information processing. So much importance was seen in such a development that if no credible domestic bids were forthcoming, his agency was prepared to consider the unusual step of subsidizing the work by foreign nationals. It should be obvious on reflection why this might be so. A quick survey of the world's land masses prompts the question: "What proportion of the total terrain is negotiable by jeep or tractor? What proportion is negotiable by horse, mule, camel, llama, or elephant?" Some people view automobile technology as having reached a plateau, with nothing but small optimizations here and there to be expected. Nothing could be more profoundly wrong. It only looks that way because until supporting technologies for a new leap forward have been developed, no one can ever envisage the leap. Wheeled transport did not require the microprocessor revolution as a precondition. Legged transport does. This is because the control required to coordinate the legs is a highly complex task of information processing.[6]

There is an interesting precedent. Readers may have seen artists' reconstructions of prehistoric birds in books on evolution. One in particular, the Archeopteryx, had a magnificent flowing tail (Figure 54). A contemporary observer (who would have had to be an extraterrestrial, since our own ancestors were not yet up to ratiocinations of this kind) might have remarked that this wonderful flying frame had been highly optimized for aerodynamic stability. Indeed it had, but it was not maneuverable. The development of the brain gave later birds a different kind of stability through the new principle of feedback, and by degrees dispensed with the long tail. A stuffed Archeopteryx could have been used as a glider. A stuffed seagull cannot. Yet when its brain is engaged, the seagull's ability to glide is unsurpassed, as is its ability to maneuver. In the same way, microprocessors make practicable a whole new generation of versatile land vehicles using legs.

Such lessons had also been drawn and pondered by AI workers at the USSR Academy of Sciences' Institute of Applied Mathematics and Information Transmission, in collaboration with Moscow State University. They now have an impressive variety of six-legged robots under test. This too was brought by McGhee to the attention of Proxmire's senate committee. The saddest point of the story, however, is that the successful rebuff to ignorant persecution was achieved by arguments that McGhee regards, as do many, as being entirely beside the main point. The quick-fire rejoinders lay ready to hand and they did the job, but McGhee's instinctive reply, before his university's public relations office came to his aid, was: "Basic research is for producing knowledge, not new products." But how to convey this thought to those who have charge of such matters?

Figure 54. Archeopteryx

YELLOW PERILING

Scientists are often faced with this dilemma: should they try to explain their real technical concerns, knowing that their reward may be fidgets, yawns, and puzzled frowns, or should they use the knee-jerk tactic and hit where they know they can get a response? Reference to scientific goals, and attempts to explain them, are often wasted breath. Hitting the technology button, on the other hand, seems to buy us something. The knee-jerk tactic is known in the AI business as Yellow Periling. Everyone, after all, can understand that intelligent robots could be useful in the industrial struggle against Japan. But to understand why the scientists themselves consider the work important—that is not easy to convey to busy people. But it is often just not appropriate for scientists to justify their work in terms of immediately visible benefits.

The Dutch government's advisory group on the social impact of microtechnology has been afflicted with a similar worry. The group noted that "the speed of innovation makes it increasingly difficult for governments to follow developments."[7] Except that the statement covers only a small part of what could be said, scientists may well feel: "At last someone has said it."

To those concerned to see that the potential of the synthesis of new knowledge by computer is fully exploited this situation presents a major obstacle. Substantial investment of money and political commitment is going to be needed to make the creative computer happen. The field of Artificial Intelligence specifically has had particular difficulty in gaining acceptance in the political and scientific establishments. Its existence over the last twenty-five years has been punctuated by influential cries that the whole exercise is an infantile disorder. In 1972–73, the British Science Research Council received two reports on long-range policy for computing science and machine intelligence. One, the careful work of experienced computer professionals, said, "Build it up!" The other, which said, "Wind it up!" came from an outsider, Sir James Lighthill: distinguished as a fluid dynamicist, a controversial government expert, and the departing occupant of Cambridge University's Lucasian Chair of Applied Mathematics.

Advice to government has traditionally emanated from past holders of this chair, some of it of uneven quality. Professor Sir George Biddell Airy once advised Queen Victoria that if the royal salute were fired outside the Crystal Palace, the building would collapse. More pertinently to us, Airy's advice secured the withdrawal of government support for Charles Babbage's Difference Engine.

BEARS AND BALLS

We must believe that Lighthill's advice did not spring from shallow roots. Some of it was, however, a little strange. In considering the question "Why build robots?" he remarked:

We have to remember the long-standing captivation of the human imagination by the very concept, as shown by its continual prominence in literature, from medieval fantasies of the Homunculus through Mary Shelley's "Frankenstein" to modern science fiction. To what extent may scientists consider themselves in duty bound to minister to the public's general *penchant* for robots by building the best they can?

Incidentally, it has sometimes been argued that part of the stimulus to laborious male activity in "creative" fields of work, including pure science, is the urge to compensate for the lack of the female capability of giving birth to children. If this were true, then building robots might indeed be seen as the ideal compensation! There is one piece of evidence supporting that highly uncertain hypothesis: most robots are designed from the outset to operate in a world as like as possible to the conventional child's world as seen by a man; they play games, they do puzzles, they build towers of bricks, they recognize pictures in drawing-books ("bear on rug with ball") . . .[8]

The "bear on rug" reference was to a paper on computer vision published in 1972 by Harry Barrow, Pat Ambler, and Rod Burstall.[9] One of the simple pictures used to test their program had "Bear on rug with ball" as its caption. Lighthill continued:

Nevertheless, the view to which this author has tentatively but perhaps quite wrongly come is that a relationship which may be called pseudomaternal rather than Pygmalion-like comes into play between a Robot and its Builder.

Lighthill divided the field of AI into: A—Advanced Automation; C—Computer-based research into the workings of the central nervous system; and B—Bridge activities intended to link A and C, or alternatively, Building Robots. He asserted that while progress in A and C had been disappointingly slow, they were nevertheless legitimate areas for research. B on the other hand, he argued, was getting nowhere and ought to cease. It had "grandiose aims" which it had failed to reach, he said, adding that, "This raises doubts about whether the whole concept of AI as an integrated field of research is a valid one.''

The nature of Lighthill's misunderstanding is at root the same as that encountered by Robert McGhee. As was pointed out at the time, B should really stand for "Basic," the fundamental research that constitutes the heart of the subject. It was as if Thomas Hunt Morgan and his colleagues who pioneered modern genetics had been told: "You have the mathematical theory of Mendel to play with. You have breeding work to do for the community's good in improving crops and farm animals. You are also free, and we will even fund this modestly, to investigate the broader matrix of biological processes in which the genetic phenomena are embedded. But frankly, we see no need to be breeding fruit flies. Better switch to cows!" Being able men, Morgan and his colleagues would doubtless have made more than adequate cattle breeders and could indeed have found one or two shrewd applications of already formulated principles of academic genetics. But the chromosome theory of heredity would have had to wait, and everyone, including farmers, would have been the losers.

THE HORIZONS OF DELPHI

Lighthill also accused AI workers of making wild predictions. Is that charge justified? The best-known exercise in AI forecasting was a "Delphi" survey published in 1973 by four scientists from Stanford Research Institute and Lockheed. The Delphi technique of taking a survey of a substantial number of people about their views of the future is widely used in industry to forecast new products and technologies. The 1973 predictions are summarized in Figure 55.

Nothing has happened or failed to happen in the intervening years that is inconsistent with this set of forecasts. Considering individual items whose dates have already passed:

P5: Convincing prototypes exist for computer identification of personnel by signature, voice, and photographs. A leading center for this work has been Case Western Reserve University, and commercial systems for all three media of identification are on the market.

Products	Median Prototype Date	Median Commercial Date
HIGH POTENTIAL SIGNIFICANCE		
P5 - Automatic identification system	1976	1980
P8 - Automatic diagnostician	1977	1982
P13 - Industrial robot	1977	1980
P1 - Automated inquiry system	1978	1985
P9 - Personal biological model	1980	1985
P11 - Computer-controlled artificial organs	1980	1990
P18 - Robot tutor	1983	1988
P16 - Insightful economic model	1984	1990
P2 - Automated intelligence system	1985	1991
P20 - General factotum	2000	2010
MEDIUM POTENTIAL SIGNIFICANCE		
P14 - Voice response order-taker	1978	1983
P15 - Insightful weather analysis system	1980	1985
P3 - Voice-actuated typewriter	1985	1992
P6 - Mobile robot	1985	1995
P4 - Automatic language translator	1987	1995
P12 - Computer arbiter	1988	1995
P10 - Computer psychiatrist	1990	2000
P17 - Robot chauffeur	1992	2000
P21 - Creation and valuation system	1994	2003
LOW POTENTIAL SIGNIFICANCE		
P19 - Universal game player	1980	1985
P7 - Animal/machine symbiont	2000	2010

Figure 55. Dates forecast in 1973 for the appearance of various computer technologies. So far, the predictions have turned out remarkably accurate.[10]

P8: Working systems exist for meningitis, congenital heart disease, lung disease, thyroid enlargements, acute abdominal pain and internal medicine more generally, urinary infections, and bacteraemia and other clinical areas.

P13: "Industrial robot" as used here implies optical and tactile sensing in addition to programmable manipulation. Several such devices have been demonstrated, and commercial systems are now on the market, notably from Unimation Corporation.

P1: Powerful prototypes have been tested that are capable of inferential question-answering, in addition to ordinary data-base retrieval.

P9 and P11: If the "median commercial dates" of these two are reversed, then today's laboratory evidence would place both developments well on course.

P14: Systems already in commercial use allow the customer to place orders by interactive terminal or ordinary push-button telephone, with computer-generated voice reply.

P15: The current budget of the UK meteorological center at Bracknell includes such "insightful" aspects. Practical implementation is likely in this case to fall behind the Delphi projection.

P3: A typewriter that converts the user's speech into printed words was introduced into the Japanese market by Nippon Electric in 1981. The Japanese "Kana" alphabet, being entirely phonetic, makes this considerably easier technically than it is for Western languages.

There is one curious item on which the seers lose—not in estimating its date, but in underestimating its commercial significance. "Universal game player" is placed as a low-importance entry, but microprocessor-driven game attachments to home television sets and hobby computers used mainly for games have constituted a whole boom industry by themselves. The arcade game Pac-Man collected $1 billion in the U.S. in 18 months, and computer games overall are now making more profits than the entire film industry.

The most noteworthy feature of the forecast was not, as AI's critics allege, prediction of things that did not happen, but rather the failure to predict things that did, such as the swing toward distributed processing now arising from the microcomputer revolution.

The farther into the future one tries to forecast, the riskier the exercise becomes. Few people would be prepared to predict when the computer in the office will really come into its own, as characterized by a little scene stemming from an idea of Nicholas Negroponte's. You will walk into your office in the morning and ask your general factotum computer, "Where is it?"

The machine replies, "Where's what?"

"*You know*," you retort.

"Ah," says the machine, and tells you.

On the other hand, Ed Fredkin of MIT has stated that although it will take at least fifteen years to create a machine equating human intelligence, it will be no longer than forty. From that it should not be too great a step to I. J. Good's predicted Ultra-Intelligent Machine, which would be, to steal words from the calypso:

Smarter than the man in every way.

BRINGING ABOUT THE CHANGE

Not so far away, an abundance of benefits are waiting to be gained from research in AI if the investment and commitment can be mobilized. One early priority must be stopping the lunatic waste of scarce human resources in our universities now, where experienced AI scientists spend much of their time teaching undergraduates other subjects instead of doing urgent AI research. This is tantamount to using water in the desert to polish the bumpers of a car.

But how to bring about the change? George Gallagher-Daggitt, an engineer at Rutherford Laboratory, has called for "innovation centers." These would "allow university researchers to join multidisciplinary teams, involving industry and possibly private inventors as well, without upsetting their promotional prospects. In this environment they would be subject to the stimulus of commercial competition and could devote their efforts to commercializing intellectual concepts arising from fundamental research carried out in universities.''[11]

Brave words: something along these lines could surely flip the switch to the ''on'' position. Work that presses against the margins of the possible requires a special environment. Academic excellence as well as technological know-how must be combined in a fluent mix of support mechanisms—contracting out, contracting in, government sponsors, industrial sponsors, research grants, graduate students, visitorships senior and junior.

As far as investment cash from the private sector is concerned, something like the Investment Allowance Scheme as tried in Australia could make a start. This was introduced in the 1960s, followed by a planned phase-out. Another dose to revive flagging investment was administered in the 1970s. To take as an example the purchase of computer terminals, the usual amortization of capital expenditure for tax relief would be 30% of the balance each year plus the residual balance after five years. Under IAS, an additional allowance would be made during the first year of 40% of the purchase price. The total allowance thus adds up to 140%, a not insignificant incentive for the investor.

First and foremost, the need is for specific projects to concentrate minds. Sectors ready to yield to determined thrusts include the following:

Parallel processing, with special reference to computer vision. New architectures promise not only breathtaking speed-ups but, more importantly, radical conceptual simplifications of complex domains. Applications of cheap reliable computer vision range from optical inspection of industrial parts and structures to the input and interpretation of diagrams from books and documents.

Automatic program synthesis, to help tackle the crisis in the production of software. An example of how industry is taking up the ideas of AI with enthusiasm is the substantial work in automatic program synthesis at IBM's Yorktown Heights Laboratory and at Schlumberger.

Expert systems: The country that first establishes an edge in interactive knowledge bases will be in a fair position to call the shots. Knowledge engineering is like genetic engineering: the principles are relatively simple, the range of applications unlimited.

Intelligent robots: Expert systems to drive industrial robots confer versatility, retrainability, and autonomous resourcefulness beyond anything yet seen in automation. The advantages for manufacturing are obvious. There could not be a better moment. Not only in the factory, mobile robots or "gofers" would have many uses, as outlined in Chapter 1. A team of intelligent gofers at Three Mile Island in radio contact with the outside world would not have come amiss. As it happens, the essential problems of robot plan-formation and of automatic program synthesis are closely related.

ROBOTS AND EXPERT SYSTEMS GET TOGETHER

The connection between the sciences of expert systems and of robotics is contentious. At the boardroom level, it is often thought that there is no connection. Moreover, the man who taps train wheels and the man who tests tire alignments will join forces to put the same view. Nor is it the slightest use to talk of the Carnot Cycle or the physics of frictional losses. Boardroom and workbench will be unanimous that clever talk does not butter the nation's parsnips.

There is one kind of person who sees the connection instantly and sees it as important. He is the R & D engineer. But whoever listened to engineers, except in wartime? So with robotics. The expert-systems approach to robotics tends to be viewed as diversionary. "Haven't we got enough to do getting reasonable performance out of dumb robots without complicating the issue with intelligence?" The answer is to conjure from the past the wild-eyed proposal that must at some definite moment have come forward for the first time: how about an internal-combustion approach to railway transport? "Haven't we got enough to do getting reasonable performance out of steam without complicating the issue with diesel?"

In the robot context, what is this precious "diesel?" It is called formalized knowledge. Standard programming methods do not allow a robot or other computing system to do any of the following:

(1) Explain what it is doing;
(2) Be taught a better way;
(3) Explain how it does the new way;
(4) Think up a better way;
(5) Explain that too.

Such capabilities will be highly valuable in an industrial robot of the future, whether anchored to a work station or free-roving. A needless gap has opened up—or perhaps it always existed—between excellent and devoted production engineers and on the other hand those whose primary interests center around the software design principles of items (1) to (5). For once the greater share of blame lies with the practical men, although in virtue of valiant and long unrewarded toil on the dirty end of the job, they have the moral right of way. So too the steam engineers had a right to call out to the diesel experimentalists: "Drop your playthings and get back into the real work!" To have said so would have signified courage, even a little arrogance—and also uninformed technical judgment.

If there is room for a production-engineering approach to robotics, then there is room for an expert-systems approach, along with contributions from software technologists, hardware designers, microelectronics specialists, and programming theorists. Interdisciplinary teams may be unfashionable in the staid world of peacetime science, but the technological struggle that lies ahead will not be easy to win any other way.

THE FOUR FALLACIES

Not long ago, efforts to get knowledge-based robotics off the ground used to encounter variations on a general theme: "These scientists want to play God." The variations took the form of Four Fatal Fallacies:

Fatal Fallacy 1: "There are no conceivable socially useful applications."

Fatal Fallacy 2: "If there were, the research would be of immediate benefit to our hard-pressed industries."

Fatal Fallacy 3: "Robotics is not an information engineer's problem. Hand it to the mechanicals and electricals."

Fatal Fallacy 4: "There is no need to mimic human ways of doing and thinking. Machine ways are best."

Happily, a more informed awareness seems astir. Fatal Fallacy 1 is now *seen* to be a fatal fallacy. Let us look at the other three.

Fatal Fallacy 2: Analysis has shown that industry is not investing nearly enough in order to be able to take up new developments. Instead, industrially relevant academic research goes to fuel the engines of Far Eastern competitors.

Fatal Fallacy 3 seems visible in today's university research. Much cash is flowing to academic hopefuls ready to do battle in the technology of industrial manipulators with the Goliaths of Mitsubishi and Hitachi. But in this war the lethal slingshots are in software. It is early days, and the balance may yet correct itself.

Fatal Fallacy 4, the danger of which has been one of the central themes of this book, is still maintained even by some first-rate professionals. A corrective is the Japanese Fifth Generation Computer Survey and Research Committee's recommendation of close study of "pattern recognition and imitation of the operation of the human brain."

SOWING THE FALLOW LAND

There is an international dimension in all this. Ed Fredkin has proposed the establishment of a world institute, perhaps in Geneva, where scientists could begin a major effort to develop this technology on a broad scale, free from political and overtly commercial pressures. The equipment and working conditions would be adequate for the job and securely established. The institute would be funded by endowment, to avoid the need to show immediate practical results, but it would have a specific long-term goal—namely, the creation of an intelligent machine. Fredkin's reasoning on this is sound. Through fear of inactivating the scientific mind by strapping it too tightly to immediate application, it is sometimes believed that the best course is to let it flap loose. This too can be counterproductive. In the history of experimental science, it is the development of well-chosen and timely goals that has opened winning lines, rather than wayward genius. Montaigne, himself a scholar of excellence, wrote in 1580:

> Just as we see that fallow land, if rich and fertile, teems with a hundred thousand wild and useless weeds, and that to set it to work we must subject it and sow it with certain seeds for our service . . . so it is with minds. Unless you keep them busy with some definite subject that will bridle and control them, they will throw themselves in disorder hither and yon in the vague fields of imagination.[12]

Such an institute is not needed just for the sake of rapid progress, Fredkin asserts. No complex computer program was ever produced without bugs, he points out, adding that "flaws in the creation of a 'super-intelligence' are frightening to consider." Thus, the project would have a brief to set standards to guard against such possibilities. Whatever the institutional basis, if properly enabled, the result of this generation's work can be, in Fredkin's words, "the development of a safe and beneficial AI for the benefit of mankind."*

*Since the words of the foregoing paragraph were written, the Turing Institute has been established in premises in Glasgow adjoining the University of Strathclyde, with which the institute has concluded an Agreement of Association. Its work is dedicated to the realization of the Fredkin concept.

POSTSCRIPT

IT IS COMMONLY THOUGHT that the aim of Artificial Intelligence is to develop a race of super-clever Daleks, unfathomable to man, that will eventually dominate the globe. In fact, what AI is about is exactly the opposite: making machines *more* fathomable and *more* under the control of human beings, not less. Conventional technology has indeed been making our environment more complex and more incomprehensible, and if it continues as it is doing now, the only conceivable outcome is disaster. AI seeks to reverse that process and return technology to its proper place as the obedient yet perceptive servant of humanity. Together, man and machine may then be able to subdue many, perhaps in time most, of the world's afflictions.

Many people fear the development of intelligent machines as an invasion by a race of conquering aliens. Instead, we should see ourselves as a beleaguered garrison who at the eleventh hour can see on the horizon the dust of the relieving column. This book is a shout from the battlements.

APPENDIX: BASIC PRINCIPLES OF COMPUTING

BY RORY JOHNSTON

A WIDELY ACCEPTED DEFINITION of the word *computer* is "a general-purpose, automatic, programmable information processing machine." "General purpose" here means that the machine can do a wide variety of tasks, not just one; "automatic," that it runs on its own once started by the user; and "programmable," that the user can specify at any time and in detail what it is he wants done. The information being processed can be numbers or words; pictures, sounds, and so on can be handled, but they always have to be reduced to numbers by some mechanism or other as, for that matter, do words. With modern computing techniques, however, this can largely be done automatically, so the user does not have to be conscious of any numbers. In essence the machine is dealing with symbols, and for that reason some people feel that a better definition of *computer* is "symbol manipulator."

Nearly all computers are surprisingly similar in the principles on which they work and surprisingly different in their detail. Fundamentally, they interact with the user by *commands*. These are English words that tell the machine what to do; the user types them on a keyboard like that of a typewriter. The response from the machine appears on a television screen or something similar. Each computer can only understand a few dozen words, and the words in use at any one time constitute its "language." There are many different languages, each suitable for different purposes. We will use for our examples the best known of these, which is called Basic. A typical command in Basic is the word PRINT, which tells the machine to display something on the screen (the word is left over from the days when teleprinters were more common than screens). For instance the command

PRINT 3 + 5

elicits the response from the machine:

8

The computer works out the arithmetical expression and "prints" the result. A sum can be very complicated:

PRINT 21*(287.35 + 89) − 44.9

The symbol * is used for "multiply," to avoid confusion with the letter X. The machine replies:

7858.45

If we try saying something to the computer that is not in its limited vocabulary:

HELLO

we get the response:

?SYNTAX
ERROR

It assumes we have made a mistake. As simple as the word is, the machine cannot make head or tail of it.

THE COMPUTER REMEMBERS

A vital part of the computer is a memory in which information can be held while it is being worked on. We can tell the machine to save a number in its memory, but to do that we must put a label on the number in order to be able to get it back again, just as in checking a suitcase. The label in this case can be a letter, any letter we choose:

LET A = 293

This means: "Store the number 293 away in the memory and call it A."

Then if we say

PRINT A

we get the response

293

The information will stay in the memory indefinitely.

The same memory can also be used to store *instructions,* and this is where the computer really comes into its own. A procedure in information processing may be so long and complicated that specifying each step as it arises would be impossibly slow. So the instructions can be saved in memory and then executed automatically in the correct sequence. As a very simple example, take the formula with which we are all familiar for working out the area of a circle: $A = \pi r^2$. Suppose we need to know the areas of a large number of circles. We can load the appropriate instructions into the computer to make it do this automatically with no further thought on our part. The procedure is to take the radius of the circle (r), square it, multiply by π (3.14), and print out the answer. The radius of course comes from the world outside the computer, so as a first step the machine has to be told to accept the "data" from the human user. The instruction for this is:

INPUT R

This tells the machine to wait for someone to type the number (the radius of a circle) on the keyboard and, when that has happened, store it away in the memory with the label "R."

Then the arithmetic is done:

LET A = R*R*3.14

This works out the area and stores it as "A." The last step is to print out the answer:

PRINT A

When typing in these instructions, we precede every line with a *number,* which tells the machine the order in which they are to be executed and helps us to refer to them later on. All together, the instructions look like this:

1 INPUT R
2 LET A = R**R*3.14
3 PRINT A

Having typed them in, we give the command RUN, which tells the machine to execute all the instructions in its memory. First it encounters Instruction 1, which makes it wait for us to type in a radius, say 2. Then, taking no appreciable time, the computer works out the arithmetic in Instruction 2 and (Instruction 3) prints out the answer:

12.56

For another circle, we type RUN again, and so on indefinitely.

SMALL STEPS FOR PROGRAMS

The three instructions constitute a computer *program,* albeit a trivial one. A program is simply a set of instructions for a computer to do one particular job. To be really useful, a computer needs a more complex task than this. Whatever the task, the programmer (a human being) has to break it down into a series of steps, each of which is small enough for the machine to handle. He then writes the steps out in the appropriate computer language. This process can be quite difficult. The programmer has to be careful to get all the steps clear and in the right order. Imagine, for instance, writing out all the steps involved in changing the tire of a car. They might be:

Apply handbrake
Get jack and brace
Remove hubcap
Loosen wheel nuts
Jack up car
Remove wheel nuts
Remove wheel
Get spare
Mount spare
Replace nuts
Lower car
Tighten nuts
Replace hubcap
Replace jack, brace, and flat tire in car

We must remember the importance of loosening the wheel nuts *before* jacking up the car. Readers might like to try the same exercise with "filling a fountain pen" or "making a pot of tea." When does the pot get warmed?

None of these sample procedures involves decisions or questions, but in real life these arise all the time. Any process that involves decisions is best shown in the form of a *flowchart,* as in Figure 55. The diamonds are decision points. Readers could try drawing a flowchart for "how to cross the road." (This is not as simple as it might seem.)

AN AVERAGE TASK

Getting back to the computer, an example of a more substantial program would be one to work out the average (mean) of a set of numbers. This is done of course by adding all the numbers together and dividing by however many numbers there are. A program to do this cannot simply say, "Add the first two"; Add the third"; "Add the fourth" . . . because it is not known beforehand

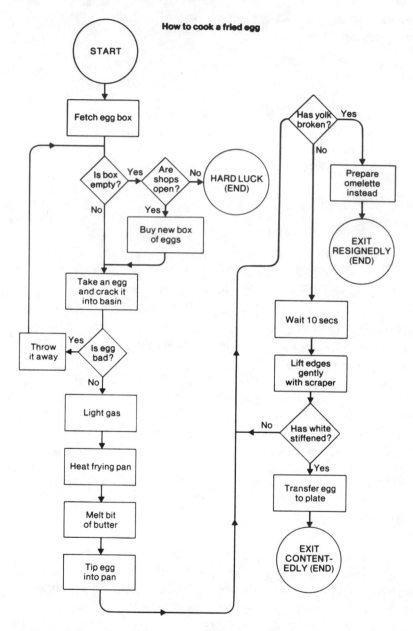

Figure 55. An example of a flowchart

how many numbers there are—it varies from one problem to another. Consequently, the program must go around in a *loop*, adding each number as it comes in to an accumulating total, until all the numbers have been received. To do this, it must first find out from the user how many numbers there are. Then it needs to count the numbers as they are fed in and stop after the last one. Then it should do the division and print the answer. This process is shown in Figure 56.

One location in the memory is used to hold the running total and another to keep the count. Each time around the loop, 1 is added to the count, and then the question is asked: "Has the count reached the required tally yet?" In other words, "Have we got all the numbers yet?" If no, the program loops back and gets another number. If yes, it does the division and displays the answer. The running total and the count both have to be set to zero at the beginning—this is a commonplace requirement in computing that is called *initialization*. All of these functions can be seen in the flowchart. A complete, carefully worked out procedure such as this is known by mathematicians as an *algorithm*, specifying exactly what to do in a mechanical way.

Making the program loop back requires two further Basic commands: One is the word GOTO, followed by the number of an instruction. This makes the program jump out of its usual sequence of instructions and carry on from whatever line is specified. For example, one can make a program jump back to the beginning and go around and around a loop forever by adding GOTO 1 on the end.

The decision in a flowchart diamond is implemented in Basic with the command IF. This can take the form, for instance:

IF X=3 GOTO 20

The program only "goes to" line 20 if X equals 3. If X is anything else, the program carries on with the next line in sequence as normal. In the averaging program, an IF instruction is used to test whether the count has reached the required number yet. If it is still less than the required number, the program loops back. Otherwise it moves forward to the closing part of the program.

The program in Basic is as follows. We give an English expla-

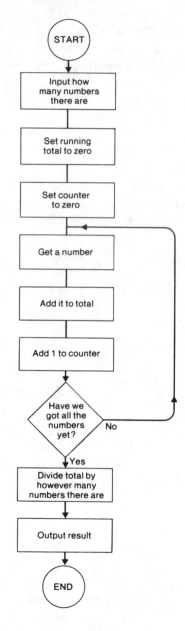

Figure 56. Flowchart for finding averages

nation of each line on the right. Note how closely the program corresponds to the flowchart.

1	INPUT N	Get how many numbers there are.
2	LET T=0	Clear running total.
3	LET C=0	Clear count.
4	INPUT X	Get a number.
5	LET T=T+X	Add it to total.
6	LET C=C+1	Add 1 to count.
7	If C<N GOTO 4	Is C less than N?
8	PRINT T/N	No—do division to find average.

The command LET $C=C+1$ looks a little strange. It is simply a neat way of adding 1 to C, by telling the machine to take the number C, add 1 to it, and make that the new value of C. LET $T=T+X$ does the same thing, adding each number in turn to the accumulating total T.

MAKING THE COMPUTER EXPLAIN ITSELF

It would be nice if the user of this program (as opposed to the programmer) did not have to understand how the Basic instructions actually worked. We would like the program to prompt the user, telling him what has to be done at each stage: that is, typing in the various numbers. We can do this by using the ability of the PRINT command to handle words as well as numbers. The words are enclosed in quotation marks. Thus the command

PRINT "CHEERS"

elicits the response from the machine

CHEERS

We add before each input command in the averaging program a PRINT instruction that will tell the user, as the program runs, what it is the machine is asking for. The sample screen display in Figure 57 shows this, together with a run of the program.

```
1 PRINT "AVERAGE FINDER"
2 PRINT "HOW MANY NUMBERS";
3 INPUT N
4 LET T=Ø
5 LET C=Ø
6 PRINT "NUMBER";
7 INPUT X
8 LET T=T+X
9 LET C=C+1
1Ø IF C<N GOTO 6
11 PRINT "THE AVERAGE IS ";
12 PRINT T/N

RUN
AVERAGE FINDER
HOW MANY NUMBERS? 4
NUMBER? 12
NUMBER? 37
NUMBER? 25.6
NUMBER? 2
THE AVERAGE IS 19.15
```

Figure 57. Typing in and running the averaging program on a computer

Real-life computer programs tend to be much bigger and more complicated. At the next level up from the averaging example could be: a perpetual calendar—that is, a program to work out the day of the week for any given date; or a program to find the prime factors of any given number. For averaging you do not really need a computer; for finding prime factors of a large number you certainly do. Readers interested in finding out more about programming should see one of the books listed in the notes.

Many practical applications of computers involve no clever programming at all—the computer is useful simply because so much data is handled. Examples might be invoicing, payrolls, or stock control. On the other hand scientific number-crunching, weather forecasting, and the control of airline-reservations systems and large data banks can be very complex. These latter examples generally require very large computers, while business applications use medium-sized machines and the control of factory equipment and assembly-line robots can be done with minicomputers or microcomputers. Likewise, languages vary according to the application. There is a bewildering array of languages, differing mainly in how much of the programming donkey work they handle and how much they leave to the programmer. "Low-level" languages are fast and versatile, but they require the programmer to specify the task in minute detail. "High-level" languages are more like English and easier to use, but are more limited in what they can do because the programmer has less control over exactly how the machine handles the job. High-level languages include Basic, Fortran, Algol, Pascal, and many others.

BUGS AND HOW TO FIND THEM

Programmers, being human, make mistakes. If these are simply typing errors, such as PRIMT instead of PRINT, the computer will fail to recognize the command and will respond:

?SYNTAX
ERROR

In other cases, however, an instruction given will be perfectly valid but will still be the wrong one for achieving the desired result. For instance, the instruction PRINT A-B could be written when it should be PRINT B-A. The computer has no way of knowing it is wrong and will carry out the instruction happily, giving the wrong answer to whatever problem it is. The programmer will need to notice this and do some detective work to find the error or "bug" in the program.* In the same way, failure to remove the car hubcap or to loosen the wheel nuts will make the operation of changing the car tire unsuccessful. When people say, "The computer made a mistake," it was invariably not the computer but the programmer or the operator who made the mistake. When the electronics themselves fail (and this happens quite often), the machine virtually never gives the wrong answer; it simply gives no answer at all. This highlights the fundamental distinction in all computing between the electronic and mechanical equipment, known collectively as "hardware," and the programs, parts of programs, and collections of programs that are called collectively "software" because of the ease with which they can be changed.

The absolute predictability of a computer can sometimes be a nuisance. When the machine is playing a game, we want it to be able in effect to "throw dice." Space invaders need to arrive unpredictably. In planning, say, a timber plantation, the trees should be laid out irregularly rather than in straight lines, to reduce soil erosion. For such purposes as these, computers have special software routines to generate random numbers on demand. Since everything the machine does is deterministic, the numbers are not really random—they are worked out from a very long division calculation and so could be predicted by someone who went to a lot of trouble. They are called pseudo-random and are good enough for most purposes.

When a permanent record of a computer's "output" is needed, it can be produced on paper by various devices ranging from an ordinary teleprinter to a massive "line printer" capable of generat-

*According to Commodore Grace Hopper USNR, the first bug was exactly that. While troubleshooting the Mark I computer at Harvard in 1945, she found a two-inch moth inside, playing havoc with the circuits. She has kept the moth in her laboratory notebook as proof of her claim to this piece of jargon.

ing twenty or thirty pages a minute. The speed with which a computer can disgorge information contrasts starkly with the slowness of feeding it in. Every character (letter, figure, or punctuation mark) has to be entered on a keyboard by a human being. This process is called data entry, and companies have large rooms full of people who do nothing else all day long, copying from handwritten forms or what have you. This bottleneck of "input" remains a major obstacle in the development of computing.

YET MORE STORAGE

The internal memory of the computer (the workings of which we explain below) is limited in capacity. Thus separate devices are needed for storing information in bulk. These are commonly magnetic tape or rotating magnetic disks, both working on the same principle as sound-recording tape. It takes much longer to get information from either of these than from the computer's internal memory, and tape is slower still than disk because of the time spent in winding tape back and forth. Keeping track of where information is stored on disks and tapes, retrieving it when required, and erasing and reusing storage areas no longer needed is a very complicated task, and for this purpose a special program called an *operating system* is provided. With this, the user can take all the information on one particular topic, give it a name, and store it away and retrieve it without having to think about what its actual physical location is on the tape or the disk.

On large computers, operating systems also perform functions such as "timesharing." For a long time computers were too expensive to devote to just one application at a time, and a timesharing operating system would enable several dozen users to be connected to the machine simultaneously. These people can be some distance away, using screen-and-keyboard units, called *terminals,* connected to the computer by wire. The machine spends a few milliseconds dealing with one user's task, then a few milliseconds on the next, and so on around in a loop, so quickly that each user thinks he has the machine's undivided attention. The pressure on cost of the central processor is no longer so great, but timesharing is still widely used, especially where resources such as large data bases and expensive printers need to be shared. Large operating systems are among the most complex artifacts in existence. It is not surprising therefore that they can be unreliable and prone to mysterious failures. Many large computers cannot run for more than a few days without an operating system "crash" in which everything grinds to a halt, requiring a complete restart.

LIFTING THE LID ON THE COMPUTER

A typical computer in schematic layout looks like this:

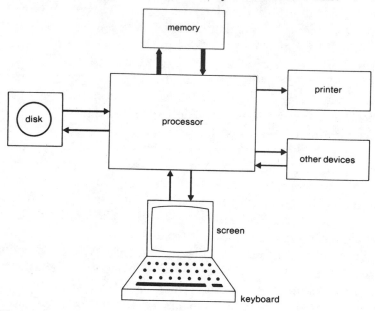

Figure 58. Schematic layout of a computer

Internally, the computer works entirely with numbers. These numbers are all held in electronic circuits called *registers*. The physical size of a register determines the largest number it can hold—typically, this might be 65,535. (The reason for this curious number will become apparent later.) Usually, all the registers in a particular model of computer are the same size, and it is this size that to a large extent determines the architecture of the machine. Giant computers have large registers, while microcomputers in general have small ones. We will describe the workings of an imaginary computer; real computers nearly all work on these principles but are more complicated in detail.

Within the central processor are three special-purpose registers: the Program Counter, the Instruction Register, and the Accumulator. The Program Counter controls the flow of the program, the Instruction Register deciphers the instructions, and the Accumulator is where the data is actually processed. The computer's memory consists of several thousand identical registers, or "cells." These are numbered sequentially so that the processor can refer to them—each cell's number is called its "address," as a natural word for specifying location. All this is shown in Figure 59. The memory holds both the program and the data on which it is to work. These are indistinguishable, so the computer has to keep track of where the program is and where the data is. Each instruction in a program, like everything else, is a number, and the program occupies a series of consecutive cells in memory.

The Program Counter contains the address of the instruction to be executed next. The processor goes to that cell in the memory, reads the number contained therein, and loads it into the Instruction Register. The instruction is carried out, the address in the Program Counter is increased by one, and the process is repeated with the next instruction of the program. The machine thus works in *cycles* of two parts: the first half, called Fetch, in which the instruction is read out of memory, and the second half, called Execute, in which the instruction is carried out. One cycle typically takes about a millionth of a second.

VERB AND OBJECT

The instruction as it sits in the Instruction Register has two parts: an operation and an operand. We can see these as corre-

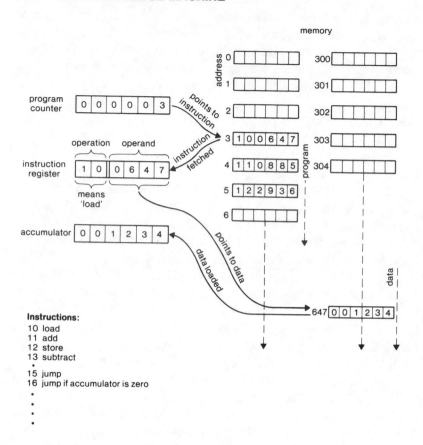

Figure 59. How a computer works internally

sponding to the verb and the object in an English sentence (all instructions are imperatives, so there is no subject stated). Suppose the operation is the number 10 and the operand the number 0647. Operation 10 could mean "Load." Thus the whole instruction means: "Read the number stored in memory cell 0647 and put it in the Accumulator." Operation 11 could mean "Add." Then the instruction 11-0885 would mean: "Add the number that is in memory cell 0885 to the number that is currently in the Accumulator and put the result in the Accumulator." Instruction 12 could signify "Store" and 12-2936 would say: "Take the number that is in the Accumulator and store it in memory location 2936." (Whatever was previously in that location gets thrown away.) The processor would have a dozen or so major instructions like these, including "Subtract" and "Clear the Accumulator to zero." Some simple computers do not even have a "Multiply" instruction—they require a programmer to write a short routine to multiply by repeated addition.

It is important to see that these instructions are not the same as Basic commands, nor are the memory addresses the same as Basic line numbers. More on that point later. To move about in the program in the manner of a Basic GOTO, the computer has a "Jump" instruction. If "Jump" is instruction code 15, a whole instruction could look like: 15-0073, meaning, "Carry on executing the program from memory cell 0073." The mechanism for this is very simple: the processor just takes the operand part of the instruction (which is the address to be jumped to) and forces it into the Program Counter, like this:

This causes the program to carry on from that point. If a jump is made to an area of memory that contains data rather than program, the processor will try to execute the data as if it were instructions and will go completely haywire.

For making decisions, there is a *conditional* Jump instruction, saying "Jump to the address indicated *if the Accumulator is zero.*" This way a question box on a flowchart can be implemented by having a test on a particular piece of data: if it is zero, the program jumps; if it is not, the program carries on in the normal sequence of steps. All questions have to be reduced to the form: "Is something or other equal to zero or is it not?" Thus, to ask "Is number A equal to number B?" the program has to subtract one from the other and test to see whether the result is zero.

There has to be one other set of instructions, and that is for input and output. One instruction would mean: "Accept a character that has been typed on the keyboard and load it (yet again encoded as a number) into the Accumulator." Another command could be: "Take the character held in the Accumulator and send it to the screen." All other input and output devices such as the disk store and the printer have their own Input/Output commands.

PUTTING THE INSTRUCTIONS TO WORK

The instructions we have described are really very crude, but by putting together long sequences of them, it is possible to make the computer perform very complex tasks. Each step the computer takes is a very small one, so a great many steps are involved in any useful operation. As a result, even though one millionth of a second may seem a miraculously fast time for one processor cycle, it is none too fast when it comes to tackling real-world tasks. The fact that every step has to be carried out one after the other in strict sequence is also a serious hindrance—this is known as the "von Neumann bottleneck," after the pioneer of this design of computer.

The numerical instructions make up what is known as the computer's "machine code." It is possible to program the machine entirely in these numbers, but it is extremely tedious, as numbers are hard to remember. This is why computer languages have been devised. The English words of whatever language it is are translated into the machine code by a special program loaded into the computer for this purpose. In the case of low-level languages, this program is known as an "assembler," and for high-level languages it is a "compiler" or "interpreter." Obviously, the person who wrote the original assembler had to write it in machine code. Each command in a low-level language corresponds to one machine-code instruction, and for this reason low-level languages tend to be specific to particular models of computer. In contrast, one command in a high-level language is translated by the compiler into typically several dozen machine-code instructions. For example, a Basic PRINT command will carry out a calculation and then cause a whole series of characters to appear on the screen, while one machine-code Output command will transfer only one character.

High-level languages are more or less standard across different computers, and a choice of compiler programs will normally be available for any one machine, so it can be used with Basic one day and Pascal the next if desired. The user simply has to load the appropriate compiler and feed in his program written in the corresponding language. The process of translating a high-level language is extremely complicated, and compilers are large and cumbersome programs that, like operating systems, are seldom free from errors.

MAKING NUMBERS OUT OF ELECTRICITY

How then are these functions of a computer actually implemented in electronics? Since everything inside the machine is a number, the first problem is how to represent numbers in some physical form. The earliest electronic computers used varying voltages to do this: the stronger the voltage, the larger the number. This method of working, called "analogue," is awkward and unreliable and was soon superseded by "digital" computers, which use circuits that are either on or off—there is nothing in between. Using these on-off circuits to hold numbers requires counting in twos rather than in tens as we do normally. This is not as odd as it may seem. Instead of the digits being labeled:

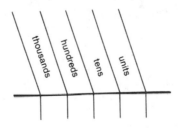

they are:

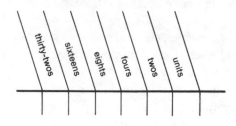

This is called the "binary" system, as opposed to the usual "decimal" system. As one example, 101 in binary is

$$
\begin{array}{r}
1 \ \text{four} \\
0 \ \text{twos} \\
\text{and } 1 \ \text{unit} \\
\hline
\end{array}
$$

making 5 in decimal

This is what the decimal numbers from one to ten look like in binary:

sixteens	eights	fours	twos	units		
				1	= 1	decimal
			1	0	= 2	
			1	1	= 3	
		1	0	0	= 4	
		1	0	1	= 5	
		1	1	0	= 6	
		1	1	1	= 7	
	1	0	0	0	= 8	
	1	0	0	1	= 9	
	1	0	1	0	= 10	

One binary digit (0 or 1), also called a "bit," is the smallest possible unit of information. A common size of register for a computer is sixteen bits, so the largest number that can be held in one of these is 1111111111111111 or 65,535.

The effect of counting in binary is that numbers are much longer than in decimal, but only two different symbols are needed (0,1) instead of ten (0,1,2,3,4,5,6,7,8,9). "0" can easily be represented by "Off" and "1" by "On." A digital computer therefore is nothing but an assemblage of on-off switches. The switches, though, cannot be actuated by a human being's finger like household switches—the machine has to be automatic, so it must be possible for the switches to be turned on and off *by other electric currents*. Such devices have existed for many years, and they are known as "relays." These consist of a switch with the coil of an electromagnet alongside:

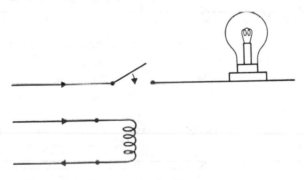

When current flows through the coil it becomes magnetized, the arm is pulled down, and the switch goes on. At first, digital computers were built with relays, but they are slow and prone to mechanical failures so they were soon replaced by electronic vacuum tubes. These have no moving parts, but they still have the drawbacks that they are expensive, take up a lot of room, and generate a great deal of heat. The computer did not really become a practical proposition until the invention in the late 1940s of the transistor, in which the electric charges themselves act as a switch, using a microscopically small junction in pieces of exotic materials called semiconductors. From being built out of separate transistors soldered together, computers have progressed to the stage where entire processors consisting of thousands of transistors are made all in one piece on a single sliver or "chip" of the element silicon. These "integrated circuits," as they are called, can be mass-produced very cheaply and it is this that has brought about the micro-electronic revolution of recent years.

Until fairly recently computers had memories made out of thousands of tiny magnets—magnetization in one direction meant "0" and in the other meant "1." Nowadays it is cheaper to use transistor circuits that are off for "0" and on for "1"; a separate circuit is required for each bit stored. These have the disadvantage that all the information in a memory is lost when the power is shut off, but information that needs to be kept is usually held on magnetic disks or tapes anyway.

GATES FOR LOGIC

Central to the workings of the switches in a computer is a system of logic invented in the 1850s by George Boole. In this, all statements have one of two values—True or False—and there are three connectors—And, Or, and Not. These enable one to construct descriptions of the world such as: "I will play soccer tonight IF there is nothing good on television AND the weather is fine." The truth of the statement "I will play football tonight" can be established by finding out the truth of the two following clauses and linking them with the logical And operation. "Or" works like this: "We will have a goalkeeper IF Bill turns up OR Bob turns up." It is of course possible for both of them to turn up, and "Or" is taken to include that possibility. Finally, "Not": "We will play IF the field is NOT taken by somebody else."

These can be easily implemented in electronic circuitry. True corresponds to On or "1" and False to Off or "0." "And" is two switches in series:

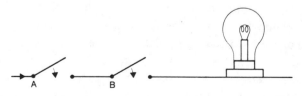

The light will go on only when *both* switch A *and* switch B are on.
An arrangement of switches like this is called an "And gate."
  "Or" is two switches in parallel:

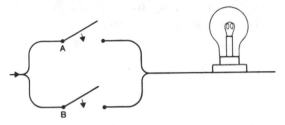

The light will go on if either switch A *or* switch B is on, or both.
This is an "Or gate."
  "Not" is a switch with a contact on the "released" side:

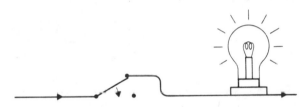

When the lever is pushed down, the light goes *off*.
  Interestingly enough, all the functions required in a digital
computer can be implemented using combinations of these three
types of gates. As a single example, consider the instruction
"Jump if the Accumulator is zero." The Accumulator consists of
one circuit for each binary digit (say sixteen of them). For the
condition for a jump to be fulfilled, *all* the digits have to be zero,
so for this instruction all the circuits are connected together in a
series of Nots and And gates. Only if the digits are all zero will
current pass through the And gates and activate the "Jump" circuitry:

Each of the other functions of the processor has its own set of circuits that are brought into play when the appropriate instruction is in the Instruction Register: one set for Loading, another set for Adding, and so on. It is easy to see from this why a practical computer needs many thousands of circuits.

ACKNOWLEDGMENTS

Parts of this book originally appeared in *Computer Weekly,* and in *Microelectronics and Society,* edited by Trevor Jones, Open University Press, 1980. These, and extracts from Alan Turing's lecture to the London Mathematical Society and the poem "Pavan for the Children of Deep Space," are reproduced by kind permission of the copyright owners.

For assistance in numerous ways we would like to thank: Keith Abbs, Malcolm Abbs, Igor Aleksander and his colleagues at Brunel University, Sir Alfred Ayer, Dominic Boreham, Chris Briscoe, the British Computer Society, Paul Brown, the Lewis Carroll Society, Becky Cohen, Harold Cohen, Chris Crabtree, Paul Davies, Edsger Dijkstra, Susan Dowell, David Em, Richard Gregory, Joyce Hannam, Larry Harris, Jean Hayes, Hervé Huitric and Monique Nahas, Edward Ihnatowicz, Margaret Jackson-Roberts, Doug Lenat, Ryszard Michalski, Lord Miles, Bob Muller and his colleagues at SPL, Alvary Parkinson, John Race, Robin Shirley, Nicky Singer, Aaron Sloman, Brian Reffin Smith, Alan Sutcliffe and David Whitfield.

FURTHER READING AND NOTES

FOR EACH CHAPTER, we have listed suggestions for further reading relevant to the general topic of that chapter, followed by specific references. Some of the books and articles here are popular, some more technical. The latter, which are distinguished in each case by an asterisk, require some prior acquaintance with the sciences of computing and/or cognition.

Chapter 1: *Brute Force and Ignorance*

General:

The best introduction to the field of Artificial Intelligence is still: Margaret Boden, *Artificial Intelligence and Natural Man* (Brighton: Harvester Press, and New York: Basic Books, 1977). Boden sees AI as a fundamentally humanist study. She brings to bear the perspective of a professional philosopher who specializes in problems of cognition, including the social aspect.

Also of note are: P. H. Winston, *Artificial Intelligence* (Reading, Mass.: Addison-Wesley, 1977); *The Computer Age: A Twenty-Year View,* ed. Michael Dertouzos and Joel Moses, (Cambridge, Mass.: MIT Press, 1979), a stimulating and authoritative collection of essays by many of the most eminent people in computing and the philosophy touching on it.

One of the most influential treatments there has been of the social significance of computing is: Joseph Weizenbaum, *Computer Power and Human Reason* (San Francisco: W. H. Freeman, 1976). Weizenbaum, a professor of computer science at MIT, is eloquent and moving in his condemnation of excessive faith in technology but, as far as AI is concerned in our view, wrong.

1. T. A. Dolotta, *Data Processing in 1980–85* (Chichester: Wiley, 1976).

2. C. E. Shannon, "Programming a Computer for Playing Chess," *Philosophical Magazine* 7th Series, Vol. 41, 1950, pp. 256–275.

3. Joseph Weizenbaum, "ELIZA—A Computer Program for the Study of Natural Language Communication between Man and Machine," *Communications of the Association for Computing Machinery,* Vol. 9, No. 1, January 1965, pp. 36–45.

4. Larry Harris, "The Four Obstacles to End-User Computer Access," proceedings of the conference The Fifth Generation, London, July 1982, SPL International, Abingdon.

5. G. G. Hendrix, E. D. Sacerdoti, D. Sagalowicz, and J. Slocum, "Developing a Natural Language Interface to Complex Data,"* proceedings of the Third International Conference on Very Large Data Bases, October 1977, p. 292.

6. John Krutch, *Experiments in Artificial Intelligence for Small Computers* (Indianapolis, Ind.: Howard Sams, 1981), pp. 93–104.

7. J. Y. Lettvin, H. R. Maturana, W. S. McCullough, and W. H. Pitts, "What the Frog's Eye Tells the Frog's Brain," *Proceedings of the Institute of Radio Engineers,* Vol. 47, 1959, pp. 1940–1951.

8. M.J.B. Duff, "Parallel Architecture and Vision,"* proceedings of the conference The Fifth Generation; Duff, "Seeing Machines," in *Intelligent Systems: the Unprecedented Opportunity,* ed. J. E. Hayes and D. Michie (Chichester: Ellis Horwood and New York: Halsted Press, 1983).

Chapter 2: *Computers Join the Experts*

General:

*Introductory Readings in Expert Systems,** ed. D. Michie (London and New York: Gordon and Breach, 1983).

Intelligent Systems: the Unprecedented Opportunity, ed. J. E. Hayes and D. Michie (Chichester: Ellis Horwood and New York: Halsted Press, 1983). (This book ranges widely and touches on many subjects beyond expert systems.)

*Expert Systems in the Micro-electronic Age,** ed. D. Michie (Edinburgh: Edinburgh University Press, 1979).

1. E. H. Shortliffe, *Computer-Based Medical Consultations: MYCIN** (New York: Elsevier/North Holland, 1976).

2. V. L. Yu, L. M. Fagan, S. M. Wraith, et al., "Antimicrobial Selection for Meningitis by a Computerized Consultant—a Blinded Evaluation by Infectious Disease Experts,"* *Journal of the American Medical Association,* Vol. 242, 1979, pp. 1279–1282.

3. E. A. Feigenbaum, "Expert Systems in the 1980s," proceedings of Expert Systems: Management Tutorial, December 1981, British Computer Society, p. 114; J. Osborn, L. Fagan, R. Fallat, D. McClung, and R. Mitchell, "Managing the Data from Respiratory Measurements,"* *Medical Instrumentation,* Vol. 13, No. 6, November 1979; E. A. Feigenbaum, "Themes and Case Studies of Knowledge Engineering," in *Expert Systems in the Micro-electronic Age,* pp. 3–6.

4. Richard Duda and John Gaschnig, "Knowledge-Based Expert Systems Come of Age," *Byte* magazine, Vol. 6, No. 9, September 1981, pp. 259–262; R. O. Duda, J. G. Gaschnig, and P. E. Hart, "Model Design in the Prospector Consultant System for Mineral Exploration,"* in *Expert Systems in the Micro-electronic Age,* pp. 152–167; J. G. Gaschnig, "Development of Uranium Exploration Models for the Prospector Consultant System,"* final report, SRI Project 7856, SRI International, Menlo Park, California, 1980.

5. Duda and Gaschnig, *Byte* magazine, p. 262.

6. John McDermott, "R1's Formative Years," in proceedings of Expert Systems: Management Tutorial, p. 67; also in *AI Magazine,* American Association for Artificial Intelligence, Vol. 2, No. 2, Summer 1981, p. 29.

7. P. H. Winston, *Artificial Intelligence* (Reading, Mass.: Addison-Wesley, 1977), pp. 145–147.

8. Duda and Gaschnig, op. cit., p. 274.

9. Ibid., p. 246.

10. John Gurd, "Developments in Dataflow Architecture,"* proceedings of the conference The Fifth Generation.

Chapter 3: *The Human Window on the World*

General:

Social dangers emerging from the extension of "brute force" computing to complex human affairs are analyzed in: D. Kopec and D. Michie, *Mismatch between Machine Representations and Human Concepts,* FAST series No. 9, EUR 8426 EN, Commission of the European Communities FAST Programme, Brussels, 1983. The authors review the Three Mile Island and other cases and propose remedies.

1. J. G. Kemeny, *The Need for Change: The Legacy of TMI,* report of the President's Commission on the Accident at Three Mile Island, Washington, D.C., October 1979, p. 11.

2. Metropolitan Edison interviews with TMI operators, reprinted in Bill Keisling, *Three Mile Island * Turning Point* (Seattle, Wash.: Veritas Books, 1980), p. 161.

3. U.S. Congress, Subcommittee on Energy and Environment, "Accident at the Three Mile Island Nuclear Power Plant," hearings 9, 10, 11, and 15 May 1979, Washington, D.C., 1979, p. 111.

4. T. B. Malone et al., *Human Factors Evaluation of Control Room Design and Operator Performance at Three Mile Island-2,* Essex Corp., Alexandria, Virginia, prepared for U.S. Nuclear Regulatory Commission, NUREG/CR-1270, 1980.

5. Hedley Voysey, "Problems of Mingling Men and Machines," *New Scientist,* Vol. 75, No. 1065, 18 August 1977, p. 417.

6. *New Scientist,* Vol. 86, No. 1207, 26 June 1980, pp. 375–376.

7. Plato, *Phaedrus,* trans. Walter Hamilton (Harmondsworth: Penguin, 1973), p. 96.

8. Alan Turing, "Computing Machinery and Intelligence," in *Minds and Machines,* ed. Alan Anderson (Englewood Cliffs, N.J.: Prentice-Hall, 1964).

9. *Fifth Generation Computer Systems,** proceedings of the conference in Tokyo, October 1981, ed. T. Moto-oka (Amsterdam: JIPDEC/North-Holland, 1982), p. 8; *Outline of Research and Development for Fifth Generation Computer Systems,* Institute for New Generation Technology, Mita Kokusai Building, 21st Floor, 1-4-28, Mita, Minato-ku, Tokyo 108.

Chapter 4: *Thinking About Thinking*

General:
The first, and still the most authoritative and most readable, review of relevant limitations of the human brain is: George Miller, "The magical number seven plus or minus two," *Psychological Review,* Vol. 63, 1956, pp. 81–97.
Some of the implications for intellectual skills such as chess are discussed in: *Computer Game-Playing,* ed. M. Bramer, (Chichester: Ellis Horwood, and New York: Halsted Press, 1983).

1. Julian Symons, *Bloody Murder* (London: Faber and Faber, 1972), p. 80.
2. R. A. Miller, in *Psychology Review,* Vol. 63, 1956, pp. 81–97; J. M. Stroud, in *Ann. N.Y. Academy,* 1966; sources cited by W. G. Chase and H. A. Simon, in *Cognitive Psychology,* Vol. 4, 1974, pp. 55–81.
3. Jean Hayes, "Children's Visual Descriptions,"* *Cognitive Science,* Vol. 2, 1978, pp. 1–15.
4. Harry Lorayne, *How to Develop a Super-Power Memory* (Wellingborough: A. Thomas, 1979).
5. Alfred Binet, *Psychologie des Grands Calculateurs et des Joueurs d'Échecs* (Paris: Hachette, 1894); A. de Groot, *Thought and choice in chess,* ed. G. W. Baylor (translation, with additions, of Dutch version of 1946), (The Hague and Paris: Mouton, 1965).
6. I.M.L. Hunter, "An Exceptional Talent for Calculative Thinking," *British Journal of Psychology,* Vol. 53, 1962, pp. 243–258.
7. R. L. Gregory, *Eye and Brain* (London: Weidenfeld and Nicholson, 1966); R. L. Gregory, *The Intelligent Eye* (London: Duckworth, 1970).
8. Arthur Koestler, *The Sleepwalkers* (London: Hutchinson, 1959).
9. Michael Polanyi, *Personal Knowledge* (London: Routledge and Kegan Paul, 1958), pp. 12–13.
10. Richard Hofstadter, *The American Political Tradition* (New York: Vintage Books, 1948), pp. 130–133.
11. Colin Tapper, *Computer Law* (London: Longman, 1978), pp. 118–148; Rory Johnston, "Data Protection Laws: the Real Threat," *Computer Weekly,* 8 March 1979, p. 4.
12. R. Firth, *We the Tikopia: a Sociological Study of Kinship in Primitive Polynesia* (London: George Allen & Unwin, 1936; republished New York: Beacon paperback, 1963).

Chapter 5: *Experience and Discovery*

General:
For an early accomplishment of the transfer of know-how and the sharing of skill acquisition between man and machine, see: D. Michie and R. Chambers, "Man-machine Cooperation on a Learning Task,"* in *Computer Graphics: Techniques and Applications,* ed. R. Parslow, R. Prowse, and R. Elliott-Green (London: Plenum Publishing Co., 1969).

A volume that contains much that is of relevance to the concept of the creative computer is: *Machine Learning: an Artificial Intelligence Approach,** ed. R. S. Michalski, J. G. Carbonell, and T. M. Mitchell (Palo Alto, Calif.: Tioga Publishing Company, 1983).

1. Donald Michie and Roger Chambers, "Boxes: an Experiment in Adaptive Control,"* in *Machine Intelligence 2,* ed. E. Dale and D. Michie (Edinburgh: Edinburgh University Press, 1968), pp. 137–152.

2. Ryszard Michalski, "Pattern Recognition as Rule-Guided Inductive Inference,"* *IEEE Transactions on Pattern Analysis and Machine Intelligence,* Vol. PAMI-2, No. 4, July 1980, pp. 349–361.

3. Cited in M. H. Halstead, *Toward a Theoretical Basis for Estimating Programming Efforts,* Technical Report CSD-TR 143 (Lafayette, Ind.: Purdue University, 1975).

4. L. L. Conant, *The Number Concept* (New York: Macmillan, 1896), p. 2.

5. Ibid., p. 4; Tobias Dantzig, *Number: The Language of Science,* 4th edition, (New York: Macmillan, 1954), p. 1.

6. Martin Gardner, "On Playing New Eleusis, the Game That Simulates the Search for Truth," *Scientific American,* Vol. 237, No. 4, October 1977, pp. 18–25.

7. Michael Berry, "APL and the Search for Truth: a Set of Functions to Play New Eleusis,"* in proceedings of the APL Conference 1981 (Boston: I. P. Sharp Associates), pp. 47–53.

8. Douglas Lenat, "The Ubiquity of Discovery," *Artificial Intelligence,* North-Holland, Vol. 9, No. 3, December 1977, pp. 257–285, also in proceedings of the National Computer Conference 1978, American Federation of Information Processing Societies, pp. 241–256; Douglas Lenat, "On Automated Scientific Theory Formation: a Case Study using the AM Program,"* in *Machine Intelligence 9,* ed. J. Hayes, D. Michie, and L. I. Mikulich (Chichester: Ellis Horwood, and New York:

Halsted Press, 1979), pp. 251–283; article in *Machine Learning: an Artificial Intelligence Approach.**

9. Douglas Lenat, "The Nature of Heuristics,"* *Artificial Intelligence,* North-Holland, Vol. 19, No. 2, October 1982, pp. 189–249; Douglas Lenat, "Theory Formation by Heuristic Search,"* *Artificial Intelligence,* Vol. 21, Nos. 1 & 2, March 1983, pp. 31–59; Douglas Lenat, "Eurisko: a Program that Learns New Heuristics and Domain Concepts,"* *Artificial Intelligence,* Vol. 21, Nos. 1 & 2, March 1983, pp. 61–98.

10. R. S. Michalski and R. L. Chilausky, "Learning by Being Told and Learning from Examples: an Experimental Comparison of the Two Methods of Knowledge Acquisition in the Context of Developing an Expert System for Soybean Disease Diagnosis,"* *International Journal of Policy Analysis and Information Systems,* Vol. 4, No. 2, 1980, pp. 125–161.

11. E. A. Feigenbaum, "Themes and Case Studies of Knowledge Engineering," in *Expert Systems in the Micro-electronic Age,* pp. 13–14.

12. R. S. Michalski, R. E. Stepp, and E. Diday, "A Recent Advance in Data Analysis,"* in *Progress in Pattern Recognition,* Vol. 1, ed. L. N. Kanal and A. Rosenfeld (Amsterdam: North-Holland, 1981); R. S. Michalski, "Inductive Learning as Rule-Guided Generalization and Conceptual Simplification of Symbolic Descriptions,"* Workshop on Current Developments in Machine Learning, Carnegie-Mellon University, Pittsburgh, July 1980.

13. L. D. Erman, F. Hayes-Roth, V. R. Lesser, and D. R. Reddy, "The Hearsay-II Speech-Understanding System: Integrating Knowledge to Resolve Uncertainty,"* *ACM Computing Surveys,* Vol. 12, No. 2, June 1980.

14. Herbert Spencer, *Social Statics* (London: John Chapman, 1851, republished by Gregg International Publishers, Farnborough, Hants., 1970), p. 274.

Chapter 6: *The Creation of New Knowledge*

General:

A comprehensive and thoroughly readable account of information theory is given in: Fred Attneave, *Applications of Information Theory to Psychology,* (New York: Holt, Rinehart and Winston, 1959).

1. C. E. Shannon and Warren Weaver, *The Mathematical Theory of Communication* (Urbana: University of Illinois Press, 1949); Gregory Chaitin, "Randomness and Mathematical Proof," *Scientific American,* Vol. 232, No. 5, May 1975, pp. 47–52.

2. Douglas Lenat, "The Ubiquity of Discovery," *Artificial Intelligence,* North-Holland, Vol. 9, No. 3, December 1977, p. 274, and also in *Proceedings of the National Computer Conference 1978,* American Federation of Information Processing Societies, p. 250.

3. A. Shapiro and T. Niblett, "Automatic Induction of Classification Rules for a Chess End-game,"* in *Advances in Computer Chess 3,* ed. M.R.B. Clarke (Oxford: Pergamon Press, 1982), pp. 73–92.

4. Donald Michie, "A Theory of Advice,"* in *Machine Intelligence 8,* ed. E. W. Elcock and D. Michie (Chichester: Ellis Horwood, and New York: Halsted Press, 1977), pp. 151–168.

5. A. M. Turing, *The Automatic Computing Engine,* lecture delivered at the London Mathematical Society, 20 February 1947, typescript in Turing Collection, King's College Library, Cambridge.

Chapter 7: *A Metaphor Upside Down*

General:
Jonathan Benthall, *Science and Technology in Art Today* (London: Thames and Hudson, 1972).
Cybernetic Serendipity, ICA exhibition catalogue, ed. Jasia Reichardt, Studio International, London, 1968.
Jasia Reichardt, *The Computer in Art* (London: Studio Vista, 1971).
Donald Greenberg et al., *The Computer Image* (Reading, Mass.. Addison-Wesley, 1982). This volume includes numerous color illustrations but is more about computer graphics than art.
Joseph Deken, *Computer Images* (London: Thames and Hudson, 1983).

1. Harold Cohen, "What Is an Image?," in proceedings of the Sixth International Joint Conference on Artificial Intelligence, Tokyo, 1979, pp. 1028–1057; Harold and Becky Cohen, Catalogue of Harold Cohen Exhibition, Stedelijk Museum, Amsterdam, 25 November 1977—8 January 1978, reprinted in *Page,* Bulletin of the Computer Arts Society, No. 41, November 1978.

2. Harold Cohen, "How to make a Drawing," paper presented at

Science Colloquium, National Bureau of Standards, Washington, D.C., 17 December 1982; *Harold Cohen*, catalogue of exhibition, Tate Gallery, London, June–July 1983.

3. Harold Cohen, *On the Modelling of Creative Behaviour*, Rand Paper P-6681, Rand Corporation, Santa Monica, 1981.

4. Brian Reffin Smith, catalogue of the exhibition *Artists, Computers, Art*, Canada House, London, 24 March–20 April 1982.

5. Harold Cohen, letter in *Art in America*, September/October 1972.

6. Harold Cohen, "When Machines can Generate Images Faster than You Can Pull an Edition, Who Will Belong to the World Print Council?," invited paper at conference of the World Print Council, San Francisco, 15 May 1982, p. 3 ff.

7. Smith, op. cit.

8. Alain Fournier, Don Fussell, and Loren Carpenter, "Computer Rendering of Stochastic Models," *Communications of the Association for Computing Machinery*, Vol. 25, No. 6, June 1982, pp. 371–384; Benoît Mandelbrot, *The Fractal Geometry of Nature* (Oxford and San Francisco: W. H. Freeman, 1982).

9. Jonathan Benthall, *Science and Technology in Art Today* (London: Thames and Hudson, 1972), pp. 75–78, 166–167.

10. Nicholas Negroponte, "The Return of the Sunday Painter," in *The Computer Age: a Twenty-Year View*, ed. Michael Dertouzos and Joel Moses (Cambridge, Mass.: MIT Press, 1979), p. 27.

11. Benthall, op. cit., pp. 78–83; Edward Ihnatowicz, "The Relevance of Manipulation to the Process of Perception," *Bulletin of the Institute of Mathematics and its Applications*, May 1977, pp. 133–135.

12. *Musical Times*, Vol. 109, No. 1508, October 1968, p. 911.

13. *Computer Weekly*, 8 January 1981, p. 16.

14. Robin Shirley, "Poet and Program," *Page*, No. 25, October 1972.

15. Melpomene (G. E. Hughes), *Bagabone, Hem 'I Die Now* (New York: Vantage Press, 1980).

16. In Nat Shapiro, *Encyclopedia of Quotations about Music* (Newton Abbot: David and Charles, 1978).

17. Marvin Minsky, "Matter, Mind, and Models," in *Semantic Information Processing*, ed. Marvin Minsky (Cambridge, Mass.: MIT Press, 1968), p. 431.

18. Smith, op. cit.

19. Marshall McLuhan and Quentin Fiore, *The Medium is the Massage* (London: Allen Lane, 1967), pp. 132–136.

20. Negroponte, op. cit., p. 22.
21. Ibid., p. 21.
22. Interview on LBC Radio, London, 1 April 1982.
23. Cohen, Stedelijk Catalogue.
24. Cohen, *On the Modelling of Creative Behaviour,* p. 14.
25. Cohen, "What Is an Image?," p. 1045.
26. Negroponte, op. cit., p. 31.
27. Jonathan Benthall, "Computer arts at Edinburgh," *Studio International,* October 1973, p. 120.
28. Negroponte, op. cit., p. 37.
29. Cohen, ". . . World Print Council," p. 5.

Chapter 8: *Coming to Model Heaven*

General:
The issues raised concerning the relationship between language and thought are reviewed in: Valerie Curran, "Cross-Cultural Perspectives on Cognition," in *Cognitive Psychology: New Directions,* ed. Guy Claxton (London: Routledge and Kegan Paul, 1980). This excellently produced paperback collects together contributions on topics central to the theme of this book.

Also relevant: Anthony Davey, *Discourse Production: a Computer Model of Some Aspects of a Speaker* (Edinburgh: Edinburgh University Press, 1978).

A classic paper on the issues of modeling is: J. McCarthy and P. J. Hayes, "Some Philosophical Problems from the Standpoint of Artificial Intelligence,"* in *Machine Intelligence 4,* ed. B. Meltzer and D. Michie (Edinburgh: Edinburgh University Press, 1969), pp. 463–502.

1. Y.-H. Pao, W. L. Schultz, S.-Y. Oh, and R. G. Fischer, *"A Knowledge Base Engineering Approach to Power Systems Monitoring and Control,"** technical report, Department of Electrical Engineering (Cleveland: Case Western Reserve University, 1980).
2. W. B. Rouse and R. M. Hunt, *A Fuzzy Rule-Based Model of Human Problem Solving in Fault Diagnosis Tasks,** working paper, Coordinated Science Laboratory, University of Illinois, Urbana, 1980.
3. Michael Arbib, "Minds and Millennia: the Psychology of Inter-

stellar Communication,'' *Cosmic Search,* Vol. 1, No. 3, Summer 1979, pp. 21–25; 47–48. (A fascinating paper.)

4. P.J.E. Peebles and S. Brand, "A Million Galaxies: Computer Photo-map of the Galaxies Brighter than 19th Magnitude Visible from Earth's Northern Hemisphere," *CoEvolution Quarterly,* Sausalito, Calif., 1978.

5. See Alonzo Church, *Introduction to Mathematical Logic,* Vol. 1 (Princeton: Princeton University Press, 1956), p. 5.

6. John McCarthy, "First-Order Theories of Individual Concepts and Propositions,"* in *Expert Systems in the Micro-electronic Age,* pp. 271–287.

7. Edward Feigenbaum, "Artificial Intelligence Research: What Is It? What Has It Achieved? Where Is It Going?," invited paper, Symposium on Artificial Intelligence, Canberra, 1974, quoted in Feigenbaum, "Themes and Case Studies of Knowledge Engineering," in *Expert Systems in the Micro-electronic Age,* p. 6.

8. Richard Ennals, *Beginning micro-Prolog* (Chichester: Ellis Horwood, and London: Heinemann, 1983); K. L. Clark, F. G. McCabe, and P. Hammond, "Prolog: a Language for Implementing Expert Systems,"* in *Machine Intelligence 10,* ed. Hayes, Michie, and Pao (Chichester: Ellis Horwood, 1983).

9. *The Lewis Carroll Picture Book,* ed. S. D. Collingwood (London: T. Fisher Unwin, 1899), pp. 264–265.

10. P. J. Hayes, "The Naïve Physics Manifesto,"* in *Expert Systems in the Micro-electronic Age,* pp. 242–270.

Chapter 9: *The Cat That Isn't There*

General:

Aaron Sloman, *The Computer Revolution in Philosophy* (Hassocks: Harvester Press, 1978).

Kenneth Sayre, *Consciousness: a Philosophic Study of Minds and Machines* (New York: Random House, 1969).

R. L. Gregory, "Consciousness," in *The Encyclopaedia of Ignorance,* ed. R. Duncan and M. Weston-Smith (Oxford: Pergamon, 1977), pp. 273–281.

R. L. Gregory, *Mind in Science* (London: Weidenfeld and Nicholson, 1981).

Several major articles on these philosophical issues, and in particular on Gödel's Theorem, appear in *Minds and Machines*, ed. Alan Anderson (Englewood Cliffs, N.J.: Prentice-Hall, 1964).

A discussion on future social upheaval is in: Ieuan Maddock, "The Future of Work," in *Intelligent Systems: the Unprecedented Opportunity*. Maddock was formerly chief scientist to the UK Department of Industry.

Also with some original thoughts on the issue is: Christopher Evans, *The Mighty Micro* (London: Victor Gollancz, 1979).

1. *Computer Weekly*, 13 November 1980, p. 13.

2. Margaret Boden, *Artificial Intelligence and Natural Man* (Brighton: Harvester Press, and New York: Basic Books, 1977), p. 420.

3. *Plutarch's Lives*, the translation called Dryden's, Vol. 2, rev. A. H. Clough (London: Macmillan, 1902), pp. 252–253.

4. Edsger Dijkstra, "The Impact of Microprocessors," paper presented at the Congress of the International Federation for Information Processing 1977, published in *GMD Spiegel*, Vol. 7, No. 4, 1977 (Bonn: Gesellschaft für Mathematik und Datenverarbeitung), pp. 8–11.

5. K. Appel and W. Haken, "Every Planar Map is Four Colorable,"* *Bulletin of the American Mathematical Society*, Vol. 82, No. 5, September 1976, pp. 711–712; "The Solution of the Four-Color-Map Problem," *Scientific American*, Vol. 237, No. 4, October 1977, pp. 108–121.

6. Sigmund Freud, *New Introductory Lectures on Psychoanalysis*, (New York: Norton, 1965), p. 95.

7. John Locke, *Essay Concerning Human Understanding*, ed. P. H. Nidditch (Oxford: Oxford University Press, 1975), Bk. II, Ch. 1, par. 19.

8. Nikki Knewstub, "A Culture Undermined," the *Guardian*, 2 June 1979, p. 9.

9. *Computer Weekly*, 21 June 1979, p. 64.

Chapter 10: *Inventing for All Mankind*

General:
Handbook of Industrial Robotics, ed. Shimon Nof of Purdue University (New York: John Wiley, 1984). It contains several contributions that evaluate the convergence of the two engineering disciplines of robotics and machine intelligence.

1. Wellington, *Despatches, Correspondence and Memoranda (New Series)*, Vol. 6, p. 529, 8 March 1830, cited in Elizabeth Longford, *Wellington: Pillar of State* (London: Weidenfeld and Nicholson, 1972), p. 205.

2. In Arthur Koestler, *The Thirteenth Tribe: the Khavar Empire and its Heritage* (London: Hutchinson, 1976), p. 40.

3. Ibid.

4. *The Times* (London), 20 January 1887, p. 8c.

5. *The Times* (London), 13 January 1887, p. 8a.

6. Robert McGhee, "Walking Machines" in *Intelligent Systems: the Unprecedented Opportunity;* Mark Railbert and Ivan Sutherland, "Machines That Walk," *Scientific American*, Vol. 248, No. 1, January 1983, pp. 32–41.

7. See *The Financial Times*, 9 June 1979, p. 2.

8. J. Lighthill, "Artificial Intelligence: a General Survey," in *Artificial Intelligence: a Paper Symposium*, Science Research Council, London, 1973, p. 7.

9. H. G. Barrow, A. P. Ambler, and R. M. Burstall, "Some Techniques for Recognizing Structures in Pictures,"* in *Frontiers of Pattern Recognition*, ed. S. Watanabe (New York: Academic Press, 1972), pp. 1–29.

10. O. Firschein, M. A. Fischler, L. S. Coles, and J. M. Tenenbaum, "Forecasting and Assessing the Impact of Artificial Intelligence on Society," proceedings of the Third International Joint Conference on Artificial Intelligence, 1973, SRI International, Menlo Park, Calif., pp. 105–120.

11. *New Scientist*, Vol. 86, No. 1201, 3 April 1980, p. 15.

12. Michel de Montaigne, *Essays*, Hazlitt's edition, 1892, reprinted 1923.

Appendix: *Basic Principles of Computing*

General:

To find out more about the broad sweep of present-day computing, see: Ray Curnow and Susan Curran, *The Penguin Computer Book* (Harmondsworth: Penguin, 1983).

For a good grasp of the techniques of programming, see: John Kemeny and Thomas Kurtz, *Basic Programming*, 3rd edition (New York: Wiley, 1980).

GLOSSARY

TERMS DEFINED IN FULL in the body of the text are not included here; for them, see the Index.

address The number that identifies the location of a cell in memory. See page 259.

algorithm A clearly defined procedure in computation, e.g., Newton's Algorithm, for finding square roots. See page 251.

analogue (adj) Using continuously variable rather than discrete quantities (to represent numbers, etc.). See page 263.

And An operator in logic that requires *both* of two elements to be true for the combined expression to be true. See page 266.

anode The positive conductor of an electronic vacuum tube.

argument In mathematics, an independent variable of a *function (q.v.)*.

associative store A computer storage device with special hardware attached for searching for information in the store sequentially and very fast. This avoids having to have the information indexed. Also called "content addressable file."

binary By twos; counting by twos. See page 264.

bit Binary digit. See page 264.

bootstrapping A program to be loaded into a computer needs to be read in from some storage device such as a disk. To carry out this reading process, the machine needs a program, called a *loader*, but how does the loader itself get loaded? There has to be some special hardware or a crude loader that can be inserted by hand. This process is called bootstrapping, from the proverbial difficulty of lifting oneself up by one's own bootstraps.

bug A mistake in a computer program. See page 256.

cards Because computers can accept information far faster than people can type it, data always used to have to be entered onto punched cards or paper tape, away from the computer. These could then be fed into the machine very fast, making the best use of computer time. It is now much more economically feasible to have terminals connected on-line to the computer, eliminating the need for cards.

Carnot Cycle The operating process of a heat engine, according to the analysis of Nicolas Carnot (1796–1832).

channel In communications, an information-carrying path. In microelectronics, a part of an integrated circuit.

chip an integrated circuit. See page 266.

clock cycle One basic step of the operation of a computer.

code The commands making up a program, be they in a high-level language, a low-level language, or numbers *(machine code q.v.)*.

compiler A program for translating programs in a computer language into *machine code (q.v.)* for execution by a computer.

composite number A number that is not *prime (q.v.)*.

computer A general-purpose, automatic, programmable information processing machine. See page 245.

curve-fitting The mathematical process of finding a function that adequately describes a curve or graph.

cytology The study of the cells of organisms.

data The information used by a computer.

data bank One or more data bases *(q.v.)* available to many users and often to the general public.

data base A large collection of information on one subject held in a computer and usually organized in a hierarchical or tabular structure.

data control The job of keeping track of the work being fed into a computer and the output recieved from it.

data entry The process of feeding large amounts of data into a computer. See page 257.

declarative semantics The meaning of a computer program when this is viewed purely as a collection of *descriptive* assertions, in isolation from any imperative or *prescriptive* interpretation.

Difference Engine A pioneering mechanical computer, designed by

Charles Babbage (1791–1871). Construction was started but never completed.

digital Of a complete system that represents all information including colors and the sizes of things in terms of discrete *numbers*. See page 263.

distributed processing The techniques of using many small interconnected computers instead of one large one.

Doppler radar system Radar designed to detect movement.

epistemic To do with understanding.

extrapolate To extend a series of numbers outside the range of the known terms by assuming that the existing pattern should continue—a process prone to error.

feedback A technique used in control systems in which a machine senses the results of its actions and adjusts further action accordingly. In other words, some output is fed back in as input. A car driver is continually using feedback, watching the road and turning the wheel by small amounts to keep the car on course.

Fermat's Last Theorem One of the most celebrated mysteries in mathematics. The theorem, or more properly "conjecture," is that the equation $x^n + y^n = z^n$ cannot be true for any values of x, y, or z if n is greater than 2. Pierre de Fermat (1601–1665) wrote in the margin of a book, "I have discovered a truly wonderful proof of this, which, however, this margin is too narrow to hold." Whether he really had found such a proof is in some doubt, as no one has been able to find it since.

floating point arithmetic package Software for performing arithmetic on mixed numbers (including fractions), not just integers, and on very large and very small numbers.

flowchart A graphical device for analyzing a procedure. See page 249.

Fortran A high-level computer language. See page 255. The name stands for "formula translation."

front end The part of a computer system with which the user deals directly, namely the terminal and associated input/output software.

function In mathematics, any quantity the value of which depends upon another, e.g., the speed of a car is a function of how far down the accelerator is pressed (and of what gear the car is in, the slope of the road, and various other factors). The position of the accelerator is an *independent variable* and the speed is the *dependent variable*.

game theory The mathematical analysis of strategy and tactics in games, and competition in general.

germanium A semiconducting metallic element used in transistors.

graphics system Hardware and software by which a computer can be used to produce pictures: line drawings, diagrams, colored patterns, etc., either on a televisionlike screen or on paper.

hardware The electronic and mechanical equipment in a computer system, as opposed to the programs, or *software*. See page 256.

high bandwidth Of an information channel with a high capacity, that is, capable of carrying a large number of bits per second. A term from radio.

high-level language A computer language relatively closer to English and further from machine code. See page 255.

high resolution Of a screen capable of showing fine detail in images.

infinite sink In physics, a sink is anything that draws something away, e.g., a heat sink keeps an electronic component cool. An infinite sink is one that never fills up. The earth is effectively an infinite sink for electric charge—hence its use in radio.

infinitesimal calculus Commonly known as just *calculus*. The branch of mathematics that deals with changing quantities by considering them as divided up into very small pieces.

infra-red Invisible rays with wavelengths only slightly longer than red light.

input/output The passing of information into and out of a computer.

integrated circuit An electronic circuit consisting of many transistors made all in one piece on a single sliver of silicon, typically around one-eighth of an inch across, and encased in a plastic housing with connection pins leading out, looking rather like a centipede.

interactive Of the mode of working with a computer in which the user gets an immediate response via a terminal, instead of having to wait for output to come, say, in the mail.

interface Where two things meet. Originally, a term from physics: e.g., where oil is floating on top of water, interesting things happen at the interface. Computing uses the word to refer to the mechanisms for linking different machines or to the way information passes between a computer and the human user.

iterative Of a mathematical process that involves repetition.

keyboard A device for feeding information into a computer, with alphabetic and numeric keys like those of a typewriter.

language (computer) The commands a computer can understand. See page 246.

light-year The distance light travels in one year, viz. 5.878×10^{12} miles.

Lisp   A high-level language used for "list processing," the manipulation of text held in structures called "lists."

listing   The text of a completed program, either printed out by the computer or displayed on the screen.

loop   A part of a program that jumps back and repeats itself. See page 251.

low-level language   A computer language close to machine code.

machine code   The numerical commands that control a computer directly. See page 262.

mass spectrometry   A technique for identifying molecules of chemical compounds by directing a beam of charged particles through electromagnetic fields and observing the varying deflections produced on molecules of different weights.

matrices   In mathematics, rectangular arrays of numbers, useful in various parts of algebra.

merging   Taking two or more ordered collections of data and combining them into one ordered collection—part of the process of sorting information on a computer.

microcomputer   A small computer incorporating a microprocessor and complete with a built-in keyboard—generally not much larger than a typewriter.

microelectronics   The technology of using miniature components in electronics, leading to *integrated circuits (q.v.)*.

microprocessor   The processing unit of a computer made in one piece as a single *integrated circuit (q.v.)*.

microsecond   One millionth of a second of time—see "numbers."

millisecond   One thousandth of a second of time—see "numbers."

minicomputer   A type of small computer that emerged in the 1960s, with a processing unit normally about the size of a record player. Some minicomputers now are as powerful as full-scale computers used to be.

mnemonic   An aid to memory.

multiprocessor   A computer consisting of many separate processing units, all working together.

network   In communications, a system of computers and terminals linked over long distances by telephone lines or other transmission systems.

node   A place where lines in a network meet or where a tree branches.

Not   An operator in logic that requires an element to be false in order for the expression to be true.

Not-And The logical operation And followed by the operation Not. Also called Nand.

numbers Exponents indicate the power to which a number is to be raised, e.g., $12^4 = 12 \times 12 \times 12 \times 12$. We express some larger numbers in "scientific notation," i.e., powers of ten: 10^9 means 1 followed by nine zeroes, or 1,000,000,000. Fractions have prefixes thus:

"milli–"	= 1 thousandth
"micro–"	= 1 millionth
"nano–"	= 1 billionth
"pico–"	= 1 trillionth

on line Connected directly to a computer in "live" operation.

optical storage Very high-capacity computer storage that uses rotating plastic disks with a special film sandwiched in the middle. Microscopic holes are punched in this film by a laser beam to register binary digits and are sensed by another laser.

Or An operator in logic that requires either of two elements to be true for the combined expression to be true.

order code The instructions that make up a particular computer's *machine code (q.v.)*.

order of magnitude A factor of ten, e.g., 40,000 is three orders of magnitude larger than 40.

paper tape See "cards."

parallel Of components that are functionally side by side, or operations going on simultaneously. Compare "series."

parameter In mathematics, strictly an intermediate variable in a calculation. Now taken to mean virtually any variable, especially the values a control system is dealing with. An airline pilot is concerned with such parameters as speed, course, altitude, wind speed, air temperature, and fuel consumption.

partial differential equation A complex kind of equation that arises in the *infinitesimal calculus (q.v.)*.

Peano's axioms A formulation of the number system devised by Guiseppe Peano in 1889.

picosecond One trillionth of a second—see "numbers."

prime number A whole number that is not divisible by any whole number other than itself and 1.

probability   In mathematics, the likelihood of something happening expressed as a ratio similar to "odds"; e.g., with a six-faced die, the probability of rolling a three is 1/6; the probability of rolling an even number is 3/6 or 1/2.

procedural semantics   The meaning of a computer program when it is interpreted as a sequence of tests and imperatives, i.e., as a prescription or procedure for performing a task.

processor   The part of a computer that controls the functioning of the machine and in which operations on data are carried out.

production rule   An "IF <*condition*> THEN <*conclusion*>" program-statement, reminiscent of the stimulus-response pair postulated in studies of animal behavior, which may be *fired* whenever the system's control procedure detects a *match* of the condition with some element of a stored description of the current state-of-the-task environment.

program   The instructions that control the actions of a computer. See page 248.

programmer   A person who writes computer programs.

pseudo-random numbers   Numbers that are random for practical purposes but that are in theory predictable. See page 256.

query language   The commands used to get information out of a data base.

R & D   Research and development.

random number   A number the value of which is unknown beforehand and which is equally likely to be any number within a specified range. A die, for instance, produces random numbers in the range 1 to 6.

resolution principle   A machine-oriented generalization of Aristotle's *modus ponens* rule of deductive inference. The originator of resolution also proved it to be adequate in principle for proving any theorem expressible in first-order logic.

robot   Originally, this meant a hypothetical humanlike walking, talking machine. Nowadays it is applied to fixed computer-controlled assembly machines in factories that do not look at all like people, but as real robots become more capable we can expect to see them acquire more human characteristics such as mobility and vision, leading to hearing and speech and the ability to operate autonomously. The word *robot* is Czech and comes from the 1920 play *R.U.R.* by Karel Čapek.

routine   A part of a program.

screen See "video terminal."

second of arc A circle is divided into 360 *degrees*, each degree into 60 *minutes*, and each minute into 60 *seconds*, so one second is 1/1,296,000 of a circle.

semiconductor A material such as silicon that behaves neither as a pure electrical conductor nor as a pure insulator, used in transistors. See page 265.

series Of components that are functionally arranged, or operations that take place, one after the other. Compare "parallel."

set In mathematics, any clearly defined collection of objects or abstract entities.

silicon A chemical element, the principal constituent of sand, which happens to be a semiconductor and is widely used in making transistors and integrated circuits.

software The programs used in a computer system, as opposed to the "hardware." See page 256.

sonar A method of locating objects by analysis of sound waves emitted by them or reflected from them.

Space Invaders An electronic arcade and home video game.

taxonomy Classification.

teleprinter An automatic typewriter driven by electrical signals down wires, much used by news agencies. Originally, teleprinters were driven by a person typing on a keyboard in some remote location, but they can just as well be worked by computers sending the same electrical signals.

template A partially filled-in form in a program against which data can be matched.

terminal A device, usually a screen and keyboard, that provides access to a computer via wire, possibly from some distance away. See page 257.

theorem prover A program for working out logical deductions from complex chains of implications and axioms.

time resolution The accuracy with which a device can measure time— how close together events can be and still be distinguished.

topology The branch of geometry that concerns itself with how things are connected, ignoring size and distance. A figure drawn on a rubber sheet stays topologically constant as the sheet is stretched and twisted—hence topology is sometimes known as "rubber-sheet geometry." An ordnance survey map of New York's subway system and the schematic diagram displayed in stations, which shows the routes as a few straight-line segments, are equivalent topologically but not according to conventional geometry.

trace facility A function of a computer used in finding program errors. Each instruction is printed out as it is executed so that the programmer can see what is going on.

transistor An electronic device for allowing one current to control another, made out of semiconductors. See page 265.

video projector A television set that produces much larger pictures than are possible with a conventional glass tube, by projecting them onto a cinema screen.

video terminal A terminal on which the information from the computer is displayed on a glass screen, like that of a television set.

VLSI (very large-scale integration) *Integrated circuits (q.v.)* with many thousands of elements.

von Neumann bottleneck The restriction to serial processing of the conventional computer. See page 262.

Index